New Perspectives
on Organizational
Effectiveness

Paul S. Goodman

Johannes M. Pennings

and Associates

New Perspectives on Organizational Effectiveness

Jossey-Bass Publishers
San Francisco • Washington • London • 1981

NEW PERSPECTIVES ON ORGANIZATIONAL EFFECTIVENESS
by Paul S. Goodman, Johannes M. Pennings, and Associates

Copyright © 1977 by: Jossey-Bass, Inc., Publishers
433 California Street
San Francisco, California 94104
&
Jossey-Bass Limited
28 Banner Street
London EC1Y 8QE

Library of Congress Catalogue Card Number LC 77–82916

International Standard Book Number ISBN 0–87589–349–X

Manufactured in the United States of America

JACKET DESIGN BY WILLI BAUM

FIRST EDITION
First printing: November 1977
Second printing: August 1979
Third printing: October 1981

Code 7747

The Jossey-Bass
Social and
Behavioral Science Series

Preface

Organizational effectiveness has been the focus of increasing interest. In an era of growing dependence on organizations, social scientists as well as organization managers, government officials, and other interested parties have become intent on the problem of what accounts for organizational effectiveness. Nevertheless, the theoretical and empirical literatures on the subject are not well developed. There are no well-specified models, and the empirical literature shows little cumulative character.

The purpose of *New Perspectives on Organizational Effectiveness* is to delineate the major theoretical and methodological issues and to suggest some points of resolution. The ultimate goal is to move research on organizational effectiveness in a more analytic and cumulative direction. The book is organized around a set of original essays by major contributors to organizational theory and research. Its unique contribution is that it brings together an inter-disciplinary group of researchers who provide a direction for future research.

The interdisciplinary nature of the book should make it of interest to psychologists, sociologists, political scientists, and others concerned with evaluating the effectiveness of an organization. Also, the book focuses on many different types of organizations, so it should be of interest to those in the public sector, private sector, in production organizations, health care organizations, educational institutions, and so on.

The idea for this book was stimulated by an internal grant from Dean Arnold Weber to the behavioral science group at the Graduate School of Industrial Administration, Carnegie-Mellon University. The funds were to be spent for the intellectual development of the group and the field of organizational theory. Additional support for this venture was provided by the Office of Naval Research. Bertram King's interest and support of our work through ONR contract #N000 1475–C–0973 provided the opportunity for us to prepare our chapter in this volume.

A decision was made to focus on the area of organizational effectiveness and a workshop on that subject was planned. We selected major contributors in the field to write original essays on effectiveness. The specific design called for five major papers and five smaller papers that would react to and build from the five major essays. The latter papers were not "discussant papers"; they were to stand on their own as original papers. The contributors then gathered at Carnegie-Mellon to discuss the essays. In this workshop format, new issues were generated, which are identified in the closing chapter by Robert L. Kahn.

The unique feature of this book is the caliber of the contributors. John P. Campbell, Larry L. Cummings, W. Richard Scott, Charles Perrow, Michael T. Hannan, John Freeman, Jeffrey Pfeffer, Stanley E. Seashore, Karl E. Weick, Louis R. Pondy, and Robert L. Kahn have produced essays that will make significant contributions to the field. Their effort and cooperation in producing and revising their essays made this book possible.

Others have made important contributions to this book.

Sally Mennen did the initial editing work. The typing chores at GSIA were done by Rosaland Tallet and Cecelia Tulley.

We dedicate this book to our parents and families, who created an environment to let us grow in our professional work.

Pittsburgh, Penn.   Paul S. Goodman
September 1977   Johannes M. Pennings

Contents

The Authors

PAUL S. GOODMAN is associate professor of industrial administration and psychology at the Graduate School of Industrial Administration, Carnegie-Mellon University, Pittsburgh. Previously he was on the faculty at the Graduate School of Business at the University of Chicago (1965) and was a visiting professor at Cornell University. He was educated at Trinity College (Hartford, Connecticut), where he received a B.A. in economics in 1959. His master's work was done at the Amos Tuck School at Dartmouth College in 1961, and he received his Ph.D. from Cornell University in organizational psychology in 1966.

Paul Goodman's main professional interests are in conducting research in organizations on work motivation and attitudes, organizational design, productivity, and organizational effectiveness. Some of this research has concerned the effects of pay inequity on performance, motivation of scientists and engineers, designing organizations to retain disadvantaged workers, learning of new organizational reward systems, and the effects of new forms of work organizations on organizational effectiveness. His research has been published in many professional journals and books, including the *Journal of Applied Psychology, Organizational Behavior and Human Performance,* and *Human Relations.*

Paul Goodman is on the editorial boards of *Organizational Behavior and Human Performance* and the *Academy of Management,* and he also serves in a consulting capacity for the government and private industry. His current major research is on effects of new forms of work organization on productivity and quality of working life indicators. The results of this project are currently being put into book form.

JOHANNES M. PENNINGS is associate professor of industrial administration at the Graduate School of Industrial Administration, Carnegie-Mellon University, Pittsburgh. Prior to joining the faculty at Carnegie-Mellon in 1973, he was on the staff of the University of Alberta in Edmonton, Canada (1968–1970), and the Institute for Social Research of the University of Michigan in Ann Arbor (1972–1973). He received his education in Europe and the United States. His B.A. and M.A., both in sociology, were obtained at the University of Utrecht, The Netherlands, in 1965 and 1968, respectively. He received his Ph.D. in organizational psychology at the University of Michigan in 1973.

Johannes Pennings' research has centered around issues of organizational theory, including the organization-environment relationships, organizational design, interorganizational relationships, and organizational effectiveness. Much of this research has sought to answer questions about structural and environmental antecedents of organizational effectiveness—both from the standpoint of the total organization and the individual members. Findings from this research have been published in several professional journals and books, such as the *Administrative Science Quarterly, Human Relations,* and *American Journal of Sociology. Handbook of Organizational Design* (Elsevier, in press) contains a chapter by him on strategically interdependent organization.

Johannes Pennings is on the editorial boards of *Adminis-*

trative Science Quarterly and *Organization and Administrative Sciences.* His present research is on the relationship between interlocking directorates of large corporations and the interdependence among them to determine their effects on organizational effectiveness. This research represents one of the newer directions in organizational theory—interorganizational relationships.

JOHN P. CAMPBELL is professor, Department of Psychology, University of Minnesota.

LARRY L. CUMMINGS is professor, Graduate School of Business, University of Wisconsin, Madison.

JOHN FREEMAN is associate professor, School of Business Administration, University of California, Berkeley.

MICHAEL T. HANNAN is associate professor, Department of Sociology, Stanford University.

ROBERT L. KAHN is professor and program director, Survey Research Center, Institute for Social Research, University of Michigan.

CHARLES PERROW is professor, Department of Sociology, State University of New York, Stoney Brook.

JEFFREY PFEFFER is associate professor, School of Business Administration, University of California, Berkeley.

LOUIS R. PONDY is professor, Department of Business Administration, University of Illinois.

W. RICHARD SCOTT is professor, Department of Sociology, Stanford University.

STANLEY E. SEASHORE is professor and program director, Survey Research Center, Institute for Social Research, University of Michigan.

KARL E. WEICK is professor, Graduate School of Business and Public Administration, Cornell University.

New Perspectives on Organizational Effectiveness

Perspectives and Issues: An Introduction

Paul S. Goodman

Johannes M. Pennings

Recently, there has been a flurry of research and debate on organizational effectiveness. In the last three or four years numerous articles and monographs have appeared with "the effective organization" or "the efficient organization" in their titles. Social developments such as regulation of business, new public welfare programs, decline in labor productivity, and changing opinions in educational, gerontological, and health care domains have focused public attention on the need for optimum organizational performance in order to achieve the best allocation of society's resources.

Interest in organizational effectiveness is, of course, not a recent phenomenon. Since Adam Smith, society has tried to organize human activity to yield the highest output. Organizations are continually reporting results for which they are held accountable—traditionally by owners or stockholders and more recently by other interest groups. In addition to the interest groups associated with a particular organization, the public at large—including governmental officials and academic researchers—has become preoccupied with the factors that account for and that can be manipulated to improve effectiveness. The recent experimentation in industry with methods to improve work quality is a case in point (see Goodman and Lawler, 1977). In such pragmatic efforts, the problems consist of identifying the criteria with which to assess program or organizational effectiveness, measuring these criteria, and weighing the various outcomes in order to judge the adequacy of the organizational arrangements to attain the outcomes.

Organizational effectiveness is not only a central theme in the practical sphere; it is a central theme in organizational theory as well. In fact, it is difficult to conceive of a theory of organizations that does *not* include the construct of effectiveness—most of the central research areas eventually must deal with it to explain intra- or interorganizational variations. Investigations of the effects of different structural arrangements are needed to analyze variations in organizational effectiveness, and a researcher interested in the relationship between organizations and their environments also needs to deal with the conceptualization, measurement, and assessment of organizational effectiveness. The major theme of this book is that effectiveness is one of the most pervasive yet least delineated organizational constructs relevant to all participants in organizational life.

State of the Theoretical Literature

Although there has been a growing interest in organizational effectiveness, the literature on this topic is still in a preliminary state. There are no definitive theories. There is no agreement on a definition for organizational effectiveness; the number of definitions varies with the number of authors who have been preoccupied with the concept. In addition to the different definitions of effectiveness, there is a tendency to view effectiveness as either one-dimensional or multidimensional. Underlying these differences in conceptualization are different views of the nature of organizations, which implicitly or explicitly determine the conceptual definition of effectiveness. In one view, an organization is seen as a rational set of arrangements oriented toward achieving certain goals. From this position, effectiveness is defined in terms of goal attainment. Others take an open-system view of organizations and define effectiveness as the degree to which the organization can preserve the integration of its parts. In this view of organizations, adaptation and survival become measures of organizational effectiveness.

A main problem in the current literature is the lack of knowledge about the construct validity of organizational effectiveness. The domain of effectiveness has not been specified, and we know little about the nomological network that surrounds this concept. The effect of using different time periods (short term versus long term) also has not been examined.

Another problem concerns the role of constituencies (for example, employees, government agencies, suppliers). Constituencies determine the appropriate standards by which effectiveness can be judged. Whether one adopts the goal approach (what is the appropriate goal?) or the systems approach (what is the appropriate allocation of resources to maintain the organization?), the problem of defining the role of constituencies needs to be specified in any conceptualization of effectiveness. In the current literature this problem has not been thoroughly examined.

Another issue is that there is currently no theoretical delineation of the structure of organizational effectiveness determinants, and there has been little characterization of the relative roles of internal and external determinants of effectiveness. In addition, there is need to distinguish between determinants and components of effectiveness. For example, some writers conceive of adaptability as equivalent to organizational effectiveness, whereas others view adaptability as a determinant of organizational effectiveness.

State of the Empirical Literature

The failure to develop a coherent conceptualization of effectiveness has led to the current disarray in the pertinent research, which shows little cumulative character. Most empirical studies so far seem to have been "studies of convenience"—that is, when a particular criterion or effectiveness variable was available, it was used. There is no programmatic line in this literature. For example, although the Seashore and Yuchtman (1967) and Yuchtman and Seashore (1967) systems resource approach to organizational effectiveness is widely quoted, no coherent line of research has emerged from their provocative conceptualization of organizational effectiveness. Campbell and his associates (1974), who have conducted the most extensive review of this literature, attribute the current state of empirical research to the lack of theoretical guidance.

Critical Issues in Organizational Effectiveness

Across the diverse perspectives exhibited in this book the reader will recognize a common set of themes or issues, which represent the basic challenge to the conceptualization of organizational effectiveness. Any new framework should explicitly deal with the following six problems.

The first is the *nature of the organization*. Any theoretical development of organizational effectiveness must make explicit a view of the organization. For example, an elaboration of domains of effectiveness along the lines of Seashore and Yuchtman requires that the organization be viewed as comprising input, transformation, and output systems.

The second problem is *definition*. A precise definition of organizational effectiveness is needed. In the past, most definitions have been derived from the goal or systems approach, but these definitions are quite general. The idea of optimum allocation of resources to maintain the organization (systems approach) is at best a vague definition. It will be necessary to reconcile the roles of the goal and systems approaches in the definition of effectiveness. For example, is organizational survival or growth part of the effectiveness definition? It will also be necessary to include a precise set of dimensions in effectiveness definitions. For example, the identification of organizational effectiveness criteria, the measurement of those criteria, and a standard to judge movement along those criteria seem to be critical dimensions in any effectiveness definition.

The third problem is the *domain of effectiveness*. Little work has been done on specifying the construct space of effectiveness. A review of organizational effectiveness studies indicates that criteria such as adaptability or flexibility are frequently included as parts of organizational effectiveness. The question of whether these constitute a core set of criteria needs to be addressed. If one adopts a multidimensional definition, then the interrelationships of the criteria need to be examined. Can the criteria be ordered in some factor analytic way, or is there some hierarchical ordering among them? Do certain conditions such as greater adaptability lead to greater productivity, or are both these criteria independent components of effectiveness?

The fourth problem is that of *constituencies*. Once the properties or criteria of effectiveness have been identified, a problem still exists as to whose perspective should dominate in the use of these criteria. Is it the perspective of the owners, employees, managers, or public at large that determines the type of criteria and the level of effectiveness desired? Should it be the "official" goals, "operative" goals, or those derived by the researcher that define effectiveness? Or, for that matter, should we think of effectiveness in terms of the organization itself or in terms of its contribution to society? Switching from the organizational to societal perspective substantially changes assessment of organizational effectiveness.

The fifth problem is that of *determinants*. A framework must be developed that defines determinants of organizational effectiveness. The problem is complex since the determinants are found at individual, role, group, organizational, and environmental levels. The framework must also separate the determinants of organizational effectiveness from criteria of effectiveness. In the past, this distinction has been blurred.

The sixth problem is the problem of *research strategies*. Given the current state of the empirical literature on effectiveness, it is important to examine carefully the strategies for conducting research on effectiveness. Does research on organizational effectiveness need to be carried on at the organizational level? If so, this would require a large sample of organizations, which would probably be difficult and expensive to obtain. Or can one conduct experiments about processes relevant to effectiveness? Should one develop universal criteria of effectiveness for analysis across different organizations? Can organizations with different goals be included in a comparative analysis of organizational effectiveness? Once the theoretical specification of the organizational effectiveness construct is under way, there is a need to define a research strategy for attacking this construct.

Plan of This Book

This book was conceived to stimulate new lines of thinking and research on organizational effectiveness. We believe the first task is to examine and elaborate on the critical theoretical issues that underlie the concept of effectiveness. By identifying these issues and finding some handles to deal with them, we can begin to develop a conceptual framework of organizational effectiveness. Without such a framework, research will have no direction and will continue in its present atheoretical orientation. We do not claim that the essays in this book provide that framework. Indeed, there will be more than one viable framework. The contribution, rather, is in isolating and delineating the critical problems that underlie the concept of organizational effectiveness.

John P. Campbell begins the examination of organizational effectiveness with his essay "On the Nature of Organizational Effectiveness," in which he explores some reasons for our interest in the effectiveness construct. Campbell develops a major review of different effectiveness theories. He first examines specific models that could be classified in the *goal* or *systems* categories and then reviews the characteristics of the empirical work on effectiveness. The author asserts that many measures or indicators of effectiveness exist but that no particular core of indicators has been identified; that the indicators vary considerably in their generality or specificity; that they have been operationalized in many different ways;

and that they vary considerably in their closeness to any final pay-off. Moving from the general description of the literature, Campbell selects two empirical studies—the factor analytic studies by Mahoney and Weitzel (1969) and Seashore and Yuchtman's study (1967)—for further investigation. This comprehensive review by Campbell sets the stage for the rest of his essay and for the other essays in this book.

The last part of Campbell's essay presents a strategy for research on organizational effectiveness. Campbell argues that researchers need first to describe the actual decisions or courses of action for which effectiveness data will serve as an input. A basic question is whether the data are being used for incompatible purposes. Then the researcher must specify the task objectives of the organization. Once the objectives are identified, the means-ends relationships between the objectives should be delineated. Conditions that enable the organizations to undertake the objectives and the relative importance of each objective should be judged. Some specific methodologies for examining task objectives are discussed. Campbell's discussion of research strategies and procedures for conducting organizational effectiveness research is the most detailed of any of the essays.

L. L. Cummings' response, "Emergence of the Instrumental Organization," proposes a novel view of effectiveness. It argues that an organization can be conceived of as "an arena within which participants can engage in behavior they perceive as instrumental to their goals." Effectiveness of an organization is the degree to which it is instrumental for its members. In this conceptualization, effectiveness is defined at the individual rather than the organizational level.

Richard Scott's paper, "Effectiveness of Organizational Effectiveness Studies," moves from the current state of the literature to some of the substantive issues involved in conceptualizing organizational effectiveness. Scott first examines the concept of goals and its relationship to organizational effectiveness criteria. An important distinction is made between goals that are sources of control or motivation and those used to evaluate organizational performance. The nature of organizational effectiveness criteria and the establishment of those criteria are then reviewed. The author argues that we should focus on a more limited set of criteria, establish explicit normative bases for selecting these criteria, identify those constituencies that support or reject the criteria, and select criteria that will facilitate comparative organizational studies rather than searching for some specific universal criteria of effectiveness.

The second part of Scott's essay considers three areas where indicators of effectiveness could be identified: outcomes, process, and structure. *Outcomes* focus on characteristics of objects on which the organization has performed some operation (for example, quality of units produced in a business firm, student achievement in a school system, and mortality rates in a hospital). *Process* refers to the activities carried out by the organizational participants. Assessment of effectiveness follows from comparing the activities completed against some performance standard. In a hospital, for example, one could examine the completeness of laboratory tests ordered for a particular patient. In a factory, one could examine whether worker behavior complied with stated safety practices. *Structure* refers to organizational or participant characteristics that may bear on organizational effectiveness. The qualifications of the medical staff in a hospital or the age distribution of management in a company would be examples of structural indicators that could be used for assessment of effectiveness. Scott's discussion of possible indicators of effectiveness provides an important insight into how the domain or construct space of organizational effectiveness can be delimited.

In the last part of his essay, Scott suggests explaining determinants of effectiveness not in terms of general models but through an "attempt to develop and test more precise predictions relating particular measures of effectiveness to particular features of organizations or systems of organizations." Current research by the author on hospital effectiveness is described to highlight the issues under discussion.

Charles Perrow's "Three Types of Effectiveness Studies" builds from the Scott paper and delineates three different rationales for studying effectiveness. Each rationale has different implications for determining which perspective should be used to define effectiveness and what might be some of the appropriate indicators of effectiveness. An underlying theme in this essay is the relationship between power and the definition of effectiveness.

Michael Hannan and John Freeman, in their essay "Obstacles to Comparative Studies," deal with methodological issues involved in studying organizational effectiveness. The problems of weighting multiple goals and short- versus long-term payoffs are discussed. The authors also examine the problem of defining the appropriate system boundaries for assessing effectiveness. Here the problem is to isolate the subsystem so that the effects of structure on effectiveness criteria can be separated from other effects. A related issue is defining the level of analysis. Should an organization's outputs be evaluated at the level of the organization or of the larger system to which the organization belongs? This issue is illustrated by a discussion of school versus school district effectiveness.

A major problem seen by Hannan and Freeman in the comparative study of organizational effectiveness is the need for comparison of interorganizational utilities. These utility functions and their precise form are often not well known. It is not clear, for example, that the same increase in profitability to two firms yields equal utility. The problem is further complicated as one considers that organizations have multiple goals and different constituencies within and outside the organization attaching different preference functions to these goals. Hannan and Freeman's basic argument is that one cannot do comparative organizational analysis based on organizational effectiveness. Organizational survival is proposed as an alternative approach to organizational effectiveness.

Jeffrey Pfeffer's essay, "Usefulness of the Concept," rejects the Hannan-Freeman thesis that organizational effectiveness is not subject to scientific investigation and that one cannot conduct comparative research on organizational effectiveness. A basic theme in this essay is that effectiveness is central to all organizational research and that the methodological problems posed by Hannan and Freeman characterize all comparative studies and are of interest in their own right. Pfeffer builds from this careful analysis to identify a series of provocative research problems concerning goals as legitimating devices and guides to action, the process by which organizations control others' assessment of them in order to insure continued resources, the causes of permeability in organizational boundaries and its effect on organizational effectiveness, and the factors contributing to different time horizons in defining effectiveness.

"Toward a Workable Framework," by Johannes Pennings and Paul Goodman, attempts to synthesize and extend the conceptualization of organizational effectiveness. Their essay adopts various aspects of the strategic contingency theory (for an example, see Hickson and others, 1971), and it defines organizations as being composed of several units that differentially affect each other's performances and that of the total organization. The importance of a unit for an organization's effectiveness depends on the unit's ways of coping with uncertainty, its substitutability, and its centrality. Organizations are also conceptualized as consisting of internal and external constituencies that negotiate a complex set of constraints, goals, and referents—the major elements of organizational effectiveness. Since the constituencies are likely to have incompatible positions in specifying effectiveness, the dominant coalition is posited as the mechanism for reconciling competing demands and for defining the perspective from which organizational effectiveness will be assessed. The nature of external actors both as constituencies and as determinants of effectiveness also is delineated. A definition of effectiveness is then proposed based on the concepts of constraints, goals, and referents. Organizations are effective to the degree that relevant constraints can be satisfied and organizational results made to approximate or exceed a set of referents for multiple goals. *Goals* are desired end states. *Constraints* are conditions that need to be satisfied. *Referents* are the standards against which outcomes are evaluated. The nature of different referents used in assessing effectiveness is then discussed.

Extending the framework of effectiveness, the authors consider the relationship between effectiveness and efficiency, the effect of time parameters in assessing effectiveness, and the meaning of effectiveness in reference to the organization's input acquisition and output disposal. The role of determinants and constituencies in establishing constraints, outcomes, and referents is also examined. The last part of the essay contrasts the proposed framework with conceptualizations of organizational effectiveness by Argyris, Mohr, Price, Katz and Kahn, and Seashore and Yuchtman.

Stanley Seashore's essay, "An Elastic and Expandable View-point," begins by extending the framework for organizational effectiveness proposed by Pennings and Goodman. Particular attention is given to the distinction between goals and constraints and the role of the dominant coalition in mediating the demands by competing constituencies in the definition of organizational effectiveness.

Karl Weick's "Re-Punctuating the Problem" explores eight sets of conditions that are associated with effectiveness. Taking a novel approach to the topic of organizational effectiveness, Weick tries to show that the concept of organizational effectiveness can be punctuated by the following concepts: *garrulous, clumsy, haphazard, hypocritical, monstrous, octopoid, wandering,* and *grouchy.* Such punctuation contrasts sharply with more traditional punctuations of organizational effectiveness such as profit, member satisfaction, and integration.

Weick's basic thesis is that increases in these eight conditions within an organization can contribute to organizational effectiveness. For example, some degree of intentional randomization of action (haphazard condition) can contribute to organizational effectiveness by making organizational members more likely to break up old ways of thinking and increasing their ability to combine novel events—two factors that enhance the organization's adaptability. Similarly, effective organizations are hypocritical to the extent that selective discrediting contributes to organizational effectiveness. Condoning and preserving deviance ("monstrous" behavior) is another way organizations can ensure effectiveness. The basic focus of this essay is on adaptability rather than on goal attainment as a measure of effectiveness. The discussion of these eight conditions represents one of the most provocative statements on the nature of organizational effectiveness in the literature.

In "Effectiveness: A Thick Description," Louis Pondy responds to Weick's paper by presenting four new words—*loops, acorns, eoliths,* and *play*—to describe the eight novel punctuations proposed by Weick. Pondy attempts to provide a context for interpreting Weick's new conceptualization of effectiveness, particularly in terms of the latter's theoretical work on organizing. Pondy also breaks new ground in the discussion of optimum adaptability, the role of instrumentality concepts in adaptability theories of effectiveness, and the need to place theories such as Weick's in a contextual framework.

The final chapter—an overview and integration by Robert Kahn—describes the basic themes running through the essays and examines the diversity of viewpoints. Future directions for theoretical and empirical work are suggested.

2

On the Nature of Organizational Effectiveness

John P. Campbell

😂😂😂😂😂😂😂😂

The background for this chapter comes from an attempt by some of my colleagues and myself (Campbell and others, 1974) to examine the literature on organizational effectiveness and to say something systematic about it. The aim, now as then, is to suggest how criterion measures of organizational effectiveness should be developed so that they can be used to compare organizations, evaluate the effects of organizational development efforts, and determine what characteristics of

organizations are significantly associated with organizational effectiveness.

More specifically, after some introductory discussion of related topics, this chapter will (1) argue that organizational effectiveness is a construct and, as such, must be located in some kind of theoretical context for it to make any sense; (2) outline some alternative theories of the "construct" and suggest where they lead in terms of the meaning of organizational effectiveness and how it should be researched; (3) summarize the helter-skelter "state" these alternative models seem to have produced; (4) discuss briefly matters of value versus matters of fact in the determination of organizational effectiveness; and (5) advocate steps that might be taken in the future to make things a little clearer.

Topics Related to Organizational Effectiveness

The topic of organizational effectiveness closely resembles a number of other domains in social and behavioral science. Many of its problems are the problems of several other fields, and it would be a mistake to take too parochial a view. For example, in looking over the organizational effectiveness literature, it was startling to discover how much of the ontogeny of the development of organizational effectiveness criteria recapitulates the phylogeny of the individual performance "criterion problem." It would be worthwhile for those who are serious about this problem to review carefully the major milestones in the search for *individual* performance criteria. Several will be mentioned in this chapter.

Another closely related area is that of "evaluation" research, which in turn translates into two main themes. One theme concerns evaluations of social programs (for example, Head Start, WIN, MTDA, and others) aimed at determining whether these programs have worked or not (Rossi and Williams, 1972). Such evaluations are often mandated by federal funding agencies and are the responsibility of the contractors who implement the programs. The second theme comes principally from colleges of education and has to do with curriculum evaluation. In this context, evaluation takes on the characteristics of a discipline in its own right. It is now pos-

sible in a number of universities to obtain a Ph.D. in "evaluation." Evaluation appears to be a growing field.

Related literature dealing with the evaluation of training in business and industry (see Campbell and others, 1970; Goldstein, 1975), though older and less extensive than education evaluation research, has a few nuggets of its own that are worth looking at. Additional insights can be gained from such unlikely bedfellows as general systems theory (Von Bertalanffy, 1968) and human resources accounting (Brummet, Flamholtz, and Pyle, 1968). How these theories can aid the general explication of organizational effectiveness will be mentioned later. Here we need simply note that although the topic of organizational effectiveness undoubtedly has a number of unique characteristics, many of the problems and issues are not unique and are being actively discussed in other fields. We should not neglect them.

Theories, Facts, and Values. An underlying assumption of this chapter is that no definitive definition of organizational effectiveness can be given. *The* meaning of organizational effectiveness is not a truth that is buried somewhere waiting to be discovered if only our concepts and data collection methods were good enough. As with theories in general, a particular conceptualization of organizational effectiveness may be useful only for certain purposes.

The usefulness of a particular formulation is a function of both the values of the user and the facts of organizational life. Regardless of what theory is used, a value judgment must be made about what the goals of the organization should be. Such a statement can take many forms; but, even if never made explicit, goals under which the organization operates will be reflected in the behavior of its members. Neither the people in the organizations nor the outsiders studying them can avoid the value judgment of what the goals of the organization should be. To anticipate an argument made later, even the so-called "natural systems approach" to organizational effectiveness (Ghorpade, 1971) deals with the question of goals. It just does so in a different way. The same can be said of a very sophisticated attempt by Georgiou (1973) to preempt the issue of goals by looking at organizations as collections of individuals, each with a particular reward structure. This approach merely argues that individual people have goals, and the demon is still with us. In sum, the value judgment concerning what goals the organization should adopt and the process by which that judgment is made (for example, by default) can lead to widely differing methods of assessing organizational effectiveness.

Another value judgment concerns the purpose for which the assessment of organizational effectiveness is to be used. This judgment, which could affect greatly the way effectiveness is conceptualized and measured, will be discussed in more detail later in the chapter.

Once the goals of the organization and the purpose for which effectiveness is to be assessed are selected, then it becomes possible to consider matters of "fact." Such facts revolve around the validity of the assessment, the reliability of the measures, the costs of measurement versus the yield of information, the breadth or narrowness of the effectiveness assessment, and so on. Most discussions of organizational effectiveness and most research studies attempting to measure it jump to the factual domain much too soon, and it will be argued later that one large area of research should be the explication of value questions, including research on why individuals try to avoid these questions.

Uses of Organizational Effectiveness Measures. Why should anyone be concerned about organizational effectiveness? Perhaps a useful way to answer this question is to adopt a rather simpleminded decision-making approach and ask, For what kinds of decisions or for what choices between alternative courses of action would information about organizational effectiveness be required? It is instructive that research in personnel selection did not come to grips with the real problems until a decision theory point of view was adopted (see Cronbach and Gleser, 1965; Dunnette, 1966). For example, statements about the validity of a personnel selection tool mean relatively little until the decisions for which it is to be used are defined precisely and the economic and political conditions in which it must operate are taken into account.

There are at least six kinds of decisions for which organizational criterion data could be used. The first four, and perhaps the fifth, involve the practical problems of organizations; the sixth is the concern of the scientist trying to understand how organizations operate. For the most part, people in this field have concentrated on the first and last kinds of decision, leaving the rest to speculation and informal follow-up studies.

1. It might be necessary to decide whether some aspect of a system is in a "good" state or a "bad" state. Turnover rates are an example of an indicator that might pinpoint such a decision. Profitability, or return on investment, would be another. Frequency of racial incidents would be yet another.
2. A "diagnosis" might be required to determine *why* the system is in the state it is. For example, what is causing the high turnover rates, why is profitability high or low, why are there so many racial incidents?
3. Planning decisions often have to be made concerning what actions should be taken to change the state of the system. That is, what should be done to lower turnover or lower the frequency of racial incidents?
4. Comparison of organizations is sometimes necessary for public decision making. That is, state, local, and federal governments develop and implement numerous statutes that influence organizations. In the course of some of this law making, it is necessary to compare organizations on various indices. For example, the Bureau of Labor Statistics collects data on absenteeism, lost time due to accidents, and so on.
5. Organization change specialists might wish to use an organizational effectiveness measure to evaluate the effectiveness of an organizational development effort, be it concerned with behavioral, structural, or technological change.
6. Scientists often wish to rank order organizations on some measure, or measures, of effectiveness so as to study the antecedents of effectiveness. That is, what organizational characteristics seem to be associated with or "predict" the effectiveness criteria? There are numerous reasons why effectiveness criteria developed for scientific purposes may not be useful for practical purposes, and vice versa. For example, individual judges may provide useful ratings of organizational effectiveness when the data are for research purposes but not when there is real money riding on it.

A related consideration is who is going to use the criterion data. The identity of the decision makers will also influence the strategy used to measure effectiveness. For example, the traditional dichotomy between the technical quality of a criterion and its acceptance by the people who must use it (Maier, 1963) operates here—with a vengeance. If the people involved will not use a particular kind of criterion data, there is no sense in collecting the data. Why build indicators of organizational health if they are going to be ignored? Why develop new measures of financial performance if no one trusts them? To get a bit closer to home, academic researchers may not use a particular criterion measure because they believe journal editors will not accept research that uses it as a dependent variable.

Organizational Effectiveness As a Construct

To ask a global question about whether an organization is "effective" or "ineffective" is virtually useless. Effectiveness is not *one* thing. An organization can be effective or ineffective on a number of different facets that may be relatively independent of one another. Organizational effectiveness criteria undoubtedly can be dimensionalized with regard to an even greater number of facts than individual performance. Also, the number of situations in which multiple criterion measures should be combined into an overall measure seems fewer for organizational effectiveness than for individual performance, where such a procedure is looked at with suspicion (see Schmidt and Kaplan, 1971). In fact, I cannot think of one decision made about organizations that requires an overall measure of organizational effectiveness. Perhaps a better way to think of organizational effectiveness is as an underlying construct that has no necessary and sufficient *operational* definition but that constitutes a model or theory of what organizational effectiveness is. The functions of such a model would be to identify the kinds of variables we should be measuring and to specify how these variables, or components, of effectiveness are interrelated—or *should* be interrelated. A fully developed construct or model would also tell us how measures of the individual components of effectiveness can be used.

Strictly speaking, it is not possible for anyone concerned with organizational effectiveness to avoid using it as a construct or to avoid operating via some kind of theory. Without a theory of some sort, even if it has never been made public, it is not possible to say that one organization is more effective than another, or to say that variable X is a measure of organizational effectiveness and variable Y is not, or to plan ways to "change" an organization. It is incumbent on all those concerned to make their "theories of effectiveness" as explicit as possible.

At this point, it would be useful to examine the major conceptual themes that seem to account for the variety of ways that the construct of organizational effectiveness has been used. These themes seem themselves to form a two-tiered hierarchical structure with two general factors and a number of more specific factors subsumed under each.

Two General Models of the Effectiveness Construct. At the top of the hierarchy there are two relatively well-known points of view concerning what organizational effectiveness means and how it should be assessed. They have been given various labels, but the most popular are the *goal-centered* view and the *natural systems* view (for example, see Ghorpade, 1971). The term *system* is used here somewhat differently than it is used by those who deal with systems theory in a formal or mathematical sense.

The goal-centered view makes a reasonably explicit assumption that the organization is in the hands of a rational set of decision makers who have in mind a set of goals that they wish to pursue. Further, these goals are few enough in number to be manageable and can be defined well enough to be understood. Given that goals can be thus identified, it should be possible to plan the best management strategies for attaining them. Within this orientation, the way to assess organizational effectiveness would be to develop criterion measures to assess how well the goals are being achieved. There are a number of variations of the goal-centered view. The management by objectives tradition (for example, Odiorne, 1965, 1969) tends to fall into this category. The recently renewed interest in cost-benefit analysis (Rivlin, 1971) is an ambitious attempt to assess the actual utility of accomplishing specific goals. The attempt during the 1960s to derive overall measures of military readiness (Hayward, 1968; Popper and Miller, 1965) is yet another variation. These and other examples of this model will be discussed shortly.

The natural systems view makes the assumption that if an organization is of any size at all, the demands placed on it are so dynamic and complex that it is not possible to define a finite number of organizational goals in any meaningful way. Rather, the organization adopts the overall goal of maintaining its viability or existence through time without depleting its environment or otherwise fouling its nest. Thus, to assess an organization's effectiveness, one should try to find out whether an organization is internally consistent, whether its resources are being judiciously distributed over a wide variety of coping mechanisms, whether it is using up its resources faster than it should, and so forth. One implication that this orientation does not always recognize is that to be effective the organization needs some theory or model specifying the coping mechanisms to be built and kept lubricated. It cannot prepare itself for literally everything. One clear example of a natural systems model that incorporates specific a priori notions of what system variables should be assessed is the one developed at the University of Michigan Institute for Social Research (ISR) by Likert and his associates (Likert, 1961, 1967). In the beginning, the basic systematic variable was the degree to which subordinates participated in making the decisions that affected them, or put another way, the degree to which supervisors shared their control. By implication, an organization in which decisions were made participatively was a healthy and capable organization. The list of variables has since been expanded to include communication factors, motivational practices, and the like. The focus is on "people" factors and not on the state of the organization's technology or its physical structure. The current state of the organization is measured via a questionnaire. Taylor and Bowers (1972) and Franklin (1973) have described the most recent formalization of the model and the current measurement instrument. Other examples of systems models are those outlined by Argyris (1964), Blake and Mouton (1968), and Katz and Kahn (1966). These and others will also be discussed later in more detail.

One principal inference to be made here is that if an organizational consultant were invited by a particular organization to assess its effectiveness, the assessment approach would depend in part on which of these two points of view he or she had internalized. The goal-oriented analyst would immediately seek out the principal power centers or decision makers in the organization and ask them to state their objectives. If the consultant were worldly wise, he or she would also employ techniques to reveal the actual operative goals of the organization as well as the publicly stated ones. For example, the president's formally stated goal might be to "promote the long-term growth of the organization"; however, the operative goal might be to "show a high return on investment this year so as not to be forced to resign." Thus, certain funds might be shown as profit rather than invested in long-term research and development, making the formally stated goals and the operative goals not precisely the same. For better or worse, once the consultant had the goals defined he or she would proceed to develop criterion variables that would measure how well the objectives (of either kind) were being met. The validity of a particular criterion for assessing the degree of attainment of a particular goal would be an issue to consider. We should keep in mind that goals are not criteria. One is a desired end state and the other is an operationalized continuum representing the degree to which the desired end state is being met. If an analyst were called on who espoused the natural systems view, the questioning would not center around what the organization was trying to accomplish. Rather, the analyst would make inquiries about such things as the degree of conflict among work groups, the nature of communications, the level of racial tension, the percentage of jobs that were filled by people with the appropriate skill levels, the job satisfaction of the employees, and the like. At the outset, the consultant would be concerned not with the specific tasks the organization was trying to perform but with the overall viability and strength of the system. He or she would have some a priori notions of the characteristics of a strong system and would center the questioning around those.

    If both types of analysts took their logical second steps, their efforts should tend to converge. That is, the goal-oriented analyst seeking to explain the organization's success or lack of success in meeting its goals will soon have to investigate the system variables. For example, perhaps the organization did not perform well in a given period because of racial tension. If the natural systems analyst wonders how various system characteristics affect task performance, he or she will have to identify the tasks on which performance should be assessed. Unfortunately, in real life these second steps are often not taken. The goal-oriented analyst tends not to look in the black box, and the natural systems analyst does not like to worry about actual task performance unless pressed.

We should note in passing that the above dichotomy appears not infrequently in other types of research. It is very similar to the general notion of process versus outcome research. Research on the employment interview is an example. For years the emphasis was on the interviewer's final judgment and its reliability or validity. Only recently have investigators looked at the process through which the final decision is actually made. Another example would be process and outcome research pertaining to the effects of participation. Virtually all of the empirical research on the effects of participation in decision making is that of the outcome variety (see, for example, Coch and French, 1948; Morse and Reimer, 1956). That is, some kind of participation versus nonparticipation experimental treatment is instituted and the mean difference between the groups in productivity or some other dependent variable is noted. Process-type questions about what the parameters of participation really are, how they are perceived by the group members under various conditions, how the group members react to the opportunity to participate, and so forth, are questions that are seldom asked. Thus, we have no really good information about why participation works or does not work. There is a moral here for the study of organizational effectiveness, which we shall return to later.

Specific Examples of the Goal
Model of Organizational Effectiveness

The examples cited in the following discussions of the goal model and the systems model of organizational effectiveness are intended to give a sample of the major varieties of each type. Some of them are taken out of their original context (for example, management by objectives); nevertheless, they illustrate how the specific model of effectiveness adopted can significantly influence the way in which organizational effectiveness is ultimately measured (either by design or by default).

Industrial/Organizational   (I/O)   Psychology   Criterion

Model. In the context of measuring individual performance, the criterion problem has a large and honorable niche in the literature concerned with industrial and organizational psychology (for example, see Blum and Naylor, 1968; Campbell and others, 1970; Dunnette, 1966; Schmidt and Kaplan, 1971; Wallace, 1965). Defined as this literature defines it, a criterion is a measure of the degree to which an individual is contributing to the goals of the organization. This definition, in the context of organizational effectiveness, places the criterion securely within the goal-centered view of the construct.

In the criterion model, overall effectiveness is not *one* thing but is made up of a finite number of relatively independent component criteria. *The* criterion was laid to rest some time ago. The specification of individual criterion components flows from a detailed and systematic job description. That is, the first step in criterion development is to describe concretely the major tasks the individual is to perform.

The empirical relationships among the component criteria should also be determined. That is, a fairly large number of individuals should be assessed on each criterion component, and multivariate analysis techniques (for example, factor analysis) should be used to examine the pattern of relationships among the components. Empirical analyses should be performed to find out if changes in individual component scores or their patterning represent changes in the true scores or changes in error scores (unreliability).

The way in which individual criterion component scores are combined or otherwise used to make *specific decisions* about individuals (for example, termination, need for training, promotions, and so on) is determined by expert judgment. The proper experts are those who have the greatest knowledge of the job, the decision to be made, and the organizational objectives that the decision is meant to serve. Thus, criterion combination quite properly is based on value judgments, and there is no algorithm or higher-order truth to which we can appeal.

Criterion measures should represent an assessment of accomplishments that are directly under the individual's control. Variability in criterion scores across individuals or across time should be due to individuals' performances, not to extraneous influences. Performance refers to the concrete, observable things people do that can be evaluated in terms of their contribution to the goals the organization has for the job. As a result of performance, certain outcomes are produced. For some jobs there is a product that can be counted or clients who are satisfied or dissatisfied. For managers there are outcomes such as profits, work group turnover, and the like. The point here is that such outcome measures are not *completely* determined by the individual's performance. For example, the profitability of a retail store is determined to a great extent by its location, and a manager who has performed well may not appear very effective in terms of the profit outcome, or vice versa. It goes without saying that criterion measures should be feasible in terms of the effort and costs involved in collecting data on them.

If we were to use the criterion model in considering organization effectiveness, we might do the following: First, we would conduct an organizational job analysis to establish what the major tasks of the organization are. We should not assume that we know without a careful examination at a relatively atomistic level. To accomplish this we might consider the feasibility of using techniques of job analysis such as those described by Blum and Naylor (1968) or Dunnette (1966). The critical incident technique is one example. After some potential criterion measures are developed, we must try them out on a large number of organizations so as to examine the psychometric properties of the components. Finally, we need to assure ourselves that the component measures are indeed assessing variables over which the organization has some control. In sum, the criterion problem model assumes that qualified experts can use one or more of several techniques to infer criterion measures from a description of tasks to be performed. It then demands a multivariate analysis of data collected on a large number of observations.

Cost-Benefit Analysis. Cost-benefit analysis has traditionally been applied to the evaluation of the relative effectiveness of different training programs, different methods for developing products, and so on. That is, it is most often used to measure the relative effectiveness of *alternative* courses of action toward some goal rather than the effectiveness of an entire organization. This implies that there are actual alternatives to compare, or that expert judgment could be used to develop an "achievement standard" against which the cost-benefit ratio of an existing course of action could be compared.

Inherent in the cost-benefit model is the notion that the components of both the numerator and the denominator can be reduced to a single composite score for each and that the ratio itself has at least interval scale properties. The formal use of cost-benefit analysis to evaluate alternative organizational strategies really got its biggest push from the U.S. Department of Defense (for example, see Hitch, 1965) in the form of the Planning-Programming-Budgeting System (PPBS). The use of PPBS methodology and the cost-benefit model subsequently spread to the evaluation of social programs as well as to a wide variety of other programs, and these attempts at further application served to highlight more fully the strengths and weaknesses of the model (Rivlin, 1971).

The cost-benefit model has led to a much more analytical and thorough analysis of action strategies. A great deal of effort has gone into developing conceptual schemes and measurement methods for assessing both the cost side and the benefit side (for example, Levin, 1975). Another positive feature of cost-benefit analysis, not so often recognized, is the reminder that we can, perhaps, learn something about the relative effectiveness of different strategies by comparing their *marginal* rather than *average* cost-benefit ratios (Glennon, 1972). For example, the benefits derived from producing a certain kind of technical school graduate (type A) could virtually cease after a certain number have been produced. Then type B graduates are needed to do the more complicated tasks (which were irrelevant while the type A's solved the basic problems). If the average cost-benefit ratio of having all type A's versus all type B's were compared, the type A school would look more cost effective. However, comparing the ratios via a marginal analysis would reveal that an effective training organization would switch strategies at a certain point.

Management by Objectives (MBO). Although Odiorne (1965) views management by objectives as a complete system of management planning and control, it could also be viewed in a more restrictive context as a model of organizational effectiveness. The details concerning the practice of management by objectives have been well described elsewhere (see Humble, 1970), as have its limitations as a management technique (for example in Carroll and Tosi, 1973), and we need not repeat that.

However, with regard to MBO as a model of organizational effectiveness, it perhaps bears repeating that the measure that the model specifies as the primary criterion of effectiveness is whether or not the organization has accomplished the concrete tasks that were previously identified as necessary. It represents the ultimate in a goal-oriented model of effectiveness. Thus, rather than evaluating the organization on a single abstracted continuum such as the cost-benefit ratio or on several criterion continua that are in some sense abstractions from specific task behaviors (for example, productivity or profit), MBO says that effectiveness is some aggregation of specific, concrete, and *quantifiable* accomplishments and failures. Either an organization accomplishes a specific task that it is supposed to or it does not.

The MBO model yields a definition of effectiveness that is *unique* to each organization. For a particular time period, each organization must specify in concrete detail the specific things it wishes to accomplish. The relevant measure of effectiveness is then an accounting of which objectives were accomplished and which were not.

Behavioral Objectives (BO) Model. There is a recurring theme in a number of different domains of psychological and educational research that speaks to the general problem of measuring effectiveness and that has taken on many of the characteristics of a Kuhnian (Kuhn, 1962) paradigm. Although the basic idea has never really been applied to the problems of measuring organizational effectiveness, it appears frequently enough in other places to warrant consideration in the present context. The basic message, almost trite in appearance, is this: In judging the effectiveness of an "intervention," or some kind of experimental treatment designed to change behavior, it is necessary to specify beforehand the specific behavioral objectives of the intervention. The term *behavioral objectives* is used in a very atomistic sense. That is, we are talking about a comprehensive list of *all* the specific changes the program is meant to accomplish, and we would expect such a list to be quite long for an intervention of any complexity. The list of BOs constitutes the precise definition of what we want the intervention to accomplish in specific observable terms.

This theme arises in several different contexts. Probably its first major articulation came from research and development on programmed instruction (PI) techniques. Researchers in this area use the term *terminal behaviors* to refer to the specific things the learner should be able to do when the PI sequence is successfully completed. The terminal behaviors define what is to be learned, and their specification is the first, and most important, step in the design of an instructional program.

The programmed instruction model has been expanded into a comprehensive behaviorally oriented model for designing and evaluating almost any instructional effort. The seminal contributions were those of Gagné (1962), Briggs (1968), and Glaser (1969). The basic first step is still the specification of the behavioral objectives of the program, or the specific content of what is to be learned. In a classic statement, Gagné (1962) argued that if we cannot clearly specify what is to be learned, then it is almost axiomatic that we cannot design the training program itself or evaluate its effects. By analogy, if we cannot clearly specify what we want an organization to do, then it is very difficult to design its structure and functions, to staff and develop its human resources, or to assess how effective it is, in any systematic way. Gagné's dictum produced a revolution in training and curriculum development because it argued that the straightforward descriptive question of what is to be learned is far more important than application of psychological or educational *theory*. By analogy, theories of formal organizations will not help us too much in the assessment of organizational effectiveness. What will help is the unexciting and difficult task of deciding what the task objectives of the organization should be.

Another domain in which this theme surfaces is in individual performance measurement. Smith and Kendall (1963) used Flanagan's (1954) critical incident technique to develop a method for defining individual performance in terms of specific behaviors. The technique is referred to as Behavior Expectation Scaling (BES) and works something like this: A panel of judges knowledgeable about the job in question develop what they think is the optimal description of the major performance factors that make up the job's total performance. Such lists typically include five to fifteen factors. Based on their experiences, the judges are then asked to describe specific examples of effective and ineffective performance that illustrate a particular performance factor. Several hundred such incidents may be described. Another panel of judges then considers the entire pool of illustrative incidents and attempts to "retranslate" or assign each incident to the performance factor it best represents. To the extent that the incidents can be correctly reclassified into the factors they came from, we may infer that the performance factors are "understood" and are used consistently. Also, the kinds of classification errors made by the judges provide information about which factors are poorly defined, overlap with others, and so on.

Related to the adoption of the BES technique is the push in educational achievement measurement toward criterion referenced testing. Criterion referenced testing is usually contrasted with the more traditional procedure of norm referenced testing, which interprets an individual's test score according to its relative standing (for example, percentile) in a norm group. By contrast, criterion referenced testing defines a score in terms of the actual skills or knowledge it represents (for example, being able to identify the seventeen most common auto maintenance problems). No mention is made of relative standing in a norm group. Test items are selected such that the score reflects the level of competency directly. It should be obvious that to generate such test items the test developers must understand the subject matter very well in terms of what represents different levels of skills. This method of evaluation is also beginning to generate a very different kind of psychometric theory (Carver, 1974).

Again, it is important to note the common theme running through these techniques. Individual competence, or performance, can only be assessed by reference to a long list of highly specific behavioral objectives. Specification of these objectives serves as a rigorous definition of what it is we want the individual performer to be able to do. By analogy, the way to assess organizational performance would be to force the appropriate "experts" in the organization to specify a complete catalog of organizational objectives. According to the curriculum development literature (Briggs, 1968), these objectives should have three characteristics: (1) They must be *concrete, observable* things that organizations do. (2) The *conditions* under which the organization should be able to do them must be specified. (3) The *degree* to which each objective must be satisfied must also be specified.

Specific Examples of the Systems Models of Organizational Effectiveness

The first model discussed in this section has principal components from both major points of view. The others are more clearly in the systems category.

Operations Research (OR) Model. In some respects, the Operations Research model represents both the goal-centered and the systems view of effectiveness. Ackoff and Sasieni (1968) describe Operations Research as an applied discipline with three essential characteristics: (1) a system or executive orientation; (2) interdisciplinary teams; and (3) scientific methods applied to problems of control. They define OR as "the application of scientific method by interdisciplinary teams to problems involving the control of organized (man-machine) systems so as to provide solutions which best serve the purposes of the organization as a whole" (p. 6).

Ackoff and Sasieni (1968) state that OR's method is to build formalized models of the systems with which the decision makers are concerned. The models that have been developed vary considerably in their mathematical complexity, but they all start from virtually the same deceptively simple formula:

$$U = f(Xi, Yj)$$

where U is the overall utility or value of the system's performance, Xi are the variables that can be controlled, Yj are variables (and constants) that are not controlled but do affect U, and f is the relationship between U and Xi and Yj. OR does not have a model of the firm that allows it to optimize U in the above equation. Instead, the OR approach uses "multiple models, each representing a part of the system, [and these are] made to interact with one another so as to obtain approximately optimal solutions to planning problems" (p. 444). This tactic of breaking down the overall problem of optimizing organizational effectiveness into optimizing the performance of subsystems as they interact has led to the practical definition of a number of prototype problems. The following two examples should illustrate their nature.

The *replacement* problem is the problem of making efficient decisions about the replacement or maintenance of equipment used by the organization. There are three types of such problems: (1) replacing or maintaining major capital equipment sometimes used indefinitely but at a steadily increasing cost (with age); (2) replacing equipment in anticipation of complete failure; and (3) selecting a preventative maintenance scheme designed to reduce probability of failure.

The *queuing* problem "consists of either *scheduling arrivals* or *providing facilities,* or both, so as to minimize the sum of the costs of waiting customers and idle facilities" (Ackoff and Sasieni, 1968, p. 249, italics theirs). Customers are not necessarily people but can be letters requiring signatures, cars needing gasoline, airplanes requiring passengers, and so on.

Overall, then, the OR approach is to study an organization (system), break it down into subsystems, define models for those subsystems, solve these models for optimal performance, and implement the indicated procedures. Over the years, modeling techniques and solutions for frequently occurring situations have been developed for each of the problem areas.

Several common themes seem to run through much of the OR literature (for example, Ansoff and Brandenburg, 1971a, b).

One is that since ultimate criteria of organizational functioning are so hard to conceptualize and measure, the next best thing is to measure variables representing the state of the system. Thus, the model of organizational effectiveness implicit in the OR approach seems to have both goal-oriented and systems-oriented elements, although, as we shall observe later, the nature of the systems variables felt to be important is considerably different from that of variables posited by the behavioral science OD orientation. Variables like morale, satisfaction, participatory decision making, managerial skills, size, technology, climate, and so on, are not addressed. Instead, only those variables that appear to be directly related to a readily measured criterion outcome and that can be manipulated by management are considered. Furthermore, there appear to have been few attempts to systematically identify just what these variables might be in any taxonomic sense.

OR methods, as outlined in texts and journals, are aimed at the control problem of organizations rather than the humanization problems (Ackoff, 1973). The general OR point of view is a decision-making optimizing one, concerned almost totally with upper-management problems. The typical OR approach is to define the goals of an organization subsystem and then to determine ways of improving operation of the system set up to attain those goals.

The construct of organizational effectiveness usually is not directly addressed. Rather it is finessed by using a mathematical model of some sort, in which the parameter values are often set by expert judgment to combine whatever specific indices are used. OR does, however, have an extensive literature dealing with optimal solutions of specific problems encountered by organizations. This constitutes an effective *intervention* technique, and anyone hoping to improve an organization's performance would be well advised to take advantage of these solutions.

Organizational Development (OD) Model. The term *organizational development* means different things to different people. In the most general sense, it could refer to any activity designed to effect some change in an organization and thus would include the efforts of psychologists, economists, industrial engineers, computer technologists, and many others. However, for present purposes, a delineation similar to that of Bennis (1969) will be used, which restricts organizational development to a class of behavioral science type intervention techniques derived from the pioneering work in T-group and sensitivity training at the National Training Laboratories during the 1950s (Bradford, Gibb, and Benne, 1964). A central concern of such techniques is to provide mechanisms by which organizational members can examine their behavior in the "here and now." Team building (French and Bell, 1973), process consultation (Schein, 1969), confrontation (Beckhard, 1969), the Managerial Grid (Blake and Mouton, 1969), and laboratory education (Bennis, 1969) are all variations on this basic theme. Intervention techniques such as job enrichment (Ford, 1969) and the Scanlon Plan (Lesieur and Puckett, 1969) do not fall into the same category.

OD has just been delineated in terms of strategies (independent variables) used to bring about change; but researchers and practitioners in the field also have theories, implicit or explicit, regarding the dependent variables for which they are trying to effect changes. Although the OD model of organizational effectiveness is not always clearly stated, it is reasonably apparent that it conforms to a systems rather than a goal view. Very seldom are effectiveness outcomes mentioned by OD writers, researchers, or practitioners. If such things as profit, turnover, and the like are mentioned at all, it is in a fairly unsystematic and casual way and only after much discussion of such factors as increased individual openness, better communications, greater individual self-actualization, and other indicators of what is considered a healthy system.

Further, in both theory and practice, OD practitioners typically go beyond general statements and seem to have a fairly specific kind of system in mind that can be used as a standard of an "effective" organization. Although there is certainly not complete unanimity among organizational development specialists regarding the characteristics of this "ideal" system, there does seem to be a consensus, rough though it may be, regarding a normative model of people and organizations that permits a description of an OD construct of organizational effectiveness.

Beckhard tried to reflect this consensus by presenting a synthesized list of characteristics that define an effective or healthy organization (Beckhard, 1969, pp. 10–11). They include the following: (1) The total organization, the significant subparts, and individuals manage their work against *goals* and *plans* for achievement of these goals. (2) Decisions are made by and near the sources of information regardless of where these sources are located on the organization chart. (3) Communication laterally and vertically is *relatively* undistorted. People are generally open and confronting. (4) There is a minimum amount of inappropriate win-lose activity between individuals and groups. Constant effort exists at all levels to treat conflict and conflict situations as *problems* subject to problem-solving methods. (5) There is a shared value, and management strategy to support it, of trying to help each person (or unit) in the organization maintain integrity and uniqueness.

Considering the assumptions and normative goals implicitly

or explicitly portrayed in this example, a picture of the "effective organization" according to OD begins to emerge. Such an organization will be aware of, open to, and reactive to change. It will be searching for new forms and methods of organizing. It will have an optimistic view of its members, allowing them room to self-actualize and trusting them with the responsibility for their own efforts. It will also seek to insure the satisfaction of its members, since that is its reason for existence. To these ends, conflict will be confronted, not avoided, and communication will occur freely and effectively.

Perhaps the following summary statements about the OD model are appropriate. OD concentrates its efforts on achieving a normative state whose worth is accepted on a priori grounds. That is, the OD model assumes that if an organization can achieve the state characterized by a list such as Beckhard's, it will be effective as an organization and will be optimally equipped to carry out its missions. Most of the variables of the OD model are concerned with the human resources of an organization rather than with technological or material aspects of the organization. These human variables predominantly have to do with phenomena of intra- and intergroup behavior.

Likert-ISR Model. In somewhat of a class by itself is a systems model of organizational effectiveness attributed to a cohesive group of researchers and practitioners at the University of Michigan Institute for Social Research: Floyd Mann, J. R. P. French, Stanley Seashore, Rensis Likert, David Bowers, and others. Since Likert has written the most influential statement of this model (Likert, 1961, 1967), it will be labeled as his, even though he is not the sole contributor.

The basic variable defining an effective system, drawn from the classic study by Coch and French (1948), is participation in decision making, or shared power. That is, to the extent that individuals can truly participate in making the decisions that will affect them, the organization will be more effectively equipped to accomplish its mission. Over the years, continued research and consulting work at Michigan (for example, Katz, Maccoby, and Morse, 1950) have added to the list of systematic variables believed to constitute an effective organization.

In his 1967 statement, Likert used the term *Systems 4* to

label what he considered to be the standard for a healthy and effective organization. The actual state of an organization was assessed via a questionnaire intended to measure the perceptions of organizational members. The principal organizational characteristics tapped by this instrument are as follows: (1) the nature of the leadership processes that are used—that is, whether superior-subordinate relationships are characterized by mutual trust, confidence, and consultation; (2) the character of the organization's motivational practices—that is, whether the compensation system was developed via participation and whether personnel at all levels feel joint responsibility for achieving the organization's goals; (3) the character of the communication processes—that is, the extent to which communication is frequent, flows in all directions, is accurate, and is genuinely listened to; (4) the character of interaction or influence processes—that is, to what extent they are friendly, extensive, and cooperative; (5) the character of decision-making processes—that is, to what extent decisions are well integrated throughout the organization in a system of overlapping groups, to what extent technical and professional knowledge is used in an optimal way, and to what extent subordinates are involved in decisions related to their work; (6) the character of goal setting—that is, to what extent goal setting is carried out by group participants and to what extent goals enjoy wide acceptance; (7) the character of control processes—that is, to what extent responsibility for control is widespread, shared across many levels of management, and supported by informal organizations, and to what extent control data are used for self-guidance and group problem solving; (8) the level of performance goals and adequacy of training—that is, to what extent performance goals are high and to what extent individual job training is thorough and proficient.

There is obviously a great deal of similarity between the Michigan characterization of an effective organization and the OD characterization as portrayed by Beckhard's list, and many of the same summary statements apply. However, at least two differences should also be noted. First, the Michigan group is much more research oriented and its members have devoted more effort to developing measures of their systems variables and to linking these variables with outcome measures such as profitability and turnover.

As a result, their variables are more concretely defined, although some would argue (Argyris, 1968) that the concreteness is illusory. Second, the Michigan list is not quite so heavily oriented toward interpersonal and self-actualization type variables.

Summary of Alternative Models of the Effectiveness Construct

It is probably not time well spent to make comparative statements about which of these various models is better or worse for some purpose. The models provide a means for looking at different parts of the effectiveness construct, and, rather than choose among them, we might better take advantage of their complementary insights. Perhaps surprisingly, the systems models make the clearest pronouncement as to the specific nature of an effective organization. For example, the OD model asserts that an effective organization is one that scores high on variables such as those discussed by Beckhard (1969). In contrast, the goal models suggest that the first task of research might be to develop methods for identifying organizations' task goals, and the second, to develop criterion measures of the degree to which the goals are being achieved. For the goal model, the criterion measures have a much less normative flavor than for the OD model.

A later section will use various points of view to map out a composite strategy of reasonable procedures for assessing organizational effectiveness. To make such a discussion as meaningful as possible, we should examine briefly the available empirical literature on attempts to measure organizational effectiveness. It is a record of some success but much heartache and does not overwhelm one with optimism.

Empirical Research Concerning Criteria of Effectiveness

Although not voluminous, there is a certain amount of *empirical* literature dealing with criterion measures of organizational effectiveness. The research was generated from a variety of different perspectives and this makes it a bit hard to summarize. For example, some studies have been done expressly for the purpose of developing the criterion measures themselves. Others have focused on predicting organizational effectiveness by using some set of independent variables; in this case the investigator's primary interest was in the predictors (for example, type of technology or style of leadership), and the effectiveness measures chosen as criteria were matters of convenience. Another source of diversity is the unit of analysis. Sometimes it is a large organization with personnel located at many places, sometimes it is all the people under one roof, and sometimes the unit of analysis is an organizational subunit corresponding to the immediate work group.

Not too many years ago, Campbell and others (1974) went through this literature and attempted to make a list of the criterion measures of organizational effectiveness that have been used. This comprehensive list, adapted from Campbell and others (1974, pp. 38–133) follows. The entries in the list are not orthogonal and not all of them have appeared in research studies. The intent was to include all variables that have been proposed seriously as indices of organizational effectiveness.

1. *Overall Effectiveness.* The general evaluation that takes into account as many criteria facets as possible. It is visually measured by combining archival performance records or by obtaining overall ratings or judgments from persons thought to be knowledgeable about the organization.
2. *Productivity.* Usually defined as the quantity or volume of the major product or service that the organization provides. It can be measured at three levels: individual, group, and total organization via either archival records or ratings, or both.
3. *Efficiency.* A ratio that reflects a comparison of some aspect of unit performance to the costs incurred for that performance.
4. *Profit.* The amount of revenue from sales left after all costs and obligations are met. Percent return on investment or percent return on total sales are sometimes used as alternative definitions.
5. *Quality.* The quality of the primary service or product provided by the organization may take many operational forms, which are largely determined by the kind of product or service provided by the organization. They are too numerous to mention here.
6. *Accidents.* The frequency of on-the-job accidents resulting in lost

time. Campbell and others (1974) found only two examples of accident rates being used as a measure of organizational effectiveness.

7. *Growth.* Represented by an increase in such variables as total manpower, plant capacity, assets, sales, profits, market share, and number of innovations. It implies a comparison of an organization's present state with its own past state.

8. *Absenteeism.* The usual definition stipulates unexcused absences, but even within this constraint there are a number of alternative definitions (for example, total time absence versus frequency of occurrence).

9. *Turnover.* Some measure of the relative number of voluntary terminations, which is almost always assessed via archival records. They yield a surprising number of variations and few studies use directly comparable measures.

10. *Job Satisfaction.* Has been conceptualized in many ways (for example, see Wanous and Lawler, 1972) but the modal view might define it as the individual's satisfaction with the amount of various job outcomes he or she is receiving. Whether a particular amount of some outcome (for example, promotional opportunities) is "satisfying" is in time a function of the importance of that outcome to the individual and the equity comparisons the individual makes with others.

11. *Motivation.* In general, the strength of the predisposition of an individual to engage in goal-directed action or activity on the job. It is not a feeling of relative satisfaction with various job outcomes but is more akin to a readiness or willingness to work at accomplishing the job's goals. As an organizational index, it must be summed across people.

12. *Morale.* It is often difficult to define or even understand how organizational theorists and researchers are using this concept. The modal definition seems to view morale as a group phenomenon involving extra effort, goal communality, commitment, and feelings of belonging. Groups have some degree of morale, whereas individuals have some degree of motivation (and satisfaction).

13. *Control.* The degree of, and distribution of, management control

that exists within an organization for influencing and directing the behavior of organization members.

14. *Conflict/Cohesion*. Defined at the cohesion end by an organization in which the members like one another, work well together, communicate fully and openly, and coordinate their work efforts. At the other end lies the organization with verbal and physical clashes, poor coordination, and ineffective communication.

15. *Flexibility/Adaptation* (Adaptation/Innovation). Refers to the ability of an organization to change its standard operating procedures in response to environmental changes. Many people have written about this dimension, but relatively few have made attempts to measure it.

16. *Planning and Goal Setting*. The degree to which an organization systematically plans its future steps and engages in explicit goal-setting behavior.

17. *Goal Consensus*. Distinct from actual commitment to the organization's goals, consensus refers to the degree to which all individuals perceive the same goals for the organization.

18. *Internalization of Organizational Goals*. Refers to the acceptance of the organization's goals. It includes their belief that the organization's goals are right and proper. It is *not* the extent to which goals are clear or agreed upon by the organization members (goal clarity and goal consensus respectively).

19. *Role and Norm Congruence*. The degree to which the members of an organization are in agreement on such things as desirable supervisory attitudes, performance expectations, morale, role requirements, and so on.

20. *Managerial Interpersonal Skills*. The level of skill with which managers deal with superiors, subordinates, and peers in terms of giving support, facilitating constructive interaction, and generating enthusiasm for meeting goals and achieving excellent performance. It includes such things as consideration, employee centeredness, and so on.

21. *Managerial Task Skills*. The overall level of skills with which the organization's managers, commanding officers, or group leaders perform work-centered tasks, tasks centered on work to

be done, and not the skills employed when interacting with other organizational members.

22. *Information Management and Communication.* Completeness, efficiency, and accuracy in analysis and distribution of information critical to organizational effectiveness.

23. *Readiness.* An overall judgment concerning the probability that the organization could successfully perform some specified task if asked to do so. Work on measuring this variable has been largely confined to military settings.

24. *Utilization of Environment.* The extent to which the organization successfully interacts with its environment and acquires scarce and valued resources necessary to its effective operation.

25. *Evaluations by External Entities.* Evaluations of the organization, or unit, by the individuals and organizations in its environment with which it interacts. Loyalty to, confidence in, and support given the organization by such groups as suppliers, customers, stockholders, enforcement agencies, and the general public would fall under this label.

26. *Stability.* The maintenance of structure, function, and resources through time, and more particularly, through periods of stress.

27. *Value of Human Resources.* A composite criterion that refers to the total value or total worth of the individual members, in an accounting or balance sheet sense, to the organization.

28. *Participation and Shared Influence.* The degree to which individuals in the organization participate in making the decisions that directly affect them.

29. *Training and Development Emphasis.* The amount of effort the organization devotes to developing its human resources.

30. *Achievement Emphasis.* An analog to the individual need for achievement referring to the degree to which the organization appears to place a high value on achieving major new goals.

One can see that these potential indicators vary on a number of dimensions. First, there are simply a lot of them, and there have been precious few attempts to weed out the overlap and get down to the core variables; but this may be for good, if not sufficient, reasons. That is, within a particular model of the organizational effectiveness construct it is proper to demand such things as internal consistency, completeness, and parsimony for the dependent variables the model outlines. However, different people adhere to different models, and there is no correct way to choose among them. Thus, when a list is put together from different conceptual points of view, the composite list will almost inevitably look messy. A proposed procedure for clarifying it a bit is presented later. Second, the entries in the list vary considerably in terms of generality or specificity, and some may legitimately be subsumed under others. Third, they vary considerably in terms of the methods used to operationalize them. Archival records, direct "on-line" recording, retrospective ratings by independent observers, and suggested self-perceptions have all been used.

A fourth general characteristic of these variables is that they vary on a continuum we might call closeness to the final payoff. For example, is job satisfaction the continuum on which the real payoffs are made or is it a means to an end? Which of these are means and which are ends calls for value judgment on somebody's part. It is made implicitly or explicitly in organizations every day and cannot be avoided. Also, if the decision is that a particular variable is a means and not an end, is it then necessary to demonstrate empirical relationships between that variable and the outcomes of real interest, or should those relationships be assumed, since the outcomes of real interest are usually so difficult to specify and measure? It is here that the goal model and the natural systems model diverge. Most theorists, researchers, and practitioners who adopt the natural systems point of view appear to accept the basic assumption that the systemic variables contained in their model are significantly related in a causal fashion to accomplishment of a variety of organizational missions. In contrast, the goal model demands data, and its adherents will naturally feel guilty if they cannot produce such data.

In the best of all possible worlds, it would be nice to have some overall hierarchical map of how the criteria fit together in terms of their generality-specificity and means-end relationships. Almost by definition such a map will be impossible to construct, except perhaps within the confines of a particular theory of organizational effectiveness that provides a procedure for determining such a criterion structure.

Empirical Attempts at Criterion Organization

There have been only two really rigorous empirical attempts to examine the structure of effectiveness criteria. Both of them have used the traditional multivariate analysis approach derived from the industrial/organizational psychology model. That is, the model dictates that an investigator should amass a large sample of similar organizations or independent organizational subunits, measure each one on all thirty of the variables cited in the list previously, obtain a matrix of empirical similarities (for example, correlations) for all pairs of variables, and submit the matrix to a factor or cluster analysis (for alternative methods see Weiss, 1976). Such an approach demands a large number of observations and reliable measures of each major facet of organizational effectiveness. If such conditions are satisfied, then some clues as to the structure of effectiveness and its internal consistency can be obtained. However, we are still left with the often cited gaps inherent in the factor analytic approach. First, the picture of the more basic structure can be no better than the original sample of measures. The problem is compounded when archival measures for such things as productivity are used, since such measures never seem to be defined the same way across organizations. Second, if all the organizations or units being measured are not sampled from the same population, we cannot know the extent to which the factor or cluster solution is equally characteristic of each subpopulation. Third, a factor or cluster analysis solution also gives no clues as to the relative importance of each factor.

One of the studies using this approach was done at the University of Minnesota Industrial Relations Center by Mahoney, Weitzel, and others (Mahoney and Weitzel, 1969) and the second is the well-known effort by Seashore, Yuchtman, and others at the University of Michigan Institute for Social Research (Seashore and Yuchtman, 1967).

The Minnesota study used a questionnaire format to obtain

ratings on the effectiveness of 283 departments or subunits sampled from over a dozen different firms. The ratings were made by managers at least one step removed from the direct management of the subunit, and the questionnaires included 114 items gleaned from the literature as being potential indicators of effectiveness. The correlations among the 114 items were factored and 24 effectiveness factors were labeled and defined. Eight of the factors are described below; they are intended to be representative of the full set.

- *Development.* Personnel participation in training and development activities; high level of personnel competence and skill.
- *Democratic Supervision.* Subordinate participation in work decisions.
- *Reliability.* Meets objectives without necessity of follow-up and checking.
- *Diversity.* Wide range of job responsibilities and personnel abilities within the organization.
- *Emphasis on Results.* Results, output, and performance emphasized, not procedures.
- *Understanding.* Organization philosophy, policy, directives understood and accepted by all.
- *Planning.* Operations planned and scheduled to avoid lost time; little time spent on minor crises.
- *Productivity-Support-Utilization.* Efficient performance; mutual support and respect of supervisors and subordinates; utilization of personnel skills and abilities.

In general, the Mahoney and Weitzel (1969, p. 358) factors are meant to be descriptive and not prescriptive relative to the functioning of organizational subunits. They cover a fairly broad range on the means-ends continuum, and whether a high rating on a factor is good or bad is a value judgment on the part of the organization. As one way of "recovering" these value judgments, each subunit was also rated on "overall effectiveness," and a major additional step was to compute a multiple regression equation regressing the 24 factors against the overall rating. The regression analysis was done for different types of subunits, for organizations of different sizes, and for organizations employing different technologies. In general, the factors that account for the greatest variance in the overall effectiveness rating are not the same across the various breakdowns of the total sample of subunits. That is, the composition of overall effectiveness is different for production versus research and development units, for mass production versus unit production, and so on.

The ten effectiveness dimensions identified by the ISR group in a factor analytic study of the performance of seventy-five insurance agencies (Seashore and Yuchtman, 1967) are listed below. The basic data for this Michigan study were not questionnaire responses or subjective ratings but archival records of sales and personnel data.

- *Business Volume.* Number and value of policies sold related to size of agency.
- *Production Cost.* Cost per unit of sales volume.
- *New Member Productivity.* Productivity of agents having less than five-year tenure.
- *Youthfulness of Members.* Frequency *and* productivity of members under thirty-five.
- *Business Mix.* A combination of three conceptually unrelated performance indices, interpreted as reflecting the ability of agencies to achieve high overall performance through any of several strategies.
- *Manpower Growth.* Relative and absolute change in manpower levels.
- *Devotion to Management.* Sales commissions earned by agency managers.
- *Maintenance Cost.*
- *Member Productivity.* Average new business volume per agent.
- *Market Penetration.* Proportion of potential market being exploited.

Based on his own data and related experiences, Seashore (1972) has drawn several negative morals concerning effectiveness criteria. Liberally paraphrased, they are as follows: If several raters are asked to rank order a number of organizations or organizational subunits in terms of their overall effectiveness, the interrater agreement can be quite low. Unless they are all of extremely like mind, different raters tend to focus on different facets when making their judgments. And subjectivity is not the only problem. In the real world, criterion measures sometimes correlate negatively when they aren't supposed to. Worse yet, in the real world so-called hard data or objective criterion measures usually turn out to be quite soft. No one needs to be reminded that in almost all cases any number of artifacts and biases operate to water down the fidelity of objective measures such as profit, costs, turnover and retention rates, number of missions flown, and so on. There is no refuge in objectivity. Seashore's final moral is that in the real world it is probably a mistake to think of effectiveness criterion variables, regardless of how many there are or at what level they are, in terms of continuous and linear functions. For example, higher and higher retention rates may be "good" up to a point and then become "bad." Notice the perspiration that begins to flow when we ponder the implications of such nonmonotonic functions.

Hierarchical Versus Nonhierarchical Solutions. The two studies cited above considered multiple criteria in terms of a non-hierarchical, factor analytic model. There apparently is no research that has attempted to determine directly the *hierarchical* relationship among a representative set of criterion variables. The relationships among criteria could be hierarchical in perhaps two basic ways. One possible kind of arrangement would be a functional one. That is, the measures at one level are simply composites of measures at some lower level, and the basic functional properties of the variables are retained as one goes up the hierarchy. In a sense, the argument over the meaningfulness of a variable labeled "total performance" (Dunnette, 1966; Schmidt and Kaplan, 1971) is an argument about whether a two-level hierarchical model is appropriate. Mahoney and Weitzel implied such a two-level model was appropriate when they sought to determine via regression analysis the functional role of their individual criterion variables in accounting for the variance in the overall performance of a unit.

A second way to look at a hierarchical arrangement is in terms of the cause and effect relationships that exist, if any. For example, is morale causally related to quality of production, or vice versa, or is there some more complex reciprocal relationship? This is a critically important set of considerations since it gets at the heart of the difference between the goal and systems models of organizational effectiveness. If the causal or means-end relationship could be specified, we could go a long way toward reconciling these two points of view.

Object Lessons from Previous Research

Based on considerations of organizational effectiveness as a construct and on previous empirical research, the following generalizations seem appropriate: It is probably counterproductive to follow the multivariate approach in the development of effectiveness measures. That is, although it sounds like a good idea to assemble a large sample of organizations, measure each of them on a set of potential criteria, and then examine the pattern of relationships among the measures, it is simply not physically or economically possible to do such a study in ways that will yield useful information. To date there have been only three or four such attempts, and all of them have fallen short of the mark. Remember that each organization is only one degree of freedom, and we need lots of degrees of freedom. Also, archival or objective measures never seem to be defined the same way across organizations and this sometimes leads to rather strange-looking correlations between variables.

Searching for so-called objective measures of organizational effectiveness is a thankless task and virtually preordained to fail in the end. The conventional wisdom says objectivity is good, but a perhaps more accurate wisdom says an objective criterion is a subjective criterion once removed. For example, one might think that the number of units produced is an objective measure of an automobile assembly plant's effectiveness. However, a specific volume of production means nothing until some metric or standard is applied that informs us what numbers are good and what numbers are bad. Many subjective judgments go into the development of such standards (for example, where should production be three weeks after the model year starts) and also into the quality control judgment as to whether a unit is fit to sell or not. Similar kinds of subjective judgments can be found in *any* so-called objective measure of effectiveness, which makes using "available" objective measures (where the subjectivity is unknown) as criteria in a research study very risky business.

At this stage of the game, it is probably a mistake to concentrate our scarce research resources on attempts to develop results-oriented measures, that is, measures of the more terminal outcomes of organizational functioning, such as return on investment, productivity, and the like. These measures are often a function of many things (for example, the state of the economy) besides what the organization does (for example, the economy of its operation), and teasing out those parts which are under the control of the organization itself is a difficult task.

A number of the variables listed earlier in the chapter are aggregated individual perceptions (for example, job satisfaction, morale, and climate). Most organizations are complex enough that averaging over everybody in the organization covers up so many individual differences as to make the indicator almost useless (Seashore, 1972).

Recommendations for Assessing Effectiveness

Given the different perspectives outlined above and the rather helter-skelter nature of the effectiveness literature they have produced, is there any way to make the effort devoted to this problem yield more information than it has in the past? Here are some recommendations in that direction.

Since it is difficult to do massive studies on huge samples of organizations over long periods of time, we should recognize our limitations as researchers and devote our resources to questions and problems upon which we can have some impact. Also, there is no algorithm of science that will specify the variables that should be labeled as criteria of organizational effectiveness. That activity begins as a series of value judgments, which are usually conflicting, and ends in what is essentially a political decision. As a consequence, it seems fairly obvious that the thing for the behavioral scientist to do is to study the *process* by which people in organizations can come to some resolution of the effectiveness question. It is here that we can make a contribution.

The argument so far is that to assess organizational effectiveness one needs to adopt an explicit model or theory of effectiveness. Unless we are going to limit ourselves to conversations about basic research, it is not enough for the investigator to develop such a model; the organization must do it also. Thus, one major area for research concerns how to teach organizations about the necessity for such a theory and how best to assist them in developing their own. The core of such instruction might be something like the following, which borrows mainly from the behavioral objectives model of curriculum development, with light touches from industrial psychology and organizational development.

The people involved must first describe in very explicit terms the actual decisions or courses of action for which the effectiveness data will serve as an input. The list cannot be a cosmetic one. It must reflect the actual decisions to be made, no matter how banal, uncomfortable, or painful. As both the model and measures of effectiveness are developed, the list must always be kept in public view. To cite another example from the individual domain, the military has always had a problem with officer fitness reports (that is, performance appraisals). The distribution of rating is very negatively skewed and almost everyone looks absolutely great. However, the fitness report serves several ends, not all of which are compatible. That is, for promotional purposes it would be nice to distinguish clearly among individuals. However, a commanding officer often uses high ratings for his subordinates to create high morale in the group. Also, the higher the overall ratings of his subordinates, the better he looks to his superiors. Obviously, the same data cannot serve such conflicting demands very well, and they should not be required to do so. No amount of psychometric sleight of hand will overcome the conflict. The warning is the same for determining organizational effectiveness. At every stage in the process, two questions must be asked: Will the data base toward which we are moving really be useful for the purposes we have in mind? Are we inadvertently asking the same data to serve conflicting aims?

The next major ingredient is the specification of the task objectives of the organization or organizational subunits under consideration. Such objectives must be stated in terms of observable things the organization must do, as per the earlier discussion. The list would be quite long, highly specific, and a lot of work to generate. Obviously, this is a rejection of the notion that organizations are too complex to know what they are trying to do. It is assumed here that it is good for an organization to know what it is trying to achieve. If it does not, then it really does not know how to structure or staff itself or assess its performance. Delving into the precise form of such a list of objectives would take another thirty to forty pages and would include specific questions that only future research can answer. As a start, the reader is referred to Briggs (1968) and Mager (1962).

Once the list of task objectives is specified, the "model" now under consideration says that several judgments must be made about it. The major ones are these: First, the organization must decide which objectives are to be considered *means* and which are to be considered *ends*. Is a particular objective a dependent variable in its own right or is it really an independent variable that the organization hopes will cause certain changes in some more terminal outcome? Expressed job satisfaction is the classic example about which such a judgment must be made. To reiterate a point made previously, the systems model emphasizes "means" objectives and the goal model emphasizes "ends" objectives. In reality, they are both goal oriented. After objectives have been distinguished as means or ends, the *conditions* under which the organization should be able to accomplish a particular objective must also be spelled out to the fullest extent possible. Changes in regulatory statutes, economic conditions, and the available labor supply are examples of things to be considered. Finally, the relative *importance* of each objective should also be judged. For all the objectives considered to be bona fide "ends," or dependent variables, the organization must judge what takes precedence over what. This is, again, a value judgment. By contrast, if the status of a particular outcome (for example, high job satisfaction) is as a means to an end, then its importance is an *empirical question*.

If the above judgments are made in a thorough and systematic manner, the real conflicts in the organization will be identified. Such conflicts must be recognized and dealt with. Complete unanimity is too much to expect, and if the organization internalizes this particular theory of effectiveness, it will not have such an expectation. It is also obvious that from this point of view strategies of conflict resolution will play an important part in the assessment of organizational effectiveness.

The overall specification of organizational effectiveness, then, is the degree to which the task objectives judged to be "ends" should be accomplished, given the prevailing conditions in which the organization must work. It is at this point, and not before, that the question of how to *measure* the degree of goal attainment becomes operative. Too frequently we have jumped immediately to the question of what questionnaire or criterion measure to use before considering these prior, and perhaps more important, questions. In the training and educational field, from whence this model came, this is analogous to seizing upon a training technique before deciding what it is we want to teach.

The methods of assessment will vary according to the objectives being considered. Some objectives may require simple head counts, others (for example, job satisfaction) may require special instrumentation, and still others may require subjective ratings. However, measurement problems pale in comparison to the questions discussed previously, and if a systematic analysis of task objectives can be made, the measurement problems will be substantially solved.

One vexing problem that arises at this point has to do with *comparing* organizations in terms of their effectiveness. There may indeed be situations in which effectiveness data would be used for this purpose, though the above model tends toward an idiosyncratic definition of effectiveness. However, from a concrete decision-making point of view, such comparisons would be made only if the organizations indeed have tasks in common. If no set of common tasks can be identified, then there is something strange about wanting to make comparisons among them.

There is another use to which the catalogue of objectives can be put. Each objective can be carefully examined in terms of what antecedents *might* control its accomplishment. To accomplish a particular objective, must the organization's technology be changed, its capital resources, the skill level of its employees, or what? In the individual performance domain, the analogous question is of the form, would we "train for" or "select for" a particular kind of task performance? Even such a simplistic portrayal as the above suggests the kind of research activities that would be necessary. They are outlined briefly below.

Organizational Task Goals and Approach-Avoidance Conflict. The specification of goals cannot be avoided, no matter what implicit or explicit theory is espoused. To show a philosophical bias for a moment, *all* behavior is goal directed and organizational behavior can be no exception. Even if people cannot state their goals in any coherent explicit fashion, it should be possible to infer their goals from their behavior. Although it is difficult to support this assertion with data, many people in organizations appear to avoid making the organization's goals explicit. At the same time, they appear uneasy about not having done so. Such behavior suggests an approach-avoidance conflict. Many organizations *do* develop planning documents and written goal statements. However, these are often very general and oriented toward either global economic outcomes or a bit of momism and apple pie.

If it is true that people in organizations avoid making goals explicit, then researchers should explore the following questions: (1) What kind of goal setting now goes on in organizations? Dull though it may seem, a certain amount of effort devoted to purely descriptive research would be worthwhile. It would be useful to get some idea of the major kinds of goal-setting activities and the places in the organization where they occur. (2) From an operant point of view, what reinforcers maintain the avoidance behavior? That is, it would be desirable to observe very closely what rewards and punishments influence the behavior of the goal setters. Such research should *not* consist of making up a questionnaire that asks individuals if they are goal setters and, if so, what reinforcements act upon them. Participant observation, nonparticipant observation, simulation, or some other method of independent measurement must be used.

Description of Task Goals. An important set of research questions revolve around how the catalogue of task goals can be produced. What is needed is something akin to an organizational task analysis. There are various methods for approaching such an analysis and some research exploring their relative usefulness would be desirable. Some alternatives to explore, all borrowed from the job analysis literature, are as follows.

A panel of experts could simply write down a list of task goals. Perhaps it is not terribly unreasonable to expect the powers that be in an organization to have some idea of what the organization should be doing, in specific and concrete terms. One question concerns how best to facilitate the process. The Delphi or Nominal Group Techniques, as described by Delbecq, Van de Ven, and Gustafson (1975), would be a good place to start.

The existing goal descriptions could be examined, much in the way a job analyst pours over training manuals, existing job descriptions, and so on. In the organizational context, the existing policy and planning documents could be searched as well as the existing literature on effectiveness criteria cited earlier in this paper. For example, taking the literature on "organizational climate," someone should really review all the measures item by item, weed out the overlap, and produce a total listing of all the unique items. The people in a particular organization could then decide which constitute relevant goal statements for them.

Both participant and nonparticipant observers could be used to observe and record what the organization appears to be trying to do. There have been very few observational studies of what organizations actually *do*. Perhaps this is a very mistaken impression, but behavioral scientists interested in organization (with the exception of some sociologists, perhaps) seem to have lost their powers of observation. We are neck deep in questionnaires, but observations of actual behavior are rare.

Critical incident methodology (Flanagan, 1954) could also be used to develop the content of the task goals. Critical incidents can be recorded in a diary soon after they happen. In the present context, the objective would be to describe specific episodes in which an organization (or subunit) accomplished a specific task objective or failed to accomplish an objective. As always, the individuals describing the objectives must be carefully coached in how to describe things in specific and concrete terms. The critical incident technique requires panels of knowledgeable judges, and the question of who judges is paramount. There is no straightforward answer except to say that in any situation there are probably several groups of individuals who might have different perspectives or expertise to offer. Systematic comparisons between groups of judges would reveal important differences regarding the value systems that operate in an organization and would add a great deal to the meaning of the effectiveness construct. Again, it would be profitable to explore these techniques in a research context to determine how best to produce the statement of task goals.

Problems of Data Reduction. Since there are always multivariate enthusiasts around, a reasonable question to consider next is whether or not it makes sense to cluster the set of goal statements into some arrangement of homogeneous subsets. This is primarily an exercise in multidimensional scaling. For example, a group of judges could be asked to judge the similarity among all possible pairs of goal statements. A multidimensional scaling model could then be imposed on the similarity judgments to determine the clarity with which a smaller subset of goal dimensions could be recovered. If a series of such studies were done in a variety of organizations, we could begin to get some idea of how feasible and meaningful it is to reduce large numbers of specific organizational task goals to a smaller number of homogeneous subsets.

Perhaps we should ask why all this emphasis is put on scaling technology? The answer is that in the end organizational effectiveness is what the relevant parties decide it should be. There is no higher authority to which we can appeal. On the applied level, the task of behavioral science is to assist the people in the organization to articulate what they really mean by organizational effectiveness, show where there are gaps and inconsistencies, reveal conflicts, and help in the resolution of those conflicts. This does not preclude the behavioral scientist from trying to impose his or her own value system as to what constitutes effectiveness, but such an assertion should be recognized for what it is.

Judgment of Goal Importance and Means-Ends Relationships. As noted above, an organization must make two critical judgments concerning its array of task goals: (1) which goals are means and which are ends, and (2) what is the relative importance of those goals judged to be ends. Again, there are a number of ways of making these judgments, which can perhaps be classified into direct and indirect methods.

We could, in so many words, ask a panel of judges to rate directly the extent to which each goal is a consequence of every other. A number of interesting scaling problems emerge from such a question. For example, something analogous to paired comparisons could be used to rate the extent to which A (quality of production) is a consequence of B (morale) and the extent to which B (morale) is a consequence of A (quality of production). The anguish and the inconsistencies that are revealed in this process should say a lot about how the relevant parties conceptualize effectiveness. The judges could then be asked to rate the importance of each task goal in terms of its contribution to each specific target decision. For example, how important is knowledge about voluntary turnover for deciding whether the organization is effective or ineffective. To make the rating feasible, the context of the judgment would have to be specified in a systematic way, either by specifying the conditions under which the organization must operate or by letting the judges specify the conditions relevant to their judgments.

There are a number of indirect ways one could go about obtaining the same kinds of judgments. Some of them are dependent on being able to construct a large sample of hypothetical organizations for which the degree of attainment of various task goals can be systematically varied. For example, one task for the judges would be to judge the relative effectiveness of each pair of organizations, using some form of paired comparisons procedure. Multidimensional scaling procedures (Shepard, Romney, and Nerlove, 1972) could again be imposed on the similarity judgments to determine the number of recognizable clusters of organizations that emerged. The characteristics of the organizations in each cluster could then be examined for the purposes of determining the goal accomplishments most salient for each cluster.

Varying the instructions for the similarity judgments would be a valuable source of information. For example, insights could be gained by asking for judgments both in terms of which of two organizations is more *effective* and which is more *ineffective*. The two judgments are probably not symmetrical, and it would be valuable to know what variables characterize the asymmetry.

A similar procedure could be used if it were possible to assemble a sample of real organizations with which a set of judges would be reasonably familiar. Notice that in this case the investigator would not be limited to an a priori list of variables with which to characterize the organizations in each cluster. The characteristics identifying each cluster would be searched for after the fact. Such a procedure has some obvious advantages and disadvantages. Variables that are not in the original model but that are important determinants of the similarity judgments can perhaps be identified. However, the investigator also runs the risk of inferring that certain variables are more highly characteristic of a cluster than they really are. That is, the investigator may see more distinctions than are actually there.

Two Alternative Strategies. At this point, one might legitimately ask, Isn't there any research we can do in the real world to investigate what *independent* variables actually distinguish between organizations that are effective and organizations that are ineffective? The answer is yes, but certain qualifications must be attached. First, what we mean by effectiveness must be explicated, which requires research such as that just described. Up to this point, the discussion has really been about questions of value. Questions of fact revolve around the cause and effect relationships, the empirical covariation among task accomplishments, and the like. The argument here is still that cause and effect relationships or even patterns of covariation among different variables cannot be determined by massive studies that cover many organizations and rely on multivariate analysis. A few brave researchers have tried such strategies, most notably those at Michigan (Franklin, 1973), but the payoff has been difficult to interpret.

What then can one do? There are really only two choices: (1) carefully done simulation studies, and (2) very intensive and very thorough case studies. Saying this is painful, especially since it completely violates the basic precepts of my own training gained in the midwestern empirical dust bowl. Nevertheless, using the organization as the unit of analysis forces us into such a situation.

There is already a large literature on laboratory simulations and experimentation in organizations (see Fromkin and Streufert, 1976; Weick, 1965) that offers many possibilities not yet fully exploited, perhaps because there are so few people nurtured in the experimental tradition who are also interested in these messy, molar organizational phenomena.

In this context, a *case study* refers to a very intensive longitudinal monitoring of each relevant variable in a specific organization, using a variety of observational and data collection techniques. For example, behavior observation, interviews, questionnaires, and archival records could all be used to monitor changes in supervisory practices and concomitant changes in productivity. Enough questions would have to be asked and enough data collected to enable the researcher to trace the effect, if any, of one variable on the other and to rule out specific competing explanations. All of this is no small undertaking, and as yet the organizational literature provides no good examples. Two other research paradigms come close. One is from ecological psychology, most notably the studies by Barker (1968) and his colleagues. In fact, the developing methodology in ecological psychology (Craik, 1973) would not be a bad place for organizational theorists to browse. The second comes from the operant or "behavioral analysis" literature, where there is much emphasis on within-subject design, ABAB treatment patterns, baseline measurement, and the like. It is a powerful approach for locating causality and deserves wider use in organizations. Finally, I am well aware that case studies have their problems, but I think they offer considerable potential for learning something fundamental about the interrelated facets of organizational effectiveness.

This chapter has ended with the author in a rather peculiar and uncomfortable position. First, the prevailing winds in organization theory and research are not blowing toward a highly specific goal-oriented view of effectiveness, and the arguments just presented must lean against the wind. Second, the framework presented here will entail more work to implement than almost any other strategy one could use, which is not what people want to hear. Third, it will not be much fun, the gratifications will not be very immediate and the opportunities to do something "clever" will be rare. Finally, advocating a return to the case study and $N = 1$ studies as methods of exploring causal relationships may appear to be regressing toward more ambiguity and less control in research.

A summary response to the above concerns is that (a) it is time to go against the wind since we are currently being blown into confusion, (b) a strong dose of the Protestant ethic and hard work would not be all that bad, and (c) our current research methods lack fidelity. Somehow we must develop a richer data base such that the results of a study will have a genuine impact on the people who worry about organizations and how they function.

3

Emergence
of the Instrumental
Organization

Larry L. Cummings

John P. Campbell titles his essay "On the Nature of Organizational Effectiveness," yet it is not clear what is intended by the word *structure* in the essay. Four alternatives come to mind: (1) structure as a nomological network embracing several dimensions and measurements of the subcomponents of structure; (2) structure in a hierarchical sense—that is, the aggregation process applied to levels of analysis across individuals, units, organizations, and even societies; (3) the structure of reciprocal influences within and across organizations—that is, the structure of the process by which organizations impact one another and their task environments in the development of their domains and their mandates for effectiveness (Thompson, 1967; Pfeffer, 1976); and (4) the structure of a procedure for developing and implementing measures of organizational effectiveness. The idea of effectiveness being characterized by a structure is stimulating. But Campbell's definition of structure is not clear.

In his concluding recommendations for assessing organizational effectiveness, Campbell clearly indicates his perspective (at the applied psychological level of distinction) by his comment, "On the applied level, the task of behavioral science is to assist the people in the organization to articulate what they really mean by organizational effectiveness, show where there are gaps and inconsistencies, reveal conflicts, and help in the resolution of those conflicts." Therefore, the final step in advancing the science and practice of effectiveness is conflict resolution. This is a novel twist on organizational effectiveness (Filley, 1975). Campbell's approach to this task is essentially a technical core orientation. That is, if we could imagine an organization whose mission was to define organizational effectiveness, Campbell's essay could represent the beginnings of a blueprint for the operation of the technical core of such an organization.

The essay's discussion would be enriched by placing it within a context where the construct of effectiveness is essentially negotiated within an organization, along with the measures of effectiveness and their use, and where organizations are, for the most part, neither effective nor ineffective. Rather they are allowed, or even *encouraged,* to move into and out of an arena where effectiveness is competitively determined rather than politically determined within a shielded environment. Within this sort of context, the criterion development orientation of Campbell's essay becomes more interesting and, of course, extremely practical.

Campbell asks why individuals within organizations attempt to avoid *value questions* related to organizational effectiveness. The answer to this probably derives from the missing contextual links in Campbell's essay. That is, people wish to avoid these questions because (1) the answers to such questions tend to freeze negotiation positions or imply static logics—they imply predictability and control of member A by member B, and (2) they are not really relevant to day-to-day operating within an organization. More relevant are concerns such as the *face* validity of goal statements, negotiation of freedom and latitude, and control over the measurement process (this, in turn, provides substantial control over *what* is to be measured) versus fear of being controlled by it. Our understanding of organizational effectiveness will be enhanced by recognizing the political nature of the goal effectiveness establishment process and the assessment process itself.

Campbell argues that to query whether an organization is effective or ineffective is a useless question. But this assertion does not go far enough. Effectiveness may be seen by many successful managers (those who somehow get to the top of their organizations and make the most money within their organizations) as best defined *in process*. The object is to end up being good at what is measured. There are two ways to achieve this end. One can obtain a clear photograph of the goals and then strive to meet them. Alternatively, one can engage in a continuous process of creating a movie, and when a criterion or standard emerges one can selectively recall and present behaviors and outcomes that best meet what is expected. The latter view seems descriptive of much managerial reality. Resistance to a priori definitions of effectiveness may be a logical managerial response.

Campbell concludes that it is counterproductive to follow the multivariate approach. There is little evidence to support this in Campbell's essay. Only two studies are reviewed, and these are not particularly discouraging. Furthermore, Campbell returns to multi-dimensional scaling as a possible method for clustering goal statements. Thus, the argument that multivariate approaches are not likely to be fruitful seems to be based mostly, if not completely, upon financial and convenience considerations. If future conceptualizing and research on effectiveness are to focus on the *organizational* level of analysis, then multivariate studies across organizations will be required.

Campbell further argues that it is a mistake to concentrate resources on developing results-oriented measures. Whether social scientists have any real choice but to do this in a competitive society if they wish to be listened to by organizational decision makers is questionable. Ultimately, the lack of cause and effect models and the reliance on process models without goal components lead to managerially meaningless conclusions. Campbell is not optimistic in this regard. He seems to argue that typical cause and effect analyses have not led us far and will not in the future because of physical and financial problems of design.

Campbell contends that outcome measures are not particularly appropriate because organizations may not be able to control the variables that impact the outcomes. It can also be argued, however, that those who have expectations of organizations do not ask *whether* effectiveness is under the control of the target organization. Rather, they imply that if their expectations are not met, then the target organization has the problem of bringing the key determinants under its control or inventing new determinants. Responsibility and authority for organizational action have seldom been commensurate, and there is little reason to predict that they will be.

Campbell's overall suggestion is basically one of an intervention strategy aimed primarily at the process of defining organizational effectiveness criteria. This perspective avoids, or at least begs, the basic question: Process for what purpose? The strategy suggested by Campbell has little evidence to support its effectiveness as a conflict resolution mechanism when aimed at value conflicts. The strategy may assist members in discovering and discussing their differences. But by now we certainly know that such discovery and discussion do not necessarily, or even usually, improve organizational performance.

Alternatively, perhaps Campbell is suggesting that the criteria for evaluating most organizations are sufficiently face valid for most consumers of such criteria that questions of whether we can research them are not highly relevant. Applying these face valid criteria becomes the crucial issue in managing organizations. The process suggested by Campbell may well add credibility to the self-image of management as a rational process.

The Instrumental Organization

One possibly fruitful way to conceive of an organization and the processes that define it is as an instrument or an arena within which participants can engage in behavior they perceive as instrumental to their goals. From this perspective, an effective organization is one in which the *greatest percentage of participants* perceive themselves as free to use the organization and its subsystems as instruments for their own ends. It is also argued that the greater the degree of perceived organizational instrumentality by *each* participant, the more effective the organization. Thus, this definition of an effective organization is entirely psychological in perspective. It attempts to incorporate both the number of persons who see the organization as a key instrument in fulfilling their needs *and*, for each such person, the degree to which the organization is so perceived.

Within this framework, organizational efficiency, profitability, and productivity become necessary minimal conditions for organizational survival. They are not, however, the goals of an effective organization. In order for an organization to be effective in this instrumental sense, a subsystem must be concerned with showing that performance meets the standards that external constituencies (for example, resource suppliers) monitor. This is necessary in order to provide the resources needed to make the organization instrumental for its participants. Also, an effective organization would develop a subsystem that buffers this legitimatizing subsystem from the environment in order to efficiently produce outputs that are desired by the environment. These outputs are the mechanisms through which resources are yielded to the organization so that it can become an instrument for fulfilling its participants' needs.

There are several implications of this perspective: To understand and to influence effectiveness within organizations (and of organizations), we need both perspectives, that of the core of participants and that of the legitimatizing and buffer subsystems. However, the legitimatizing subsystem is a servant of and instrumental agent for the core. The agents engaged in legitimatizing behavior do, partially, and perhaps secondarily, buffer the technical core for efficiency, but (and more importantly) their primary mandate is to allow participants to pursue their own motivational/political agendas.

Two measurement implications arise when effectiveness is defined as the percentage of participants who perceive (and the degree to which they perceive) that the organization is instrumental to the attainment of their personal valued outcomes. Measurement would need to focus on participants' perceptions of their present organization as an instrument compared with other organizations (for example, from previous experience) and on participants' perceptions of present (actual) instrumentalities compared with ideal, desired instrumentalities.

This perspective changes the societal functions performed by organizations. Organizations are best assessed as instruments of outcomes; that is, the effective organization is the organization that best serves those who perceive it (relative to other avenues) as a means to their ends. The independent variables typically studied in organizational behavior (leader behavior, structure, task design, technology) will be assessed in terms of their impact upon the proportion of participants who see instrumentalities in the organization, upon the degree of instrumentality they perceive, and upon the number of organizational mechanisms or vehicles they perceive as instrumental to their valued ends. The relevant administrative questions become: Do we design tasks to maximize instrumental perceptions? Do we structure organizations to maximize instrumental perceptions?

This perspective suggests at least two research areas worthy of exploration: One concerns the determinants of inconsistencies in perceptions of instrumentalities given agreed values and strategies for resolving conflicts. These determinants underlie the integration or the segmentation of organizations. They are crucial to our understanding of the cohesion of social units and social systems. The other concerns the determinants of differences in the perception of independent variables that are susceptible to administrative action and that cause participants to view their organizations instrumentally.

Increasingly, scholars from varying disciplines and orientations are depicting organizations as arenas within which actors play out their own agendas, or as performances without script or program. That is, organizations are seen as being enacted in process. These perspectives imply that the criterion of effectiveness and its assessment are multidimensional, time-bound and dynamic, subject to negotiation, and organizationally, or even unit, specific. One implication of these speculations is that it is increasingly likely to be profitable to use research designs of $N = 1$. Several variants of this design are likely. Two of the more prominent are the ABA reversal design utilizing either natural or contrived reversals, and intensive, longitudinal case studies.

Several constructs, each implying issues and decisions for the researcher and the assessor of organizational effectiveness, seem to describe the present state of our knowledge of effectiveness assessment. These are dimensionality; time perspectives; levels of analysis (the aggregation question); process versus content focus; comparative frame of reference (absolute versus relative); the roles of actors in relation to the organization (for example, actors as a *determinant* of organizational behavior, as agents exerting effects on organizations; actors as a *constituent*, as agents who make claims on the organization).

Each of these issues implies decisions and choices. Choices on each of the above issues must be seen as necessary for each study of organizational effectiveness. The outcomes of the choices (for example, what dimensions to measure, what time perspectives to take, what level of analysis to use, and so on) impact the design of a study in a significant manner. These are issues that are not appropriately settled once and forever. They need to be faced and decided for each new study. In fact, the outcomes of the choices may well develop as a taxonomy for classifying studies and organizing our literature over the next decade.

4

Effectiveness of Organizational Effectiveness Studies

W. Richard Scott

$\mathbf{A}$fter reviewing a good deal of the literature on organizational effectiveness and its determinants, I have reached the conclusion that this topic is one about which we know less and less. There is disagreement about what properties or dimensions are encompassed by the concept of effectiveness. There is disagreement about who does or should set

This paper was written when I was serving as Senior Researcher at the Intramural Research Division, National Center for Health Services Research. The center's support is gratefully acknowledged.

63

the criteria to be employed in assessing effectiveness. There is disagreement about what indicators are to be used in measuring effectiveness. And there is a disagreement about what features of organizations should be examined in accounting for observed differences in effectiveness.

In this essay we shall first attempt to specify what aspects of goals are (and are not) relevant to the study of effectiveness and identify the variety of parties involved in setting goals for the organization. We shall also inquire whether it is realistic or useful to continue to pursue the quest for universal criteria of effectiveness. Next we shall explore what we believe to be a relatively neglected area, namely the selection of the indicators used in evaluating effectiveness. Three types of indicators will be examined—outcomes, processes, and structures—the costs and benefits of each assessed, and their advocates identified. Finally, we shall comment briefly on current attempts to explain the effectiveness of organizations. Here, the contingency approach will be stressed and some modest suggestions made for its improvement. Illustrations will be drawn largely from a study of hospital effectiveness in which I am currently involved.

The Problem of Goals

One reason why the concept of effectiveness is in trouble is that it is necessarily related to the concept of organizational goals— one of the most complex and controversial topics in organization theory. It may be helpful to point out that goals are employed in at least three kinds of statements about organizations. First, they are often discussed as motivational factors. Thus, Selznick (1949) points to organizational goals (he refers to them as ideologies) that motivated participants to heroic efforts on behalf of the Tennessee Valley Authority (TVA), and Clark and Wilson (1961) describe

Portions of this paper draw on a study of surgical care conducted under the auspices of the Stanford Center for Health Care Research, Stanford University. I am much indebted to my colleagues in this ongoing research program, especially William H. Forrest, Jr., Byron William Brown, Jr., Wayne Ewy, Ann B. Flood, and Betty Maxwell. The research was sponsored by the Assembly of Life Sciences, National Academy of Sciences, and supported primarily by Contract PH 43–63–65, National Institute of General Medical Sciences, administered through the National Center for Health Services Research, U.S. Department of Health, Education and Welfare.

"purposive" organizations—organizations, like amateur political groups, whose goals supply incentives to participants. Clark and Wilson's typology emphasizes that most organizations do not rely on their goals to provide incentives to members—purposive organizations are only one of several types—and their analysis suggests that organizations that do so may have difficulty in maintaining a constant flow of incentives (see also Wilson, 1962). The point, however, is that some analysts focus on organizational goals as sources of incentives for participants.

Second, organizational goals are very frequently discussed as guides to participants' efforts. Simon (1964) is a prime example of an analyst who is less concerned with the motivational or cathectic dimension than with the directional or cognitive dimension of goals. He emphasizes the role of organizational goals in participants' decision making, arguing that organizational goals may be viewed as constituting a set of constraints on individual decisions. Simon (1957a and b; 1964), like March (March and Simon, 1958), is behaviorist enough to avoid overstating the rationality of organizations: He emphasizes that factors such as perceptual bias, differential location, and subgroup loyalty distort the relation between goals assignment and implementation. The presumption is, however, that organizational goals are set—perhaps through a very complex set of bargains struck by members of dominant coalitions—and that they have some influence on the behavior of participants.

The capability of organizations to set goals that direct the energies of their members, although widely accepted, is increasingly being questioned. Starbuck (1965), for example, has argued that in many cases goals are not set internally but are imposed on the organization by environmental forces. And Rosengren (1975) has recently elevated this condition into what he terms a "nutcracker" theory of organizations, insisting that organizations are increasingly subject to commonweal expectations and regarded as "general resources that may legitimately be reoriented—by force if necessary—to serve the goals and purposes of multiple external publics" (p. 277).

But it is probably Weick (1969) who has managed to stake out the most extreme agnostic position concerning the extent to which organizations set goals that direct behavior. He argues that goal statements, because of their diversity and vagueness and because of the uncertainty of the future, exert little control over participants' actions. If the concept is to be used at all, goals are better understood not as prescriptions for the future but as explanations of the past—as attempts to impose order in retrospect upon past choices and actions. A critique of these positions is not in order at this point, but we feel compelled to point out that organizational autonomy, goal specificity, goal consensus, and environmental uncertainty are all factors that vary widely across organizations, and it seems unwise to attribute to all organizations lack of autonomy, vagueness or dissensus on goals, and environmental turbulence.

These conflicting views of goals as factors that do or do not motivate and direct the behavior of participants are reviewed here primarily so that they may be set aside as largely irrelevant to our present topic. All these arguments concerning types of incentives, power contests among participants and constituencies in goal setting, and organizational rationality are sufficiently engrossing to have seduced many would-be analysts of organizational effectiveness into hopeless entanglements. But these issues are not directly related to the determination of organizational effectiveness. In focusing on effectiveness we need to emphasize a third aspect of goals: They provide criteria for identifying and appraising selected aspects of organizational functioning. In short, we must analytically distinguish between goals employed to motivate or direct participants' behavior, on the one hand, and goals used to set criteria for the evaluation of participants' or the entire organization's behavior, on the other (see Dornbusch and Scott, 1975, pp. 136–138). This distinction may seem arbitrary or artificial, or both, but it calls attention to the empirically observed circumstance that the goals set in an attempt to motivate and direct the behavior of organizational participants may not be the same as those that specify the criteria by which the organization's performance is appraised.

This approach also allows us to redraw the goal circle to incorporate some analysts who have disassociated themselves from the conventional goal models. For example, Yuchtman and Seashore (1967) reject the goal approach in favor of a system resource model, which emphasizes an organization's ability "to exploit its environment in the acquisition of scarce and valued resources" (p. 898).

However, although rejecting the notion that goals supply direction for participants' behavior, they implicitly recognize the need to identify criteria for determining effectiveness—for their model this means criteria for determining the relevant resources to be acquired. Determining these criteria is necessary in order to assess organizational effectiveness as measured by resource acquisition.

In a perfectly rational world, we would expect the goals used to motivate and direct work to be identical with those used to evaluate it—but the laws prescribing rationality have long since been suspended. Instead, we must be prepared to observe different criteria employed by those who assign tasks and those who evaluate performance. This can occur even when the same persons or groups perform both activities. Discrepancies are, of course, much more likely when these activities are performed by different parties. Necessarily, the number of persons or groups who attempt to specify criteria for evaluating the performance of an organization can be a much larger set than the number who explicitly attempt to direct its activities.

Given that goal setting and allocation and performance evaluation are not one-time events but ongoing processes, choice of criteria for evaluation at a given time may be expected to sometimes feed back on the specification of tasks at a later time. In this way we would expect evaluation criteria to influence indirectly the specification of goals that direct participants' efforts. This process gives rise to behavior that is described by Buckley (1967) as "goal-directed, and not merely goal-oriented, since it is the deviations from the goal-state itself that direct the behavior of the system rather than some predetermined internal mechanism that aims blindly" (p. 53). Clearly defined evaluation criteria can provide a basis for goal statements directing subsequent behavior. For this to occur, however, we must assume rationality of behavior, specificity of evaluation criteria, and considerable knowledge of cause-effect relations linking behavioral alternatives and goals. Therefore, we shall not presume that all organizations are goal-directed in Buckley's sense or that there is necessarily any association between the goals used to direct organizational behavior and those used to evaluate it. In summary, it is useful to recognize that goals enter into discussions about organizational behavior at numerous points, but for present purposes we shall want to concentrate attention on the use of goals to supply criteria for assessing organizational effectiveness.

Evaluation Criteria. Working within a somewhat different problem context, Dornbusch and I have attempted to explicate the elements that minimally comprise evaluation criteria. Because it appears to be useful for proceeding with the problem at hand, that analysis will be briefly summarized at this point. Three distinguishable types of decisions are required in establishing criteria for evaluating any person or product (Dornbusch and Scott, 1975). They are: (1) selecting the characteristics or properties to be assessed; (2) if more than one property is involved and an overall evaluation is to be made, determining the weights to be assigned to each property; and (3) determining the standards against which observed values on properties are to be assessed. Of course, goals vary in terms of the precision and specificity with which they select properties, determine their relative importance, and establish standards against which observed performance values can be assessed, but all of these decisions must be made in some fashion if a nonritualistic evaluation is to be made.

The setting of standards is a central component in establishing criteria for evaluating the effectiveness of an organization. Clearly, these standards are normative and not descriptive statements. As Etzioni (1960) notes in his influential paper on goal versus systems models for evaluating effectiveness, "Goals, as norms, as sets of meanings depicting target states, are cultural entities" (p. 258). These normative statements are to be compared with selected indicators of the actual behavior of organizations. This procedure, however, disturbs Etzioni, who argues that it involves "comparing objects that are not on the same level of analysis, as, for example, when the present state of an organization (a real state) is compared with a goal (an ideal state) as if the goal were also a real state" (p. 259). But surely this is a misconception of the situation. The problem is not one of comparing real and unreal states or one of differing levels of analysis. If evaluations of effectiveness are to be made, then target states must be determined, and these states, regardless of how they are arrived at, will be normative in character.

A genuine problem noted by Etzioni is the tendency for organizations to establish unrealistic standards—in his terms,

"Olympic heights of the goal" (p. 259). Simon (1957a) insists that organizations are (and should be) happy to settle for satisfactory as opposed to optimal performance speaks for more realistic standards. The problem of how standards are set is an interesting one, which has largely been neglected by sociologists. Cyert and March (1963) have attempted to adapt the psychological concept of aspiration level to explain how organizations establish goals for use as evaluative standards. They argue that "organizational goals in a particular time period are a function of (1) organizational goals of the previous time period, (2) organizational experience with respect to that goal in the previous time period, and (3) experience of comparable organizations with respect to the goal dimension in the previous time period" (p. 123). And Thompson (1967, pp. 84–98) notes that "standards of desirability" vary in their specificity from being "crystallized to ambiguous" and that the level of performance that is expected will vary as a function of the efficacy of the technology and the selection of reference groups.

Most important for present purposes is the recognition that assessments of organizational effectiveness are never purely descriptive or objective in character. The selections of properties, weights, and standards are decisions that always rest on more or less explicitly formulated normative statements or assumptions. To seek purely empirical methods for making these decisions is to pursue an illusion. A central issue then becomes, Who establishes the criteria for evaluating the effectiveness of organizations?

The distinction proposed between goals for motivating and directing participants and goals for evaluating organizational performance prepares us for situations in which those who attempt to control the organization are different from those who attempt to assess its effectiveness. The more conventional situation, of course, is that in which those who direct organizations also determine the criteria for assessing effectiveness. For a great many organizations and for a variety of analytic purposes the evaluative goals embraced by organizational directors will be of greatest relevance.

In examining the behavior of the directors of organizations, two considerations are of immediate interest. First, how much agreement is there among these individuals about the criteria to be employed; and second, how much consistency is there between the criteria employed for assessing organizational performance and the goals announced to participants in allocating work? Mohr (1973, p. 473) has argued that the notion of goal involves intent, and since only individuals, not organizations, can intend anything, we must employ aggregate rather than global measures of goal statements. Thus, the matter of agreement or consensus becomes crucial. This is especially true as the number and variety of participants in the dominant coalition increase—as generalist entrepreneurs are replaced by specialist technocrats (Galbraith, 1967). Nevertheless, in multifaceted systems such as organizations there is no reason to expect or demand high consensus on goals, either for allocating work or for evaluating it. The extent of consensus may make for important differences in the effectiveness of the organization as defined by some criteria, and so it is a variable of interest, but we should not be surprised to discover that many organizations exhibit relatively low consensus on goals.

We should also be interested in determining the extent of consistency between the goals used to direct work and the goals employed to evaluate it. Situations can be imagined in which vague criteria are used to direct task activities; very specific criteria are employed in their evaluation, with the consequence that evaluation criteria deflect attention and effort from the original stated objectives. For example, criteria may focus on the task components that are most easily measured and ignore others less readily assessed, the result being a displacement of goals, a type of situation described by Blau (1955), Berliner (1957), and Dalton (1959), among others. In my view, the proposed distinction between goals for directing work and goals for evaluating work may represent a clearer way of describing the familiar distinction between official and operative goals (Perrow, 1961).

Turning from the organization directors to other constituencies, such as rank-and-file participants, consumers or clients, regulators, stockholders, and selected publics interested in one or another aspect of the organization's functioning, we may expect all of these groups to employ special criteria in assessing organizational effectiveness. All will have goals *for* the organization, which they fondly hope will become goals *of* organization, in Thompson's (1967) language. These groups will vary in their coherence or internal consensus as well as in their relative power to promote their interests, but all will feel free to make their assessments. The actions resulting from these assessments by constituents will also vary a good bit depending on the action alternatives available and the mechanisms established for registering approval or disapproval. As Hirschman (1970) has argued in his brilliant essay on this subject, two broad classes of alternatives are available to dissatisfied parties: *exit*— taking one's business elsewhere—and *voice*—expressing one's dissatisfaction. These *economic* and *political* alternatives, which can often be exercised in various combinations, can provide important early feedback to organizations about some aspects of their effectiveness. Hirschman encourages organizations to foster these feedback loops by which publics can communicate complaints cheaply and effectively so that the "repairable lapses of economic actors" may be corrected before an organization is in serious trouble. Note that it is not necessary to assume that the constituencies and organization directors agree on the goals to be employed as evaluation criteria. If some relevant public, for example consumers, applies criteria that leads it to be dissatisfied with the organization's service or product, then it will usually be in the interests of the directors to find this out as quickly as possible. They then must determine whether and how to respond to this information.

Given the wide variety of participant groups and constituencies attempting to set criteria for organizational effectiveness, what generalizations, if any, can be suggested to guide investigation in this area? We offer three general comments. First, the criteria proposed by each group will be self-interested ones. Customers will desire higher quality at lower cost, suppliers will wish to sell more dearly and wholesalers to buy more cheaply, workers will prefer higher wages and greater fringe benefits, and managers will seek higher profits and lower costs. We should not look for heroes or villains (although there will be fools who do not clearly see where their own best interests lie). Of course, the relative power of groups to pursue their own interests will vary greatly. Second, although no criteria are disinterested—each will benefit some groups more then others—all will be stated so as to appear universalistic and objective. Pfeffer and Salancik (1974), examining the allocation of resources within a university, argue that whereas universalistic criteria govern the budgeting process, the stronger departments make certain that the criteria employed happen to favor their own position. Third, given a set of actors pursuing their own self-interests and a situation of scarce resources, we would expect little commonality or convergence and some conflict in the criteria employed by the various parties to assess organizational effectiveness. This expectation received confirmation in a study of small businesses by Friedlander and Pickle (1968), who report relatively low and sometimes negative correlations between effectiveness scores across a set of criteria of presumed importance to owners, employees, creditors, suppliers, customers, governmental regulators, and the host community. They conclude that "organizations find it difficult to fulfill simultaneously the variety of demands made upon them" (pp. 302–303).

Finally, researchers who attempt to assess organizational effectiveness are not immune to these sociopolitical processes. Which, and whose, criteria we choose to emphasize in our studies of organizations will depend on our own interests in undertaking the study. The important thing is to state clearly what criteria we wish to employ and to recognize that whatever they are, and whoever espouses them, they are always normative, will serve some interests more than others, and are likely to be controversial.

The Search for Universal Criteria. We have argued that participants and constituencies associated with an organization may utilize varied and sometimes conflicting criteria in assessing the effectiveness of the organization. Not too surprisingly, there is a similar lack of convergence among the criteria utilized by social scientists studying organizational effectiveness. In a recent survey of this literature, Steers (1975) distinguishes between studies focusing on single versus multiple properties in assessing degree of effectiveness. An unpublished paper by Campbell (1973) is described that reviewed those studies focusing on a single property. Campbell is reported to have identified nineteen different property variables that have been used as indicators of effectiveness. Steers' survey concentrated on seventeen studies employing multiple properties in assessing effectiveness. He reports: "One of the most apparent conclusions emerging from a comparison of these multivariate models is the lack of consensus as to what constitutes a useful and valid set of effectiveness measures. While each model sets forth its three or four defining characteristics for success, there is surprisingly little overlap across the various approaches" (pp. 547–549). Moreover, correlations between indicators on the various properties are often low or negative or erratic across the organizations studied (Seashore, Indik, and Georgopoulos, 1960; Katz and Kahn, 1966).

Presumably, one important reason for the variety of criteria employed by organizational analysts is that these researchers adopt to varying degrees the criteria employed by one or another group of organizational participants or constituents. Given the variety of interests involved, this explanation should account for a good deal of the variance. However, another explanation of equal or greater importance is the variety of theoretical perspectives or models that researchers have used to guide their investigations. At the risk of some oversimplification we can briefly suggest the implication for studies of effectiveness of three influential perspectives: the rational, the natural, and the open systems models.

The *rational system model* views organizations as instruments for the attainment of specified goals (Gouldner, 1959). A mechanical model is implied in which goods or services are produced by the organization for external consumption, so that emphasis is placed on measures of productivity (number of units produced in a given time period) or efficiency (number of output units produced for a given number of input units).

The *natural system model* views organizations as social units capable of achieving specified goals but simultaneously engaged in other activities required to maintain the unit itself (Etzioni, 1960). Employing an organic model, it stresses the system's capacity for survival. Although it is possible to elaborate greatly the types of goals pursued (see Perrow, 1970, pp. 133–174), most natural systems analysts are content to add a set of "support" goals, required to maintain the system itself, to the "output" goals emphasized by the rational systems model (Gross, 1968; Mohr, 1973). Specifically, attention is directed to such properties as participants' satisfaction or morale (a measure of whether inducements are sufficient to evoke adequate contributions from participants; see March and Simon, 1958, pp. 83–99), profitability (the excess of returns over expenditures), and survival.

The *open system model* views organizations as highly interdependent with their environments and engaged in system-elaborating as well as system-maintaining activities (Buckley, 1967). The approach taken is oriented much more to the study of processes than structures—examinations of input, throughput, and output processes of materials, information, and energy being central to the analysis. Effectiveness criteria implied by this model include adaptability or flexibility (the ability to adjust to externally induced changes; see Georgopoulos and Tannenbaum, 1957) and maximization of bargaining position, as reflected in the organization's ability to exploit its environment in the acquisition of scarce and valued resources (Yuchtman and Seashore, 1967).

Yet another type of factor producing divergence in assessment criteria is time, in two senses. First, the criteria employed vary depending on whether a relatively shorter or longer time frame is assumed (Gibson, Ivancevich, and Donnelly, 1973). Steers (1975) provides an example: "if current production, a short-run effectiveness criterion, is maximized at the expense of research and development investments in future products, an organization may ultimately find itself with an outmoded product and threatened for its very survival, a long-run criterion" (p. 553). Second, organizations are at different stages in their own life cycles, and criteria appropriate for one stage may not be for another. As Seashore (1962) has noted, "the meaning of growth for the health, survival, and overall effectiveness of the organization was very different at different stages of the organizational life cycle" (Katz and Kahn, 1966, p. 149).

In sum, the search for universal criteria of organizational effectiveness would appear to be in difficulty because the many parties associated with the organization assess effectiveness by means of different and potentially conflicting criteria and because organizational analysts employ assessment criteria generated by differing and somewhat conflicting theoretical models. Add to these disagreements differences in time horizon and life cycle, stir, and we have a recipe for confusion and dissensus. Given these problems, in my opinion it will be more useful at the present stage of theoretical development to formulate more limited criteria that (1) make explicit the normative basis for our choice; (2) call attention to those who support or share them and to those who oppose them; and (3) allow us to make more specific comparisons between organizations along the dimensions selected.

The Problem of Assessment

Assuming that some kind of decision has been reached about the evaluation criteria to be employed in assessing organizational effectiveness, we must next determine what kinds of information reflecting organizational performance are to be collected. Social scientists have been less concerned with this type of question than with the question of goals. However, the area is not without its problems, as we shall see.

We shall focus on the assessment of performance on output goals, although much of what we have to say is equally applicable to support goals. Most but not all of our examples will be taken from organizations dispensing medical care. We believe there are advantages to be gained from continuity of illustrative material and that more precise questions can be formulated when a specific type of organization is identified. We choose medical organizations because this is an area in which we are currently conducting research on organizational effectiveness.

What types of information must be gathered to allow us to assess organizational performance? Determining the properties, weights, and standards to be used does not fully answer this question. We must also have indicators of the values that have been attained by the organization on the selected properties (Dornbusch and Scott, 1975, pp. 140–141). Writing about the assessment of quality of medical care, Donabedian (1966) argues that such indicators may be based on three types of data: information concerning outcomes, processes, and structures. Since these categories are clearly applicable to a wide variety of organizational settings, let us examine each in turn.

Outcomes. Outcome indicators focus attention on specific characteristics of materials or objects on which the organization has performed some operation. Examples of outcome indicators for surgical procedures in medical care organizations are measures of patients' mortality or morbidity or return to function. Outcomes are often regarded as the quintessential indicators of effectiveness: Were the desired changes actually produced in the patient's health status, in the student's learning, or in the engine's performance characteristics? However, outcomes are never pure indicators of performance quality since they reflect not only the care and accuracy with which work activities were carried out but also the current state of the technology and the characteristics of the organization's input and output environments. Thus, the patient's medical status following surgery will reflect not only the quality of care rendered by the surgical staff and hospital personnel but also the development of medical science with respect to that type of problem and the patient's general physical condition and extent of surgical disease at the time of the operation.

Clearly, one does not wish to hold individual providers culpable for inadequacies in the knowledge base on which practice rests. When the knowledge of cause-effect relations required for the transformation of inputs into desired outputs is not complete, then the standards employed should not be absolute but relative, comparing the performance of several organizations performing similar work. This approach presumes that the organizations assessed can (or should) participate in the same general cultural system and have access to the same general knowledge pool. A particular organization possessing more relevant knowledge—for example, having better trained personnel—that improves its performance would be expected to perform better than one possessing less knowledge, but the use of relative standards assures that an organization is not penalized for lacking knowledge that no one has.

The problem posed by the contribution of variations among input characteristics to variations in outcomes experienced is less easily resolved. Although we can safely assume that organizations have access to the same knowledge, we cannot assume that they have access to the same client pool or supply sources. Indeed, one of the principal ways in which organizations vary is in the amount and quality of inputs that they are able to garner. Further, the patterns of inputs characterizing various organizations are not as simple as might appear on the surface. As might be expected, prestigious universities recruit highly intelligent students, as indicated by IQ scores and standard entrance examinations, and less highly regarded institutions accept higher proportions of less qualified students. By contrast, highly regarded teaching hospitals focus primarily on the care of the very sick or of those whose problems pose the greatest challenge to medical care organizations. There is an inverse relation between presumed quality of institution and patient condition. (It may be noted also in this regard that the institutions of lowest esteem, the proprietary hospitals, are commonly condemned for the practice of "creaming," or selecting only the easiest cases to process.) Understandably, organizations wish to take credit for acquiring inputs that enhance outcomes—a widely used indicator of quality for universities is the quality of the student body they are able to attract—but do not wish to be blamed for inputs that negatively affect outcomes. Thus, hospitals insist that outcomes be standardized to take account of differences in patient mix.

In order to illustrate how difficult it can be to adjust for differences in inputs that affect outcomes, I shall report briefly on the approach being pursued by our research team in adjusting surgical outcomes for patient mix differences among hospitals in an ongoing study of organizational factors affecting quality of surgical care (for details, see Staff of the Stanford Center for Health Care Research, 1976; Scott, Forrest, and Brown, 1976). The study was conducted in seventeen acute care general hospitals and included only those patients undergoing one of fifteen surgical procedures who agreed to participate. Data describing the patients' conditions prior to surgery were gathered from several sources. Information on age, sex, extent of insurance coverage, and level of stress was obtained by patient interviews prior to surgery. The anesthetists recorded the patients' preoperative physical status, cardiovascular status, and the urgency of the procedures. The surgeons answered a short list of questions pertaining to the extent or stage of disease for each patient, these questions depending on type of surgery. Still other data were obtained by chart review. The principal outcome measures employed were morbidity assessed at the seventh day after surgery or day of discharge, if earlier, and mortality measured at the fortieth day after surgery.

The general approach employed was one of indirect standardization in which expected outcomes for each patient were generated that could then be compared with observed outcomes. To develop the prediction equations, all study patients in a single surgical category were pooled disregarding hospital location. Patient characteristics—in particular, age, sex, insurance coverage, stress, physical status, cardiovascular status, emergency status, and extent of surgical disease—were associated with each type of outcome (for example, mortality at forty days) by fitting a logistic function to the data. In this manner, the probability of a given outcome for each patient, based on his particular characteristics, could be calculated. The importance of the individual characteristics as predictors of outcomes varied from one surgical category to another. For example, physical status was the most predictive characteristic of death at forty days for gastric ulcer surgery, whereas stage of disease was more predictive for surgery of major abdominal arteries. After the probability of a specified outcome was determined for each patient, these expected outcomes were summed over all study patients within a hospital, by surgical type and for all categories combined. As a summary index of outcomes for each hospital, the ratio of actual to predicted outcomes of a specified type was calculated. These ratios measured the departure, in either direction, of the actual outcomes experienced by patients in a given hospital from those that would be expected based on knowledge of the characteristics of the patients undergoing treatment in that hospital.

This procedure has been described in some detail in order to illustrate the potential complexity involved in attempting to remove the effect of input differences in order to focus on the effect of the transformation processes internal to the organization. It is considerably more elaborate than other approaches to adjusting for differences among hospitals in patient mix (compare Roemer, Moustafa, and Hopkins, 1968; Shortell, Becker and Neuhauser, 1976) and yet its degree of success remains uneven. Even though we attempted to maximize explained variance within each surgical category by developing separate prediction equations (which assigned different weights to the various patient characteristics) and by developing measures of disease stage particular to each category, our success in predicting outcomes varied greatly by surgical type. This conclusion is based on results from a related series of linear equations used to predict combined measures of morbidity and mortality variously weighted. The range is from abdominal hysterectomy with a multiple R (correlation coefficient) of only .14 to spenectomy with a multiple R of .60. Since the predictor variables were selected in close consultation with surgical specialists and anesthesiologists, we conclude that it is often difficult to determine which input characteristics are most salient for predicting outcomes.

If the outcomes of interest reflect not only changes in the state of the object processed but also depend upon their reception by groups external to the organization, then outcome measures will be influenced by the relation between the organization and its market environment. Thus, indicators of outcomes relating to sales, for products, or to placement or rehabilitation, for prisoners or mental patients, will reflect not simply organizational performance but also market conditions. Hospitals might seem to be exempt from such factors, but they may not be. For example, a hospital can be linked to a long-term care facility in such a manner that it can discharge fatally stricken patients to it, thereby reducing its in-hospital mortality rate. Assessments based on in-hospital indicators of patient outcomes should adjust for such environmental conditions. As with inputs, organizations will prefer to take credit for conditions enhancing outcomes but will insist that conditions having a negative effect be taken into account if outcomes are evaluated.

Katz and Kahn (1966) have proposed that a distinction be made between the terms *efficiency* and *effectiveness*. They employ the former term to refer to the technical ability of an organization to minimize the costs of transforming specified inputs into acceptable outputs. The term *effectiveness* is used to refer to the organization's ability to maximize returns to it by whatever means, including not only the technical efficiency of its throughput processes but the management of its input and output environments by political and other means. This distinction is useful since it emphasizes the extent to which organizational outcomes can be affected by favorable economic locations or political processes. However, it seems inadvisable to restrict the meaning of the term *effectiveness* to the accomplishment of goals of interest exclusively to organizational directors. Katz and Kahn acknowledge this limitation but can do nothing to correct it since their formulation is embedded in a managerial frame of reference.

Regardless of which criteria are used to assess organizational effectiveness, we must deal with the issue of what factors contributing to outcomes we will want to include as measures of organizational performance and what factors we will want to adjust for or attempt to hold constant. Do we wish to adjust for differences in student intelligence among universities in assessing student performance, or do we wish to regard student recruitment as an important aspect of a university's performance? Do we wish to adjust for market differences in assessing a firm's retail sales, or do we wish to consider ability to build a solid market an important component of the firm's performance? Clearly, these questions are not methodological but theoretical and require careful consideration of what outcomes are to be assessed. This question in turn is related to a more basic query: What aspects or components of the organization are we attempting to appraise? We shall return to this question subsequently.

Very briefly, many other types of issues must be addressed when outcomes are to be evaluated. One important problem relates to the availability of information on outcomes (and on those other factors to be taken into account in their assessment) and to the relative validity and reliability of these data sources. Questions of validity and reliability are especially critical when the outcome of interest involves some underlying state or process, such as changes in a patient's health status or in a student's knowledge level. Any particular indicators used (with the possible exception of death as a measure of health status) will reflect only imperfectly variations in the general underlying states. Researchers have been encouraged to utilize data compiled by the organization itself, but many types of organizations have virtually no data on outcomes achieved. In addition to the difficulties entailed in measuring changes in underlying states, many organizations lose contact with their "products"— whether human graduates or manufactured commodities—immediately after the transformation process has been completed. The collection of relevant outcome measures can become very costly indeed if it entails tracking down such products after they are distributed throughout the environment. Other types of performance records such as profit and loss statements may not be valid for comparative studies because of the variations in accounting practices and management concerns.

The absence of objective indicators of organizational outcomes has led some researchers to rely on subjective appraisals of performance. Georgopoulos, for example, in both his studies with Tannenbaum of delivery stations (Georgopoulos and Tannenbaum, 1957) and his studies with Mann of hospitals (Georgopoulos and Mann, 1962), employs such reputational measures of effectiveness. Even though fairly high levels of interrater reliability are reported in these studies, we have reason to question the validity of such subjective assessments. In both studies, raters were cautioned to take into account situational factors affecting performance, but it is questionable whether observers lacking specific types of information are capable of such mental experiments. And, the different results obtained by the use of observational as compared with reputational measures in another research area—that of community power— should put us on our guard (Walton, 1966).

Finally, yet another important matter concerns the time at which outcomes are assessed. Many educators claim, for example, that relevant outcomes can only be assessed long after the student has left the school and attempted to apply his knowledge in the "real world." As already reported, for the study of surgical outcomes data were gathered on morbidity at the seventh day after surgery or at the time of discharge, if earlier, and on mortality at the fortieth day. Choice of any specific time period for this type of assessment must, of course, be somewhat arbitrary, but we attempted to select an assessment point late enough to pick up relevant changes in health status but early enough to reasonably be attributed to the surgical episode under study. It might be argued that since we were dealing with different types of disease processes, the time at which outcomes were assessed should have been varied to take into account differences in the usual pattern of recovery. However, we found little information regarding these patterns and were reluctant to introduce yet another variable affecting the comparability of the outcome measures. The general point is, however, that selection of the time at which outcomes are to be assessed is an important decision that will have consequences for the results observed and conclusions drawn.

Partly because of these quite formidable difficulties in assessing outcomes, other types of indicators of organizational effectiveness are often preferred. These can be more briefly described.

Processes. Measures of organizational processes are widely utilized in assessing organizational effectiveness. The standards employed focus attention on the activities performed by organizational participants, and assessment consists of determining the degree of conformity to these performance standards.

Many of the measures employed monitor activities believed to affect work quality or quality control. Thus, at the individual participant level, physicians may be evaluated on the appropriateness of the laboratory tests ordered or the completeness of the medical history taken. At the organizational level, hospitals may be evaluated on their autopsy rate or the number of cases reviewed by the tissue committee. Much recent effort has gone into developing and testing protocols and audit procedures to govern in-hospital activities. As might be expected, systematic approaches to the assessment of care processes have developed and spread most rapidly among nursing units within hospitals (see Carter and others, 1972; Phaneuf, 1972; Browning, 1974), but audit procedures for physicians are currently under development (see Lembcke, 1967; Payne, 1966; American Hospital Association, 1972) and in some form must be rapidly implemented in all U.S. hospitals. This, at least, is the intent of recent federal legislation establishing professional standards review organizations to monitor in-hospital care processes (U.S. Congress, 1972).

These developments are being watched with interest by many sociologists because they involve an attempt to externally monitor and regulate the behavior of a professional group long noted for the autonomous functioning of its members. However, they are of interest to us in the present context because of the extent to which they reveal reliance on process measures to assess quality. It is important to emphasize that all process measures evaluate conformity to a given standard of performance but do not evaluate the adequacy or correctness of the standards themselves. They are based on the assumption that it is known what activities are required to ensure effectiveness. Although this assumption may be readily accepted by some with respect to medical care, it is strongly questioned by others, who point to studies showing a lack of correlation between conformity to process standards and effectiveness of care as measured by outcomes. A recent study comparing care quality measured by both process and outcome indicators concludes, "This study demonstrated that the results of an assessment of quality of care will vary with the method used to measure it" (Brook, 1973, p. 59). Those interested in improving outcomes fear that emphasis on process measures may stifle innovation, freezing practice in patterns whose efficacy has not been demonstrated, and increase the quantity, and hence costs, of services dispensed. As Brook (1973) argues: "Since it is the tendency of most professionals to overestimate the effect of their activity on health, it is likely that many process statements that are really unnecessary will be included in the final criteria list used to evaluate care. . . . It has been shown in this study that correlation between process and outcome for most parameters was nonsignificant and for others it was weak. Consequently, regulation on the basis of process information will increase costs but is unlikely to improve the component of health under control of the medical care system" (p. 57).

We have been focusing on process measures aimed at assessing *quality* of performance. Other types of process measures are widely employed to gather data on *quantity* of activities performed. Quantity measures may be used when there are no salient qualitative differences in the product or when it is difficult to assess relevant differences. In any case, organizations gather and report as indicators of effectiveness such measures as number of visits to clients by caseworkers, number of applications processed by interviewers, and number of student contact hours per faculty member. Indeed, for a large number of organizations these are the *only* effectiveness measures systematically collected.

Organizations are more likely to compile data on process measures than on outcome measures. Indicators of quantity and often indicators of quality are regularly monitored. Gathering information on work processes, however, can be problematic. Inspections based on observation of ongoing performances are both expensive and reactive—that is, likely to influence the behavior observed. Focusing on the level of the individual worker, Dornbusch and I have emphasized the importance of visibility of work—either performances or outcomes—to the making of sound evaluations. But we also have emphasized the variety of barriers to work visibility and the problems that may interfere with attempts to monitor work processes in organizations. Workers usually resist attempts to directly observe their work in process and often collectively organize to prevent such interference. Many kinds of work occur under circumstances that render routine inspection impossible; and other kinds, such as those emphasizing mental activities, are by their nature difficult to observe. Further, some aspects of work performance are visible to some evaluators but not to others. For example, the scholarly work of professors may be visible to their colleagues but not to their students, whereas their teaching activities are visible to their students but often not to their colleagues (Dornbusch and Scott, 1975).

Partly because of such difficulties, organizations sometimes attempt to rely on self-reports of activities performed. However, self-reports are also expensive because they consume valuable participant time and are likely to be biased and incomplete. Patient charts represent an interesting example of participants attempting to keep a record of their own activities. These charts are often used in the evaluation of care processes. But, as Donabedian (1966) notes, "much discussion has centered on the question of the completeness of clinical records and whether, in assessing the quality of care based on what appears in the record, one is rating the record or the care provided" (p. 177).

Reflecting on the importance of process measures for assessing performance and on the variety of difficulties noted even in this brief account, we can better understand Haberstroh's (1965) two major conclusions drawn from his review of the literature on performance measurement: "First, performance reporting is omnipresent and necessarily so. Second, almost every individual instance of performance reporting has something wrong with it" (p. 182).

Structures. Included within the category of structures are all measures based on organizational features or participant characteristics presumed to have an impact on organizational effectiveness, including administrative processes that support and direct production activities. Examples for hospitals include measures of the adequacy of facilities and equipment, the qualifications of medical staff as reflected in training and certification, and the adequacy of administrative support structures and fiscal arrangements. These are the types of measures that have formed the basis of accreditation reviews and hospital licensure systems (Somers, 1969; Porter-field, 1973). They have also been used by sociologists as quality indicators in hospital studies (see Goss, 1970; Heydebrand, 1973).

If process measures are once removed from outcomes, then structural indicators are twice removed, for structural measures index not the work performed by structures but their capacity to perform work—not the activities carried out by organizational participants but their qualifications to perform the work. As Donabedian (1966) notes in his discussion of structural indicators of medical care quality, "The assumption is made that given the proper settings and instrumentalities, good medical care will follow. This approach offers the advantage of dealing, at least in part, with fairly concrete and accessible information. It has the major limitation that the relationship between structure and process or structure and outcome is often not well established" (p. 170).

Structural indicators focus attention on organizational inputs as surrogate measures for outputs. Economists are apt to argue that quality of outputs should not be confused with quality (and cost) in inputs, but Yuchtman and Seashore (1967) are close to embracing this position in their influential paper on organizational effectiveness. They argue for defining the effectiveness of an organization in terms of its ability to acquire scarce and valued resources (for example, expensive facilities and highly qualified personnel), making the explicit assumption that an organization's bargaining position in its input environment is "a function of all the three phases of organizational behavior—the importation of resources, their use (including allocating and processing), and their exportation in some output form that aids further input" (p. 898). This is a defensible approach although it involves a very narrow criterion of effectiveness: It explicitly embraces the interests of the organizational directors and incorporates only those aspects of output "that aid further input." This criterion is broadened in those cases where we can presume that the organization's clients or customers can evaluate the outputs they receive or are able to shift their business to alternative suppliers, thus withholding resources from organizations not perceived to be serving their interests. But where these assumptions are unwarranted Yuchtman and Seashore's model of effectiveness is narrow indeed.

As was the case with process measures, structural measures of effectiveness can have negative consequences for outcomes when utilized as regulatory mechanisms. For example, personnel licensure requirements, developed to insure that only qualified staff are employed by hospitals, have become a major obstacle to innovations and improvements in the deployment of personnel. Thus, Tancredi and Woods (1972) charge that "one of the major impediments both to the optimal utilization of existing categories of health personnel and to the development of new categories of auxiliary workers is the body of state professional licensure laws" (p. 328). And Hersey (quoted in Somers, 1969) is even more critical of this approach: "The major effect of our mandatory licensing system for professional and occupational specialists in the health field is to establish a rigid categorization of personnel that tends to interfere with the organization of services by health institutions to meet the demand of patient service" (p. 91).

So, we have the interesting situation in which proposed measures of organizational effectiveness based on the assessment of both processes and structures are argued to be detrimental to organizational effectiveness as assessed by measures of outcomes. This implies, at the very least, that we should give careful consideration to our selection of the types of indicators to be employed in assessing effectiveness.

Sampling Techniques. It is necessary to determine not only what types of information to gather for assessing effectiveness but also what sampling techniques to employ in gathering the information (Dornbusch and Scott, 1975). The term *sampling* is intended to comprehend all decisions relating to data gathering, given that the type of indicator—whether outcomes, processes, or structures—has been selected. We must not overlook the impact on our conclusions of such decisions as sample size and other factors affecting representativeness of the observations made, but we wish to emphasize here the critical importance of the definition of the universe from which the sample is to be drawn.

Two types of definitions of the universe are frequently employed in assessing organizational effectiveness. The first focuses on the actual program of the organization—its structures, processes, and outcomes—and seeks to ascertain their quality or effectiveness.

The second takes a broader perspective—asking whether the organization is engaged in the right program. Never mind how good it is at what it does. Is it doing the right things? Does it possess the necessary structures, is it carrying on essential processes, or are the outcomes it achieves those for which it should be aiming as specified by these broader criteria?

For medical care organizations, this distinction is seen most clearly with regard to outcomes. Reinhardt (1973) refers to it as one of *microquality* versus *macroquality:* "A good part of the criticism directed at the existing health care sector in the United States is that, traditionally, American providers—in particular the medical profession itself—have emphasized the quality of services delivered (microquality) at the expense of the accessibility of health care to all (macroquality)" (p. 179). It can make a considerable difference in the conclusion reached as to whether the effectiveness of a medical care organization is assessed in terms of the health status of the clients who have received services or by the health status of the population residing within the organization's service area.

Preferred Measures. Each of the various types of measures—structural, process, outcome—and sampling frames—micro, macro—provides information about organizational effectiveness as related to outputs. However, we would expect to find different measures preferred by different participant and constituent groups. Generally speaking, we expect organizational directors to emphasize structural measures of effectiveness, in part because these represent factors somewhat under their control. Thus, hospital administrators have some influence over the types of facilities provided or the standards used in hiring personnel.

By contrast, we would expect rank-and-file participants to emphasize process measures of effectiveness. Skilled and semiskilled workers, who have little or no discretion in the selection of their activities, will prefer to be evaluated on the basis of their conformity to the performance program rather than on the efficacy of those programs. Even professionals, who are granted discretion in their choice of activities, will usually prefer to be evaluated on the basis of process measures—their conformity to "standards of good practice"—since inadequacies in the knowledge base mean that they lack full control over outcomes.

Clients who utilize the products or receive the services are likely to focus primarily on outcome measures of effectiveness. They will evaluate the organization's product in terms of the extent to which it has met their own needs and expectations. Did the motor run? Was something of interest or use learned? Was their pain relieved or their functioning improved? Clients who receive personal services are also likely to place considerable value on certain types of process measures having to do with promptness, courtesy, and sensitivity of treatment. And, in some circumstances, for example, where the outcomes relate to changes in underlying states and so are difficult to evaluate, process measures may receive more weight than outcome indicators. The most extreme cases may involve ritual organizations in which no outcomes at all can be demonstrated to regularly occur—although they are alleged to occur—so that both participants and recipients devote attention to evaluating conformity to established norms of practice.

All of the interest groups considered to this point—organizational directors, rank-and-file participants, and consumers or recipients of services—are likely to focus on microquality indicators. They will prefer to focus on the structures, processes, and outcomes associated with the work that the organization is actually performing. But another interest group—representatives of the public at large, including some public regulatory bodies—will be more likely to emphasize measures of macroquality. Is the organization concentrating its attention and its resources on the proper products or problems? Is the community as a whole benefiting from its operation?

There remains to be considered one final constituency. We refer, of course, to the "objective" scientific analysts of organizational effectiveness. We would hope to find this group busily engaged in analyzing all types of indicators of effectiveness, exploring their interrelation, and employing criteria variously drawn from all of the interested parties. Although I have not conducted the kind of systematic survey of the literature required to support such a conclusion, it appears to be the case that we analysts have emphasized structural or process measures of effectiveness—the types of measures preferred by organizational directors and participants—to the neglect of outcome measures—preferred by clients and the public. Both ideological and economic factors help to produce this bias. Organizational analysts are more likely to identify with organizational directors and professional participants than with client and public interests. Indeed, much of the research on organizations is conducted by those who train future managers while consulting for the present ones. Also, most of the data we have available to us for analysis are data collected by the organization itself or data based on information supplied by the organizational directors. Organizations are much less likely to collect data based on outcomes than data based on structural features and processes. If we want data on outcomes—and especially on macromeasures of outcomes—we shall have to collect them ourselves (or persuade governmental agencies to collect them for us). We should not minimize their cost, nor should we minimize their value in correcting the bias that currently exists in indicators of organizational effectiveness.

The Problem of Explaining Effectiveness

The problems of goals and their assessment, which have been discussed here at length, can be quickly summarized: (1) Criteria for evaluating organizational effectiveness cannot be produced by some objective, apolitical process. They are always normative and often controversial, and we must be prepared to defend our choice. (2) Similarly, the indicators to be utilized in assessing organizational effectiveness must also be chosen from among several possible types and the data gathered from several possible sampling frames. We should not expect much convergence of these various measures, and we should expect that our choice will influence our findings. Given these conclusions, the primary message of this last discussion can perhaps be anticipated: (3) We should not seek explanations for organizational effectiveness in general since it is not clear to what, if anything, this concept refers. Rather, we should attempt to develop and test more precise predictions relating particular measures of effectiveness to particular features of organizations or systems of organizations.

In 1968, Price had the misfortune to publish a propositional inventory of the empirical literature on organizational effectiveness that was out of date the day it appeared because it was written without knowledge of the paradigm revision under way as a result of the efforts of Burns and Stalker (1961), Woodward (1965), Lawrence and Lorsch (1967), and Thompson (1967), among others. In a very few instances, Price's propositions take into account the complexity of the organization or the professionalization of its staff, but for the most part, the predictions are developed without conditions. For example: "Organizations that have a high degree of division of labor are more likely to have a high degree of effectiveness than organizations that have a low degree of division of labor (p. 16). . . . Organizations that have continuous systems of assembling output are more likely to have a high degree of effectiveness than organizations that have batch systems of assembling output (p. 39). . . . Organizations whose systems of communication are primarily instrumental, personal, and formal are more likely to have a high degree of effectiveness than organizations whose systems of communication are primarily expressive, impersonal, and informal" (p. 175). Our reaction to these propositions as simpleminded reveals the extent to which our thinking has been transformed by the contingency model.

We mean by the *contingency model* to refer not to any specific set of substantive predictions but rather to the general expectation that what constitutes a "good" organizational arrangement will depend on what the organization is attempting to do and on the conditions under which it is attempting to do it. After the long search for "the one best way to organize," this insight was hard to come by, but now that it has been won, the contingency approach seems so obviously correct that we are not likely to give it up easily.

Indeed, having embraced the contingency model in relating organizational features to the nature of the work done, we would extend the model in our studies of organizational effectiveness to emphasize that our choice of organizational features should depend upon what measures of effectiveness we wish to use. Our previous discussion has stressed the variety of criteria, properties, indicators, and sampling frames that may be employed in assessing effectiveness. We need to know clearly what we wish to explain before we attempt to set about explaining it.

This suggests, in turn, that we should pay more attention to the outputs or effects that are to be explained, a position endorsed by Weick (1974b), who has recently admonished organizational analysts to "obsessively analyze effects" (p. 376). Weick begins with an extended quotation from Cohen and Nagel (1934), which says, in part: "When a plurality of causes is asserted for an effect, the *effect* is not analyzed very carefully. Instances (outcomes) that have significant differences are taken to illustrate *the same* effect. These differences escape the untrained eye, although they are noticed by the expert. Thus, the way in which a house burns down when an overturned lamp is the cause is not the same as when defective wiring is the cause" (p. 270). Weick (1974b) then concludes: "My argument is that we typically do a fine-grained analysis to isolate separate causes but then do a coarse-grained analysis when we examine effects. We treat effects more crudely than we do causes. If we tried obsessively to discriminate subtle differences in effects, we would probably find more single-cause, single-effect relationships than we now see" (p. 366).

The necessity of distinguishing between closely related effects is illustrated by the behavior of the outcome measures in our study of surgical care in hospitals. Outcome measures included the number of patients undergoing surgery in each hospital who died within forty days; the number who were judged to have severe morbidity at seven days after surgery; and the number who were judged to have only moderate morbidity at seven days after surgery. Each of these measures was indirectly standardized to take into account differences in patient mix among hospitals. We had expected these outcomes, as indicators of quality of surgical care, to be positively interrelated. This was the case for the measures of mortality and severe morbidity but not for the measure of moderate morbidity, which revealed only a small positive association with severe morbidity and a moderate negative association with mortality. Examination of these unexpected patterns in outcome measures revealed that different types of outcomes were dominated by different surgical procedures, suggesting that hospitals performing well in types of surgery associated with high mortality or severe morbidity may do no better, or perhaps not perform as well, on other types of surgery associated with moderate morbidity. This explanation is currently being explored. It serves here to underline the importance of carrying on a "fine-grained analysis" of the effects we seek to explain.

Although recommending that contingency theory be embraced as an intellectual style, we must also recognize that the approach is void of content or substance. To assert that in order to be effective organizational structures should be appropriate to the work performed and the conditions under which it is performed tells us nothing about (1) what aspects of the work are relevant; (2) what aspects of working conditions are relevant; (3) what is meant by "appropriate"; and (4) what is meant by "effective," a question that should sound familiar by this time.

A rapidly growing literature does exist that provides some guidance in answering these questions, but the principles developed are generally vague and need to be carefully adapted for application to specific settings. For example, there is considerable agreement among contingency theorists that when work is complex and uncertain, specification of procedures will lower work quality (see Thompson, 1967; Perrow, 1970). Although the general principle is clear, its application to a specific setting may not be. Thus, Perrow (1972) has taken Neuhauser (1971) to task for his application of this generalization in a hospital setting, as follows: "Tasks are complex on the medical side of the hospitals, so when dealing with doctors, specification of procedures should be low. But the specifications of what kind of procedures? Any, it seems. For example, he includes the number of tests required at admission . . . and the number of limitations placed upon the surgery that people can perform (a general practitioner cannot do heart surgery). Using knee-jerk theorizing, he says that if there are a lot of specifications of these kinds, quality should be low. Presumably he could have included scrubbing before surgery as a specification of procedures that would lower quality when tasks are complex" (p. 420).

The offense illustrated by Neuhauser's application of contingency theory is unfortunately all too common. We are too often in thralldom before a general principle, applying it mindlessly to situations whose complexity swamps whatever truth might have been revealed by a more thoughtful approach. Let us not be misunderstood: We need the guidance of general principles, but we also require enough knowledge of the organizations and their work to be able to select appropriate aspects of the work to be examined and valid indicators of the variables to be assessed. If we wish to explain outputs, there is no substitute for a knowledge of the specifics of the causal process linking them with relevant inputs and technologies and other organizational features (see Hannan, Freeman, and Meyer, 1976).

A recent article by Pennings (1975) reviews the literature on contingency models of organizational effectiveness and reports his own study of brokerage organizations. Based on his review as well as on the results of his own research, Pennings is pessimistic about the utility of this approach to organizational effectiveness. We observe, however, that both this study and that by Mohr (1971), who also failed to find supporting evidence, fail to provide a clear rationale for linking the correspondence between their measures of technology and structure or of environment and structure to their measures of effectiveness. In Pennings' research, for example, why should we expect to find the association between knowledge about competition (an environmental variable) and the distribution of power within the organization (a structural variable) to relate to aggregate performance of brokers (an effectiveness variable) as measured by summing the ratio of each broker's earned commission to the mean commission of his own seniority category? Perhaps there is a specific argument linking these variables that has not been spelled out. More likely, these were the indicators that happened to be available and were pressed into service to test the general expectation that uncertainty in environments associated with centralized decision making produces poor outcomes. If this was the case, then all we have learned is that the general model is not sufficiently powerful to be able to overcome deficiencies in our selection of indicators.

More encouraging results employing the contingency model have been reported by Khandwalla (1974). He reports that the association between a firm's orientation to mass-output technology and such structural features as vertical integration, decentralization of production decisions, and use of sophisticated controls is stronger for high-profit than for low-profit firms. In selecting this measure of effectiveness, Khandwalla not only has employed an indicator that may reasonably be expected to be associated with these independent variables; he also has taken care to select his sample of organizations in such a manner as to randomize the effect of differences in such features of market structure as concentration, probably the single most powerful environmental factor affecting profitability (see Caves, 1964).

We cannot report at this time the results of our research examining the relation between hospital structure and surgical outcomes because the analysis is not yet completed. However, enough has been said about the study to this point that we feel compelled to describe briefly the procedures we are following (for details, see Scott, Forrest, and Brown, 1976). Because our indicators of effectiveness relate to quality of surgical care, our approach has been to focus attention on those units and personnel most intimately associated with the care of surgical patients. These include the operating room complex, recovery room and intensive care units, wards caring for surgical patients, members of the surgical staff including anesthetists, and critical support units such as the blood bank and the radiology department. We also have measures of general hospital structure, administrative arrangements, fiscal hospital structure including administrative arrangements, fiscal characteristics, and roles in the regional division of labor that can be used as contextual variables in the analysis. Principal independent variables expected to be associated with quality of care include staff qualifications, complexity of the surgical tasks performed measured both from the standpoint of surgeons and nurses, the balance between integration and differentiation, and the power exercised by the surgical staff over its own members. Scores rating the complexity of the surgical tasks allow us to explore a contingent model in which, for example, surgeons' qualifications are expected to have a greater effect on outcomes for more complex procedures.

Our analysis will be conducted at the individual patient level, both because we believe that the causal process operates at this level and we wish to avoid the biases inherent in aggregating these data at the organizational level (see Hannan, Freeman, and Meyer, 1976) and because this will allow us to utilize more specific and accurate data. Patients in hospitals are not "treated" by the entire organizational structure and its associated staff but receive care from specific physicians and staff in particular units. Tracking data permit us to assign each patient not only to a specific hospital but to a particular surgeon, anesthetist, and surgical ward; and we have measures on our independent variables for each of these providers and units. Multiple regression techniques will permit us to examine the effect on patient outcomes, indirectly standardized for patient condition, of a variety of indicators of staff characteristics and subunit and organizational structures. In addition, we shall be able to determine the extent to which effectiveness as measured by patient outcomes is associated with effectiveness as measured by structural or process indicators.

Finally, we do not mean our pleas for better substantive knowledge of the situations to which we apply our general predictions to be taken as implying that we are content with the state of these general theoretical propositions. We are not. In particular, as stated elsewhere (Scott, 1975), we need to be more explicit about the ways in which organizational structures relate to environments and technologies with consequences for their effectiveness. Specifically, the contingency approach presumes that more successful (effective) organizations are those that better fit their technological or environmental situations. But how does this match come about? Assuming an ecological perspective, one can argue that the more poorly adapted organizations will fail to survive, but this does not help us with the problem of explaining why some organizations are better able to adapt than others. Unfortunately, the most prominent current theories guiding work on these problems explicitly assume rationality on the part of those who design the organizational structure (for example, Thompson, 1967; Perrow, 1970). Given other information on organizational functioning and, indeed, on human behavior generally, we find ourselves quite uneasy with this as a guiding assumption.

5

Three Types
of Effectiveness
Studies

Charles Perrow

⊂⊃⊂⊃⊂⊃⊂⊃⊂⊃⊂⊃⊂⊃⊂⊃

The type of effectiveness study discussed by W. Richard Scott and most of the other contributors to this volume is one that might be called the *variable analysis* type. After briefly discussing this type of study, which currently dominates organizational analysis, I would like to propose two other types of effectiveness studies: *gross malfunctioning analysis* and *revelatory analysis,* which asks the question, "effectiveness for whom?"

96

Variable Analysis

Those in this volume who are critical of effectiveness studies are referring to the variable analysis type, which is virtually the only type of effectiveness study now practiced by scholars. In its simplest form, it designates Y as a legitimate goal or output of the organization and studies the effect upon Y of changes in X or a number of X's. Y may be the adaptability or flexibility of the organization, productivity, profitability, amount of job satisfaction, growth, or wealth, to cite the most common dependent variables that Steers (1977) found. X may be training, supervisory style, authority structure, integration, coordination, specialization, or any number of things. A typical study, then, might ask, What is the effect of centralization of decision making on job satisfaction?

Hannan and Freeman, Scott, and others are rightly very critical of these kinds of studies. I need not repeat their criticisms here except to underline, with a personal reference, an excellent point that Scott makes. Scott notes that for any valid claims to be made about a causal connection, X and Y had better be pretty closely linked, and they often are not. I once believed that if organizations had a better fit between their technology and their structure they would be more efficient and thus more profitable. In a study of a number of firms in various industries I learned what should have been obvious to me at the outset: If the Y's are growth and profitability, the X's should not be the fit between technology and structure but such variables as market position, industry profitability and growth, brand identification, collusion, bribery, and falsification of accounting records. These relate directly to what pose as profitability and growth. My measures of technology and structure might perhaps have related to the cost per unit produced if an enormous number of controls were introduced, but I doubt even that. The managers I observed and interviewed often mentioned luck, accident, and chance, but I was not interested in uncorrelated residual effects at the time. Organizational theory is changing now, and some theorists are becoming quite interested indeed in what managers take for granted.

I have one solace from this experience: My faith in mainstream organizational theory appears to be no more naive than that of most who write about effectiveness. Scott is particularly correct on two counts in his critique: "We are too often in thralldom before a general principle" and fail to follow the complexities of organizational life through; and we assume too much rationality in organizations. I plead guilty to both. A strong note of dissatisfaction with the basic assumptions of mainstream theory sounds throughout Scott's essay, and I find myself in sympathy with it. Whether Scott's own variable analysis actually shakes loose many of these basic assumptions is a matter I shall return to later. At the least, his research avoids some of the most common errors, and, at the best, his essay helps chip away at conventional wisdom.

Gross Malfunctioning Analysis

It is striking that most variable analysis studies choose organizations that have a quite restricted range of variation on the dependent variable that is labeled a goal or ouput. We rarely compare failing businesses with highly successful ones, brutal correctional institutions with permissive or treatment-oriented ones. In fact, we rarely design effectiveness studies to deal with the reality of gross malfunctioning. Perhaps our real interest is in the independent variables, such as leadership, structure, or processes instead of in the outcomes for customers, clients, investors, or taxpayers. Gross malfunctioning we leave to journalists, muckrakers, investigatory bodies, or public interest groups.

Why? For one thing, we conceive of ourselves as social scientists, not as "reformers." We are interested in how organizations work, not why the worst ones are so bad and how they might be improved. The latter concern is not a "disinterested" one. Second, we operate under an implicit contract with our sites (when we do field studies), and that contract assumes we will investigate things of concern to the masters of the organizations. Gross malfunctioning is not something they wish attention called to. Access is also a factor. Failing businesses disappear, by definition (but inefficient ones are propped up), and the worst organizations are not likely to be cooperative. Finally, we find them less problematical. Ready explanations come to mind as to why Penn-Central was so incompetent, why

Lockheed could not build safe, flyable airplanes, why the Attica prison was so brutal and overcrowded, why medical clinics swindle Medicare and Medicaid, why some local governments are so corrupt. Note, however, that these ready explanations are those of the man in the street or the journalist; they deal with conventional wisdom. They are not the explanations we seek to test in our effectiveness studies. Conventional wisdom notes that people are corrupt, that everyone is out for himself, that there is no proper regulation or enforcement of laws, that Lockheed is staffed with ex-Defense Department officials and has plants in the states of powerful congressmen, that the public will not support decent prison facilities, and so on. Demonstrating the obvious is not the way to publish and thrive. Furthermore, bad organizations (even the phrase sounds strange to academic ears) are a couple of standard deviations from the mean and at the wrong end of the distribution. We are interested in deviant cases when they are at the other end—the International Typographical Union deviates because it should be oligarchic but is not.

Of course, I am a part of this scholarly consensus. When we planned a comparative study of juvenile correctional institutions many years ago, there was tacit agreement that there was no point in showing how dreadful the really dreadful institutions were. For our extreme case we picked a moderately punitive one. We were far more interested in getting quite unique and highly therapeutic institutions in our sample, and we were particularly excited by making the "stunning" contrast between the therapeutic institution that emphasized individual therapy and the therapeutic institution that emphasized group therapy. We argued that the latter was the most successful, but of what relevance was this to the thousands of brutal institutions or to the people who want to change brutal institutions?

Similarly, in hospital studies, it is my impression that we are seeking refined ways to discriminate between the very best and the next best. If such a measure works, it is then valid and can be used widely. Of course, the record has been rather dismal; we cannot produce such a sensitive device because of all the complexities, measurement problems, and so on. So we say we are unable to measure effectiveness of care. I once proposed at a conference of public health officials and doctors concerned with evaluation studies that the government stop funding research of this type and instead develop a simple, rough device that would distinguish the bottom 20 percent of hospitals from the rest, with a margin of error of 10 percent on each side. This would allow us to pick out the worst 20 or 30 percent of the offenders and concentrate on improving them rather than improving the best. The government officials and the doctors were appalled and I was publicly abused. The National Institute of Health, I gathered, was not particularly interested in the worst hospitals. Some of my fellow sociologists were not interested in "sloppy research."

I think we deceive ourselves when we argue, How can you know an organization is really bad, since there are so many criteria, variables to hold constant, measurement problems, and so on? I have a very alert mother-in-law with a low tolerance for foolishness living in New York City. She has many, many years of casual observations under her belt. When I visit I often have a clipping shoved at me from the *New York Times* reporting on some bit of organizational insanity or corruption on the part of the school board, the sanitation department, the police department, the mayor's office, business organizations, hospitals, professional organizations, or whatever. "You are an expert on organizations," she announces, with no intent to flatter. "Explain to me why such a thing could happen? Well, tell me." Vague mutters about goal displacement or lack of performance standards do not suffice. She is right; it is easy to identify gross mismanagement; the *New York Times* has many targets to pick from and much evidence from investigatory bodies and astute journalists. It is inconceivable to me that—to take just one example—a social scientist could argue that from the points of view of the recipients of care and of the taxpayers there is a problem in deciding whether many nursing homes or Medicaid programs in that city are really inefficient or not. Steers, in his book *Organizational Effectiveness,* has a very sensible list of recommendations for using a process model of effectiveness in our studies. But it would not begin to touch the problems of gross malfunctioning. It is designed to make A.T. & T. or Beth Israel Hospital a bit more effective, in terms of their goals. Over the years, partly from such prodding, I have been trying to understand why nothing works in that great city, in so many other organizations, and in my own grossly mismanaged university, and I have been trying to think of ways to change things.

I think this is an extraordinarily valuable discipline for sociologists accustomed to theoretical work. It leads one to look at the extremes of the distribution and at fairly gross variables that might make a gross difference. It is a primordial concern with effectiveness, and, in contrast to most variable analysis, which is preoccupied with the independent variables, it starts with a dependent variable—why this outcome? This shift in emphasis may appear elusive, but it moves us from the clean room of our depoliticized, antiseptic, autonomous professional concerns with leadership, technology, or structure to something the neo-Marxists like to call *praxis*.

Revelatory Analysis

If one rejects this activist view, as many will, there is still another kind of effectiveness study. Instead of starting with a dependent variable that is a presumed public good and asking why are we not getting it, as in the previous perspective, revelatory analysis asks "who is getting what" from the organization, or "effectiveness for whom?" The question presupposes a definition of organizations that is different from that assumed by many schools of thought. It sees organizations as intentional human constructions but not necessarily rational systems guided by official goals; as bargaining arenas rather than cooperative systems; as systems of power rather than crescive institutions reflecting cultural norms; and as resources for other organizations and groups rather than closed systems. If we define organizations, then, as intentional human constructions wherein people and groups within and without the organization compete for outputs of interest to them under conditions of unequal power, we have posed the issue of effectiveness quite differently than in the other two perspectives. We now have to ask, What does the organization produce? The answer can be revealing.

Take human service organizations, such as hospitals, prisons, social agencies, welfare departments, public schools, and so on. Some outputs that are probably far more critical for the organization than service to clients might be: providing employment opportunities in a society where business and industry cannot generate enough jobs, so tax money is used to employ people; segregating and controlling people who are defined as deviant while symbolically indicating something is being done for them; providing economic opportunities for legitimate business interests, political machines, and organized crime; providing employment opportunities for political parties or ethnic groups. I know of no effectiveness studies that have these as their dependent variables, yet they are not novel observations. Organizations surely vary in the degree to which each of these usages is important for some group or other.

Another set of usages concerns the employees. Employee morale figures heavily in effectiveness studies, but note how it is defined; *High morale means that people find it gratifying to do what the organization wants them to do.* I would propose a different morale scale, asking questions such as this: Do you find this a good place to have pleasant chats with others about things that interest you? Can you daydream or relax without being bothered? Can you use the organization's facilities for your own personal needs (the telephone, typists, office supplies, machine shop, personnel department, travel facilities)? Could you get a friend or a relative a job here? Can you control your work so that when you are not in the mood you do not have to work too hard? Can you hide your mistakes and advertise your successes? Can you make use of tediously acquired skills and knowledge so that you have some bargaining edge with co-workers or superiors, or some sense that what you are doing is meaningful because you have had to learn how to do it and can control it somewhat? Do you pick up any interesting tidbits about the world working here, or can you be interesting at social gatherings because of what you do here or learn here? Can you expect to have a job here as long as you need it?

I recommend this list to the Michigan Survey Research Center. I think it is an eminently reasonable version of a morale scale, one that does not assume that high morale means effective and unobtrusive exploitation by superiors and one that is a good candidate even for variable analysis effectiveness studies. It certainly will tell us something about the nature of the organization—that is, the uses to which it can be put.

A revelatory analysis of effectiveness not only will tell us more about the way the organization is used by groups within and without it, it will also indicate the very substantial limits on this resource. That is, it will *disclose ineffectiveness.* In variable analysis, if a change in X does not lead to a change in Y (better evaluation procedures do not seem to increase productivity), we may conclude that X is not important, that something else was going on to counteract the effect of the change, or that X and Y were poorly measured. A revelatory analysis might disclose that the new evaluation procedures were evaded by some of the parties, did not operate properly because they were too complex, were not in effect because of some unpredictable events, had the opposite effect of that which was intended because of misunderstanding or unexpected employee reactions, and so on. We could do the same with the predicted increase in productivity. A revelatory analysis is more likely to reveal what most managers know but social scientists cannot afford to acknowledge, namely, that complex social systems are greatly influenced by sheer chance, accident, luck; that most decisions are very ambiguous, preference orderings are incoherent and unstable, efforts at communication and understanding are often ineffective, subsystems are very loosely connected, and most attempts at social control are clumsy and unpredictable. Social systems exhibit low coherence when you look for that; it may be their means of survival given the uses to which people wish to put them. We construct a reality that is far more rational and go to great lengths to load our random dice so that our studies come out as predicted (for example, we are fond of proving relations that are nearly tautological).

I suspect that if we entertained the hypothesis that most things are not effective, we would find great support for it. It is not an unreasonable hypothesis; in fact, given the history of things that should have worked but did not, it is more reasonable than those we entertain in variable analysis.

Hospital Studies

Thus, after Scott finishes his present study, I have two more to recommend. First, let us review his present one, as described in his essay in Chapter Four. The independent variables are "staff qualification, complexity of the surgical tasks performed measured from the standpoint of surgeons and nurses, the balance between integration and differentiation, and the power exercised by the surgical staff over its members." The dependent variables are mortality and morbidity rates after several days or weeks. The contextual variables are "measures of general hospital structure, administrative arrangements, fiscal hospital structure including administrative arrangements, fiscal characteristics, and role in the regional division of labor." It is a well-conceived, elaborate variable analysis, assuming a rational organization and probably assuming, though I cannot be sure, a strong commitment to performing effective surgery.

In his next study, Scott might ask a number of hospital administrators, doctors, health officials, community groups, and perhaps even ex-patients what are the worst hospitals in the areas he is sampling from. He should then take the ones upon which there is considerable agreement and try to find out why they are bad. He should look at the way external groups and internal groups use the hospital for their own ends, since these might diverge from those of patients and taxpayers (taxpayers have a legitimate interest in private hospitals since they receive government subventions and do not pay taxes on land and other things). He should examine community variables, government controls, the county medical society, drug companies, and so on, as well as hospital employees and staff doctors. Then he should recommend what needs to be done to bring these grossly malfunctioning hospitals up to the level of those that are presumed to be adequate and publish his findings and recommendations widely.

After that, his next study should include adequate and good hospitals as well as the bad ones. He would ask who gets what from hospitals? We might find in this study that mortality rates after surgery are a minimal constraint on hospitals—they cannot be too high, but no one really knows what is too high and few people see the data anyway. But occupancy rates might be extremely important, and thus attractive facilities and conveniences for the doctors would be important because that increases their use of the hospital. In fact, the more attractive the hospital's facilities, and the more special facilities for patients—wine with meals, mobile beauty parlors, and so on—the better class of patients the hospital can attract and thus the more it can charge and the more it can sell profitable services to the sick and dying. Increasing government subventions might be another use of the hospital, leading to the emphasis upon certain kinds of facilities and services. Perhaps medical equipment firms are more successful in penetrating some kinds of hospitals than others. Perhaps communities only take an interest in the hospital when they can control hiring practices or employees may look primarily for good benefits, convenient housing close by, and easy work (this is probably true of doctors too, though other things are involved). Finally, he might find that all this goes on in a context of great ambiguity, unpredictability, misunderstandings, chance, and so on. It might sound like a Ralph Nader monograph or a Paddy Chayevsky movie script, but it would be a revelation for most hospital effectiveness studies. It would also drastically change our conception of these organizations and thus our view about the nature of all organizations. Like myself, Scott seems to be rooted in a rationalistic view; using effectiveness as a revelatory device we might free ourselves from this constraint. His work, with Dornbusch, on evaluation and my own on technology are not thereby rendered useless by any means; but they are such small parts of the whole as to render their predictive value truly minor, and of course their impact upon gross malfunctioning must be near zero.

6

Obstacles to Comparative Studies

Michael T. Hannan

John Freeman

❧❧❧❧❧❧❧❧

Effectiveness is one of the strongest and most persistent themes in the literature on organizations. Most theories of organizations introduce effectiveness considerations, and many research reports comparing organizations claim to speak to effectiveness issues (see Price, 1968, for a literature review). Despite the considerable activity, there is little evidence of any cumulation of knowledge concerning the relationship of organizational characteristics to effectiveness. The lack of cumulation may be attributed to either theoretical inadequacies or methodological deficiencies in published research, or to both (compare Steers, 1975).

We propose that the quality of both theory and methodology contributes to the lack of cumulative character in the literature on comparative effectiveness. This essay treats a number of specific problems of each type. The thrust of our argument, however, is to point to the more fundamental problem of comparing effectiveness across organizations. Most definitions of organizational effectiveness introduce some normative standard against which to evaluate organizational performance. Usually the standard is the set of goals of each organization included in the comparison; sometimes it is the researcher's view of what behavior is appropriate. These two different sets of standards introduce different conceptual obstacles to the comparative study of effectiveness.

When the standard against which performance is evaluated is the set of goals of the organization, comparative studies are hampered by logical difficulties similar to those that arise in attempts at making interpersonal comparisons of utilities. We argue that current conceptions of organizational goals do not permit the establishment of organizational preference functions with properties strong enough to justify interorganizational comparisons of goal attainment.

When the standard of comparison is the values of the researcher or critic, the methodological problem is different. As long as the standard is applied consistently, there is no obstacle to systematic comparisons of effectiveness (so-defined) across organizations. We argue that the difficulty in this case is that the information produced does not meet the minimal standards for scientific analysis. The comparisons depend intimately on the properties of the observer. Any knowledge claims that result are subjective and not falsifiable. In short, such comparisons are oriented not to constructing a scientific body of knowledge but to evaluative or engineering ends.

Definitions of Effectiveness

The literature on organizations suffers from a somewhat general failure to distinguish engineering activity from scientific activity. The problem is as old as the scientific management tradition. The goal of scientific management was an obvious form of social engineering—the use of scientific theory and procedures to solve a *particular* management problem. Yet the writings on the subject attempted to cumulate the engineering experience into *general* laws about organizations. One does not have to claim that evidence from applied studies has no relevance to basic science to object to an uncritical shifting from engineering to scientific orientations.

The very term *effectiveness* suggests an engineering focus. We suppose that materials engineers, for example, charged with the obligation of certifying whether a proposed structure will withstand certain stresses, will formulate conclusions in terms of the effectiveness of various alloys for the design. Likewise, a construction engineer may debate the effectiveness of various designs. However, no physicist uses terms like effectiveness in formulating and testing laws that explain the behavior of substances under stress. To do so would be to introduce theoretically irrelevant issues (goals) into the theory.

This is not the place for an extended discussion of the differences between basic research and engineering (or as it has come to be known in the social sciences, evaluation research). It is enough to note that the two realms of activity are oriented differently. The pure scientist seeks to formulate abstract and timeless theories that explain properties of nature. The engineer seeks to use science to modify nature. The boundaries between the two orientations are often blurred. Nonetheless, there is reason to believe that it is useful to separate the two activities whenever possible. The theorist must be able to work unconstrained by practical exigencies, which are the métier of the engineer. Likewise, the engineer cannot afford the luxury of the broad scope or cavalier unconcern with deadlines enjoyed by the basic scientist. Our point here is that there is ample practical experience implying that both science and engineering benefit when the division of labor is explicit and different standards are used to evaluate the two kinds of work.

Our general theme is that effectiveness is a concept of applications and engineering but not of abstract scientific theory and research. To introduce effectiveness considerations into attempts at formulating and testing general laws of organizational behavior confuses the two realms of activity to the detriment of both engineering and science. We have no objections to formulating organizational design issues in terms of effectiveness. All of our objections apply to attempts at formulating general theories of organizations in terms of effectiveness.

Survival Versus Goal Attainment. The term *effectiveness* is used in a bewildering variety of ways in the organizations literature (Steers, 1975). Most of these can be seen to reflect one of two distinct emphases: survival or goal attainment. From the first perspective, the organization is effective if it manages to maintain an inflow of essential resources from its environment (Yuchtman and Seashore, 1967). From this perspective, the effectiveness problem concerns relations with the environment and particularly *managing* the environment (Aldrich and Pfeffer, 1976; Hirsch, 1975). The more classical usage refers to goal attainment. An organization is effective if it meets or surpasses its goals. Most commonly the goals considered are the public goals of the organization. Sometimes the term *effectiveness* is used with reference to the organization's meeting the goals of leading coalitions or of members generally (Simon, 1957).

It is important to keep these two usages separate. They refer to different organizational processes, and both the strategies and structures involved may be quite different. Neither one is a surrogate for the other. Nothing we know about organizations suggests that organizations meeting public goals are more likely to survive or that surviving organizations are more likely to meet their publicly stated goals. Unless one can argue convincingly to the contrary, one should not slip indiscriminately from one meaning of the term to the other. This essay follows the more normal usage of effectiveness to refer to goal attainment (Etzioni, 1960, p. 8).

We have elsewhere (Hannan and Freeman, 1974, 1977) discussed the usefulness of modeling selection (nonsurvival) in populations of organizations. We have also dealt with the methodological problems that arise in such a study (Freeman, 1975). Therefore, this essay concentrates on obstacles to the comparative analysis of goal attainment-effectiveness. This analysis is followed by a brief contrast of the survival and goal attainment perspectives.

A third common meaning of effectiveness that deserves mention is adaptation (see Steers, 1975, who finds that many discussions of effectiveness use the imagery of adaptation). In one sense, adaptation is not conceptually different from survival: An organization is adaptive to the extent that it can adjust to changing environmental circumstances. In a second sense, adaptation can be seen as a dynamic aspect of goal attainment: An organization is adaptive to the extent that it can adjust output performance to meet goals under varieties of environmental circumstances. Later in this essay we discuss the need for dynamic perspectives in the study of organizations. Beyond that there is no need for a separate discussion of adaptation-effectiveness.

Effectiveness Versus Efficiency. Within the tradition that emphasizes goal attainment, effectiveness is distinguished from efficiency. There is widespread agreement that the former refers to goal attainment and the latter refers to the costs incurred in goal attainment (usually unit cost per output). That is, effectiveness considerations are not made conditional on resources committed and used, whereas efficiency introduces cost comparisons.

Having raised the question of cost comparisons, we are led to ask whether an unconditional analysis of goal attainment has much meaning. Do not all performance comparisons use at least implicit cost comparisons? The question reduces to the relevance of resources and cost constraints. Organizations that do not face resource constraints can presumably choose to stress either effectiveness or efficiency. Those that employ finite resources (either because they operate in limited environments or face competition) do not have this luxury. When resources are scarce, performance evaluations that do not take costs into account are not very useful. Organizations that do not face resource constraints must be very rare, yet it is these organizations that profit from a distinction between efficiency and effectiveness. Consequently, we have chosen not to distinguish between the two. We use the term *effectiveness* to refer to goal attainment, but insist at a number of places in our argument that resource constraints must be considered.

Conceptual and Methodological Problems
with Goal Effectiveness

In its most common usage, effectiveness refers to the degree of congruence between organizational goals and observable outcomes. Effectiveness is well defined only if both goals and outcomes are well defined and the comparison of the two is meaningful. Our position briefly stated is as follows. Organizational goals are both difficult to conceptualize and difficult to measure. Outcomes, although conceptually simpler, are also difficult to measure. Nonetheless, there is no insuperable difficulty in utilizing either concept in developing logically consistent and falsifiable propositions concerning organizational structure and behavior. The possibility that both goals and outcomes may be defined and measured adequately does not guarantee that attempts at measuring correspondences between the two will yield a scientifically useful concept. We allow that evaluations of goal attainment are meaningful when applied to a single organization whose goals are well understood. However, we claim that these comparisons are not meaningful across organizations and that propositions concerning comparative effectiveness are untestable.

Goals. A great many theorists have pointed to the difficulties involved in defining organizational goals (Simon, 1964; Etzioni, 1960). In light of these many complications, some of which are discussed below, one is tempted to formulate theories of organizations that do not employ the concept. Such a resolution to the problem is not satisfactory. Social scientists have found it useful to distinguish formal organizations from families, communities, and other forms of social organization precisely because formal organizations have explicit, specific, and limited goals (Blau and Scott, 1962). Were we to drop goals from consideration, there would be no need for special theories or formal organizational structure and behavior.

Simon (1964, p. 3) defines goals as "value premises that serve as inputs to decision making" and equates goals with preferences. Goals define both the relevant criteria and a preference ordering (at least) of outcomes on each criterion. The major conceptual difficulties arise because of the likely *multiplicity of organizational goals.* Although some organizations have single public goals (the firm is the classic example), many others have multiple ostensible and *publicly legitimated goals.* Prominent examples include universities (research and teaching), prisons and public mental hospitals (custody and rehabilitation), and tertiary care hospitals (primary medical care, medical education, and research). Virtually all public agencies and bureaus have very many public goals. For example, the number and diversity of goals of agencies like the Department of Health, Education and Welfare (HEW) and the Department of Commerce boggle the imagination.

This multiplicity is compounded by the fact that many, if not all, organizations have *private goals* (sometimes called operative goals) that diverge to some extent from public goals. Dominant coalitions often develop the goal of preserving their position of power at almost any cost to the organization. Often this leads them to pursue very cautious organizational strategies (even when the public goals call for decisive action). The classic analysis of this phenomenon is Michels' (1949) account of the subversion of the public goals of European socialist unions and parties by dominant coalitions intent on avoiding risky action. Similarly, Galbraith (1967) argues that the dominant coalitions (called the technostructure) in modern concentrated industries subvert the goal of profit maximization with its attendant risks. Instead they pursue policies of steady (and presumably safer) growth. Baumol (1959) argues that managing coalitions privately maximize sales, and Williamson (1964) claims the operative goal of managing coalitions is the maximization of executive salaries (by such strategies as maximizing the size of the organization). In none of these cases are these goals announced. But insofar as the dominant coalition controls organizational action, it leads the organization to conform to goals that are different from the public goals. Performances that may appear quite unsatisfactory relative to public goals may be quite satisfactory from the perspective of what have become operative goals.

Subunits of organizations often develop their own goals. The process may be identical to that just discussed. Leaders of every subunit may subvert organizational goals in exactly the manner in which dominant coalitions do. Members also bring their own goals to organizations, and the degree of correlation between their public and private goals is problematical. A number of theorists have argued that problems created by this disjuncture depend systematically on such variables as the "inducements" (both quality and kind) provided by the organization, the "contributions" members are called upon to provide, and the alternatives available through withdrawal (compare, Simon, 1957, 1964; March and Simon, 1958). Their analyses lend little comfort to those who claim that organizations (even firms) have simple goals.

A second broad problem concerns the *specificity* of goals. Consider the university's goal of advancing the store of useful knowledge or a police agency's goal of protecting the public safety. A very great range of more specific goals may be seen (by at least some relevant groups) as consistent with the public goals. As a consequence, the goals may differ from unit to unit. Moreover, over time any single unit may emphasize one or another of the set of goals consistent with the public goal, depending on the nature of the practical contingencies facing the organization. So even though no set of participants may be subverting public goals, each set may follow very different operative goals.

A third broad problem concerns the *temporal dimension of goals*. Just as individuals may differ in their time horizons or time discounts (their preferences for immediate versus long-term gratification), so too may organizations. Public goal statements rarely, if ever, give a clue to the relevant temporal considerations. Should we consider the short run or the long run or both? The many published empirical studies that employ cross-sectional data on samples of organizations (see, for example, Lawrence and Lorsch, 1969) tacitly take the short-run perspective. Whether or not this is appropriate depends on the nature of the goals function for each organization. To the extent that the goals function stresses quick return on investment (as in many business ventures, disaster relief organizations, military field units, and so on) the short-run outcomes should be given highest priority. For those organizations that orient toward continued production (for example, many other types of business ventures, universities, research and development organizations, and so on) the year-to-year fluctuations in performance should be discounted and the average performance over longer periods emphasized.

The conceptual problem is that we do not know how organizations discount time. Two organizations with the same goals operating with the same structure in the same environment may place a very different emphasis on speed of return on investment. One organization may capitalize on some situations in a way that

increases both the probability of quick favorable outcomes and the
risk of long-term decline. The other may eschew the quick return
in favor of long-run security. As we shall point out later, in such
cases both short-term and long-term comparisons of performance between the two organizations are misleading effectiveness comparisons.
The general point is that it is not enough to know the output
criteria in the goals function. The analyst must also know the
premium placed on speed of return.

We would not be at all surprised to find that different time
perspectives are employed at different organizational levels. In fact,
Barnard (1938) has argued that there is a positive relationship
between the length of the time perspective employed by a unit and
its place (height) in the organizational hierarchy. If so, this produces an interesting problem. Consider an organization with a single
known goal. If this organization has several layers in its hierarchy
that employ quite different time perspectives with respect to the
timing of desired outcomes, the organization has a continuum of
goals. Unless we are willing to take some kind of average of the
time perspectives of all the units as the organization's time perspective, there is no longer any simple goal.

Each of the issues we have identified points to the subtlety
of the concept of organizational goals. Each issue also poses quite
serious challenges to attempts to measure organizational goals. In
particular, we see that organizational goals are multidimensional,
often unobserved, and temporally indeterminate. Due to the nonspecificity of so many goals, it will often be unclear exactly what
organizational action or what dimensions of outputs are relevant to
goal attainment. Careful research design could in principle overcome each of the seeming problems with the measurement of goals.
But the measurements that would result would be complex (they
would consist at a minimum of vectors of value inputs). More important, they would, we believe, provide only very rough preference
orderings of outcomes.

It is appropriate, given the numerous problems with the
concept of organizational goals and with their measurement, to
reopen the discussion of the role of this concept in organization
theory. Recall that, following Simon, we defined goals as preferences. Consider the treatment of preferences in microeconomics,

where they play a fundamental role. In all consumer theory (including the logically equivalent theory of the firm) preferences and the actions of the environment (summarized in prices) are assumed to determine behavior. But preferences are not measured directly. Their role (more precisely, the role of hypotheses regarding preference functions or indifference curves) is to permit the formulation of testable hypotheses relating prices and consumer behavior.

Many of the problems we have listed are also problems in the conceptualization and measurement of individual preferences. The point is that these difficulties do not impede the use of unmeasured preferences in the formulation of individual preference theories with strong empirical implications. The same could be true of organizational goals. Goals and environmental configurations together determine organizational behavior. We suggest treating goals as unmeasured causal variables and using propositions involving goals to derive falsifiable propositions relating environmental characteristics and organizational behavior.

Organizational Performance. The second concept involved in goal effectiveness is organizational performance—usually output. The problems associated with organizational performance appear more methodological than conceptual. Therefore, we stress the methodological issues as they arise in all comparative studies of the relationship between variations in structure (or other characteristics of organizations) and outputs, whether or not effectiveness is the subject under investigation.

An important consideration in studying organizational performance is *time perspective.* In changeable environments, organizations are faced with a strategy problem. When the environment shifts unpredictably among a series of states to which any organizational structure is differentially well adapted, an organization must choose either to adopt a structure that does well in one or a limited number of environmental states (that is, to specialize for certain environmental outcomes) or to adopt a more generalized structure that is not particularly well suited to any single outcome but that does passably well in all or most of them. We have discussed the manner in which the form of environmental variation affects the optimal strategies for organizations elsewhere (Hannan and Freeman, 1974, 1977). Two issues from that discussion are relevant here.

The typical generalist strategy involves the accumulation of varieties of excess capacities (for example, stockpiling raw materials and diversifying product lines by manufacturing firms; preparation for "brushfire" and nuclear war by armies). In whatever state the environment takes at any instant, the generalist will appear maladapted. All of the excess capacities that are useful in other environmental outcomes will appear wasteful in the present environment. In contrast, any organizations that specialize in the environment prevailing at that moment will appear adaptive. That is, performance, given available resources, will be high relative to all other organizations in the field.

However, if the population ecology theory we advanced is true (this theory is a fairly straightforward application of Levins', 1968, fitness set theory), we can find environments where populations of generalists over time will outperform populations of specialists. This possibility allows that two investigators studying the same collection of organizations may draw exactly opposite conclusions from cross-sectional and time series performance comparison. On the average, specialists in their optimal environments will outperform the generalists in every cross-section. Over time, as long as the environment is changing the generalists will tend to outperform the specialists. The situation is actually more complicated than this since the specialists who do not hit their optimal environments will do even worse than generalists. Consequently, in any cross-section there should be greater variance in performance among populations of specialists than generalists. We obviously cannot deal with these complexities in the usual cross-sectional design. With longitudinal data, these considerations lead to testable hypotheses.

One of the most difficult problems in testing propositions relating structure to performance is to isolate *bounding systems,* in which the effects of structure can be distinguished from the effects of other variables (including other organizational structures). The problem, of course, is not unique to organizational analysis but is endemic to all empirical scientific activity (Blalock, 1964). Nonetheless, the problem hits with considerable force in this area.

At a minimum, one must be able to identify precisely the structures that are involved in any output performance. Organizational performance can often be analyzed into a series of discrete actions, each of which can be linked to a relevant organizational structure. A description of an organization in these terms will be a microscopic description of structure that impinges on all action within the organization. The question arises, Should one employ a microscopic or macroscopic perspective on structure in evaluating performance outcomes? Both strategies find their advocates in the literature. For example, Scott and others (1972) argue for studying structure as close to task performance as possible. Bidwell and Kasarda (1975) argue (from school organizations) that one should focus on the highest levels of organization, the levels at which policy decisions affecting the entire organization are made.

One cannot decide between these alternatives without considering the nature of the process under study. It is obvious that a microscopic perspective yields more detail and allows a finer specification of the manner in which structure enchances or impedes task activity. Nevertheless, we should not expect that a series of microscopic perspectives taken together will provide as clear a view of the overall relation of a structure to performance in any organization as will a macroscopic perspective. Absence of hierarchy (in Simon's, 1962, sense of a partial ordering of units in a set of Chinese boxes) also complicates the system closure problem. The more horizontal links one finds in organizations, the less clear will it be at the microscopic level what structures and what resources were activated in any performance.

Our interest is in the different system closure demands that the alternative strategies impose on the researcher. It seems that the more finely one divides the organization, the more difficulty one will have in isolating exactly what fractions of effort (manpower and other resources) are devoted to the task in question as opposed to other tasks. To this extent one will have difficulty in isolating the effects of elements of structure from resources. Because of this, microscopic study will probably require trade-offs between the fineness of detail on the causal structure and the difficulty in isolating the system.

Complexity of the performance also increases the difficulty in isolating the structures and resources that influenced the performance. Ordinarily, the more complex the product, the more joint is the action that produced it. Insofar as joint action extends across small-scale task organization lines, it will be difficult both to identify which structures are involved and to determine what levels of effort were expended in the performance. Any particular subunit structure may be given undue credit or blame for the contributions of joint actors.

Many of these difficulties can be avoided by considering the systems as entire production processes including all of the units involved in the process. In many cases the production will involve all units in an organization, and in other cases a single organization will contain many separable production processes. Presumably one would distinguish boundaries between production processes by examining the gradients in flows in information, personnel, and materials among positions and units. It is important to notice that a production process often extends beyond the boundaries of a legally constituted organization. Often a specialized organization is simply one component of a large-scale division of labor. Just as it is difficult to draw meaningful boundaries between subunits of a single organization, it may be difficult to do so in communities or networks of organizations (Hawley, 1950, 1968). The production of basic research provides a clear illustration of the problem. Since so much scientific knowledge is communicated rapidly through the research community, discoveries in any research institute may pay off as rapidly in other institutes (in terms of improved performance in making future breakthroughs) as in the institute that made the discovery. To the extent that information flows freely across institute boundaries it appears as though science as an institution is a more meaningful production system than the staff and facilities of any research institute. The more general point, then, is that the more permeable the boundaries of any organization (or subunit of an organization) to flows of information, personnel, and other strategic production resources, the more difficult it is to close the system at that level and the more meaningful it is to formulate and test propositions relating structure to performance at some wider system level.

A related set of issues arises in selecting a *level of analysis* at which to test propositions. Should we consider the properties of outputs as they leave the organization? Should we consider the organization's impact on the larger system? Does it suffice to employ information on average levels of output quality, or must we utilize information on distributions? The answers to these questions depend on the form of the propositions under study, the nature of the organization, and the relationship between properties of the inputs (objects worked on) and eventual outputs.

To attempt a complete analysis of these issues would require much more space than we have here. It will help compress the discussion to consider a single type of organization—schools. Suppose that the only output of schools is instruction in some subject matter and that the measure of instruction is academic achievement. Suppose, finally, that we believe that properties of students such as ability, socioeconomic background, and aspirations are important determinants of achievement. Consider the problem of testing hypotheses that relate school or school district structure to achievement. Most research that takes this form (the "school effects" literature) relates individual pupil achievement to his or her relevant characteristics and to the properties of school structure. For example, one might regress each student's achievement on his or her IQ, race, parent's SES, and the proportion of school professional work force that is not involved primarily in teaching.

Bidwell and Kasarda (1975) criticized the school effects literature for choosing the wrong level of analysis—school instead of school district. They pointed out that the structures that regulate the flows of essential inputs and that buffer the technological core from the environment are district level structures. They proceeded to use measures of district structural features *and* to study district *average* achievement rather than individual outcomes. They argued that the choice of level of system at which to measure the structural variables settles the choice of level at which to measure outcomes.

In no sense does choice of system level at which to conceptualize and measure structural variables determine the level at which one is to conceptualize and measure outcomes. Rather, the choice of each should be determined by the nature of the causal process under study. If the causal process is stated in terms of the effects of structure on the careers of individual students (as was the case with Bidwell and Kasarda's paper), the pair "district structure and individual outcome" is appropriate. Suppose, instead, that one were studying the hypothesis that a certain structure alters the correlation between ability and achievement (perhaps the structure was advertised to have such a consequence and was introduced for that reason). Could one study this process utilizing average outcomes over students? No. A test of such a proposition requires distributions of outcomes within structures (districts, in this example).

We have criticized this research on the grounds that the level of aggregation of outcomes is not consistent with the nature of the causal processes proposed (Hannan, Freeman, and Meyer, 1976). Bidwell and Kasarda (1976) have responded to our criticism by noting that aggregate events are summaries of individual events and that consequently the investigator may choose any level of aggregation according to his "design." No one will dispute that a distribution consists of information about the properties of individual events. But it is hard to imagine someone defending the view that because of this logical dependence one may shift freely from considering the distribution to considering its center (the average).

When are distributional issues relevant to tests of propositions about structural effects on output? The key to the issue is the extent to which the investigator expects properties of the inputs (children, in this case) to have impacts on outputs and the likelihood that the distributions of the relevant properties differ among organizations. If no individual properties are relevant, analyzing averages will yield the same results as analyzing individual outcomes. Further, if all of the relevant individual properties are controlled, grouping observations by district will not systematically alter results (Hannan, Young, and Nielsen, 1975). But, if some individual properties relevant to output are left uncontrolled, one can expect considerable divergence between analyses of individual outcomes (as in most sociological school effects studies) and of average outcomes (as in Bidwell and Kasarda). See Hannan, Freeman, and Meyer (1976) for substantive evidence. (Under exceptional circumstances, the bias arising from grouping observations may offset the bias due to the presence of uncontrolled individual properties—correlated with structural properties—in models used to estimate effects from individual data. See Hannan, 1976. None of the cases under consideration fits the conditions for aggregation gain.)

Choosing between the entire distribution and its average is the most subtle of the levels of analysis issues, since the language used to describe the results in each case is so similar. We have no such difficulty discovering the data requirements to test hypotheses about effects on variances, correlations, and so on.

Performance cannot always be measured internally to the organization. For example, to evaluate the performance of public health organizations in preventive medicine it is not sufficient to observe the actions of members of those organizations or the health status of persons they contact. Rather one must evaluate some measures of health status in a target population. That is, for some types of organizations the unit within which to evaluate the outcome in some populations is much larger than the population that has direct experience with the organization. In such cases, the number of uncontrolled factors that operate is presumably very large, and it is extremely difficult to distinguish the effects of organizational characteristics on the target population from properties of the population and uncontrolled effects of the environment.

To this point we have tacitly accepted the classical view of modeling performance (which is also incorporated into models of effectiveness). Performance is equated with the quantity and quality of outputs. Characteristics of the environment, the organization's technology, the quality of inputs are considered *given fixed constraints* facing the organization. It is time to consider the appropriateness of these assumptions.

Why should the qualities of inputs be taken as a fixed constraint in modeling performance? Many organizations have control over their inputs. Organizations may do well or poorly in identifying appropriate inputs and screening out those that do not fit their needs. It seems reasonable to consider this an aspect of performance (Aldrich and Pfeffer, 1976). In fact, Yuchtman and Seashore (1967) consider this the most useful defining criterion of effectiveness. Consider the action of elite private schools. Such schools may have high levels of student achievement because they have highly selective admissions policies and high demand for entrance. Controlling for student characteristics, such schools may not have high levels of performance, however. Should we conclude that these schools are not performing well? To do so ignores the success of these organizations at an essential activity: obtaining inputs. Similar considerations hold for the other factors usually considered fixed.

Many organizations have some measure of control over their technology, the quality of staff, levels of environmental support, and so on. Just as it does not appear meaningful to evaluate output performance holding input quality constant, so too with these other factors.

Once we acknowledge that all these factors are subject to organizational strategy and action, we are faced with a serious methodological problem. All of the variables that appear in the conventional analyses are endogenous, that is, causally dependent on other variables in the model. For example, the quality of inputs may be a function of the expenditure on inputs, which is a function of output performance. If none of these factors is causally prior, or exogenous, it is extremely difficult to obtain unique estimates of any relevant causal effects in the system. In the technical language of econometrics, the system is underidentified. To remedy this situation one must make a considerable number of strong assumptions concerning the details of the causal structure. Unfortunately, the existing theories of organizational performance (and effectiveness) do not provide a basis for these assumptions.

The empirical literature on output performance does not measure up well when confronted with this test of methodological complications. To some extent the apparent lack of cumulation in the empirical literature on comparative effectiveness can no doubt be traced to a general failure to solve these problems. Nevertheless, each problem discussed so far appears solvable. What is required is imaginative research design combined with careful model specification. We do not mean to suggest that the effort required is minor. It is not. It will take a considerable alteration in the way in which we approach comparative organizational research to solve the problems. But we believe that it can be done.

It is tempting to blame the lack of cumulative knowledge about comparative effectiveness on the methodological problems just discussed and on difficulties in conceptualizing and measuring organizational goals. If this were so, the picture would be guardedly optimistic. But, although these issues contribute in important ways to the lack of cumulation in the comparative literature on effectiveness, there are also more fundamental problems, which we shall turn to next, involving meaninglessness of effectiveness comparisons (goal attainment) across organizations.

Goal Effectiveness. As noted earlier, effectiveness involves comparisons of outcomes (for example, output performance) with goals. Thus, all of the conceptual and methodological problems discussed to this point also bear on the meaning and measurement of effectiveness. In our view, these are the least serious problems that arise in the comparative analysis of organizational effectiveness. Here, we treat what we consider more fundamental problems.

We have argued that organizational goals are always multiple, often unobserved, and relatively nonspecific, particularly with respect to time considerations. That is to say, the preference functions we call goals do not have very strong properties. They will usually provide no more than a very rough ordering of outcomes in terms of preference. It helps to envision a concrete example. Suppose we observe two schools (or school districts), each with three students and with the goal of maximizing pupil academic achievement. Suppose further that achievement takes on only three values—0, 1, and 2—denoting poor, moderate, and high levels, respectively. We denote outcomes to each school by a vector of the form (0,1,0), say, where the first element is the outcome to the first pupil, and so on. Clearly, the schools prefer (2,2,2) to all other outcomes and prefer any other outcome to (0,0,0). This minimal information enables us to make logically consistent comparisons of goal attainment across schools. If, for example, both schools begin at (1,1,1), and School A goes to (2,2,2) and B goes to (0,0,0), we conclude correctly that A has done a better job of goal attainment than B. These comparisons are permitted by the relatively weak goal statement because we observed change over time, and we considered only the extreme outcomes. Let us examine these two restrictions in more depth.

Suppose A has outcomes (2,2,2) and B has (1,1,1). Is A better off in terms of goal attainment than B? Not obviously. We can draw such a conclusion only when the two preference functions are comparable and measurable ("cardinal" in the usual designation). The same sort of issue arises in assessments of change. Suppose A goes from (1,1,1) to (2,2,2) and B goes from (0,0,0) to (1,1,1).

Are these equal gains in goal attainment (effectiveness)? Only if the utility functions are cardinal and interorganizationally comparable.

The comparisons are often more complex than has been indicated so far. Suppose both schools begin at (1,1,1) and A shifts to (2,1,0) while B remains the same. Are the two schools equal in effectiveness (assuming, as we probably should not, that they were equal initially)? It depends on the nature of the goals or preference functions. One organization may be indifferent to such a change; it may focus only on average outcomes across pupils. Other schools may consider such a change an improvement in the sense that having one superior outcome is preferable to having none (regardless of what happens to the distribution); others may consider this an inferior outcome in the sense that having one failure is inferior to having none. The general point is that the public goals do not provide enough information even to order (in a strict order) all of the outcomes that fall between the extremes. We think this problem is general. For many organizations (even those with single goals), public goal statements often do not provide enough detail on the nature of the preferences to do more than indicate a weak ordering (a semiorder) of outcomes. If so, interorganizational comparisons of effectiveness will be justified only for the most extreme changes.

Some of these difficulties arise, in the case of schools, because it is meaningful to consider the outcomes to each pupil. Other organizations orient only to total or average outcomes rather than to the details of the distribution across subunits or objects worked on. For example, the classical firm orients only to total profit. In such cases, comparisons of goal attainment over time are simplified in the sense that many of the intermediate cases collapse into single outcomes. If, for example, (2,1,0) and (1,1,1) denote the profits of subunits of a firm, the two outcomes are not differentiated. However, even in this simpler case, static comparisons of effectiveness are not justified. Nor can we conclude that a given change in profitability (say, a 5 percent gain) in two firms yields equal "utility" in each. To do this, we need much more information about the precise form of the preference or utility functions—we need cardinal preferences.

To this point, we have assumed single goals. Suppose the

two schools also have as public goals maximizing the socialization of certain values. That is, the set of outcomes of interest now includes both student achievement and values, or, in operational terms, both an achievement score and a values score for each pupil. Suppose that values are also measured on a three-point scale, so that the most preferred outcome is [(2,2), (2,2), (2,2)] and the least preferred outcome is [(0,0), (0,0), (0,0)]. We now have a very large number of intermediate cases. How, for example, do we compare [(2,0), (2,0), (2,0)] with [(0,2), (0,2), (0,2)]? To be able to do so requires that we know the precise weighting of each type of outcome (actually, we must know the precise weighting of each combination of outcomes). Again, *we must have cardinal preferences* in a situation in which the public goals give us no more than a very weak ordering of outcomes.

We believe this problem is quite general. Previously we argued that all organizations (firms, hospitals, and so on) can be seen to have multiple goals in the sense that different units or levels each form their own distinct goals and in the sense that timing considerations differ across organizational units and participants. For any organization, it is a Herculean task to accumulate enough information to rank order all outcomes in terms of preferences of the organization as a corporate entity, all of these collectivities and units taken together (to do so also requires that we somehow weight the preferences of the corporate organization and of all the other units). It is inconceivable that we could obtain enough information to measure also the distances (in terms of preferences) among outcomes and a zero point (required for cardinality).

The problem as we have sketched it to this point is primarily an information problem. Many economists would argue that the problem of effectiveness comparisons is more fundamental. We are considering what amounts to interpersonal comparisons of utility (where the persons may be literal persons, groups, or organizations as corporate entities). Although the matter is still the subject of some dispute, most microeconomists have long since concluded that such comparisons are not logically justified (see Arrow, 1951, for a classic statement of this position). The problem has been rendered moot (except perhaps in welfare economics; see Rothenberg, 1961) by the discovery that a satisfactory microeconomics (consumer theory,

theory of the firm, and so on) can be constructed on the basis of ordinal utilities (ordinal indifference mappings). In fact, it is possible (see, for example, Henderson and Quandt, 1971) that the modern consumer theory is unaffected by monotonic transformations of the preference functions. Therefore, there is no point in attempting to justify stronger utility arguments.

We believe that the field of organizations faces a similar situation. As we argued earlier, most organizational analysts need to employ goals (preferences) to relate environmental states to organizational action, in the same way that economists use preferences to relate price changes to consumer behavior. Comparative statements concerning goal attainment encounter all the difficulties that complicate interpersonal comparisons of utilities. In addition, goal functions for organizations are more complex. As a result of the shifting nature of goals within units of organizations, a set of additional complications arises in comparing goal attainment across organizations.

For the reasons just given, it is impossible to compare inter-organizational utilities. As a consequence, analysts of effectiveness will tend to make such choices on the basis of their own personal values or those of the people who are paying them. Because there is no objective way to determine which goals are to receive emphasis in evaluating effectiveness, researchers will fall back on the arbitrary criterion of audience. So when a business firm is evaluated for owners, profit will be the overwhelming criterion. When the same organization is evaluated from the members' point of view, member satisfactions will be emphasized.

Differences in goals also imply specifying different operating functions in determining effectiveness. In most formulations, it is assumed that some overall or typical level of performance will be used in evaluation. It is clear, however, that this logic is appropriate for some kinds of organizations but not for others. Business firms, for instance, may be evaluated by total profits or by earnings per share. From this perspective, it makes no difference whether the organization made very high profits from one sale but lost on all others, or made a small but consistent rate of return on all its ventures. Often, however, an organization's one failure may be more important than a thousand successes. Custodial prisons, for example, are evaluated on the basis of their failures not successes (Cloward, 1960). One escaped murderer costs more than a thousand successful incarcerations. Other organizations are evaluated in terms of infrequent but important successes. A research-oriented university that produces one Nobel Prize every five years will probably be judged effective, even if many of its researchers are doing pedestrian work. A competing university that does good, solid, but undistinguished research will probably be judged less effective, if for no other reason than that those who do the judging are often unaware of good but undistinguished research. Finally, we can add that whereas some organizations are judged by the typical level of success, others are judged by the *variance* of success. Any organization that is judged in terms of *justice* will be evaluated in this way. So, as Weber (1947) pointed out, the public goal of legal-rational bureaucracies is to treat each case the same. Success is defined in terms of standardized outcomes, and variation is abhorred. The logic, based upon calculability of performance, stresses this invariant performance. Consequently, a failure is not counterbalanced by a success. A letter delivered with particular rapidity does not counterbalance a letter delivered with particular delay. Consequently, organizational characteristics that encourage effective performance in one organization may hinder it in another.

All in all, we see no gain from utilizing the concept of effectiveness in comparative studies intended to test general and abstract propositions concerning organizational structure and behavior. Rather, we see an endless cycle of dispute over terminology and an inability to obtain interobserver reliability across comparative studies of effectiveness. Similarly, it is almost impossible to prevent value statements from creeping into effectiveness assessments in a way that impedes theoretical development and empirical cumulation. (It should be noted that many of the problems we have been discussing vanish when we drop the comparative focus. An investigator can certainly draw meaningful conclusions concerning effectiveness of certain elements of organizational design when interest is focused on the performance of a single organization and when the analyst has access to precise information on the nature of organizational goals. This is the situation we earlier characterized as the engineering application.)

Organizational Survival

When we began this discussion, we distinguished between goal attainment and survival as ways of conceptualizing organizational effectiveness. We believe conceptualization of effectiveness in terms of survival fails to solve the problems that concern us. If we define the failure to survive as structural dissolution, it is *not* true that organizations that fail to achieve their goals or fail to make progress in that direction will fail to survive. Nor is it necessarily true that organizations that achieve their goals will survive. (We are ignoring for the moment all that we have said about how difficult it is to assess the degree of goal attainment.) In fact, goal attainment and survival are often inimical, as Michels (1949) pointed out. Being too successful may result in a loss of mission, which results in survival failure. For example, corporate apologists sometimes declare that breaking up monopolists is "punishing success." All of these issues are explored in depth in Hannan and Freeman (1977) and Freeman (1976).

This is not to say that the goals concept is irrelevant to organizational research in general or to survival studies in particular. The *pretense* of goal attainment is fundamental for acquiring legitimacy and other resources. Whether the organization in question actually pursues the goals is significant primarily as it serves as possible support for the pretense. In this sense, the conceptualization of organizations as goal-directed devices is useful. Organizations are social systems whose creation is accomplished through a public affirmation of goal-seeking behavior. This announcement of intention serves as a legitimating device and as the basis of a claim on resources including participation.

We do not believe that we profit very much from assuming that loss of inputs results in failure to survive. Of course the absence of inputs will eventually have such a result. But most organizations that fall apart do so long before they reach this point. Some resources are more important than others and some are easily made up by conversion processes. Money, for example, is an extremely general resource, which is translatable into many other scarce system inputs. We can say, however, that when there is a *simultaneous decline* in the various resources used by the organization, its existence is imperiled.

One set of circumstances under which this general decline is to be expected involves legitimacy crises. When organizational activities are normatively proscribed by the social system within which they take place, the consequences are likely to be many and varied. For example, the United States Army experienced such a catastrophe during the late 1960s when the Vietnam War received widespread criticism. It became difficult to obtain money for new weapons systems or to attract personnel; allies abroad began withholding cooperation. The consequences to be expected are very much the same as those Stinchcombe (1965) described with the term "liability of newness." It is in this sense that the goals basis of the effectiveness definition retains its importance. When organizations are founded, a claim on resources is attempted through a statement of purpose. When the purposes are new or unique, when the method of pursuing them is different, or when alternative channels for achieving that purpose already exist, the claim will receive a rough reception.

As these remarks suggest, organizations with diffuse goals should be best able to protect themselves from adverse assessments. When the success of a given kind of organization is difficult to assess internally, it will also probably be difficult to assess from the outside. In particular, organizations with diffuse or multiple goals can always attempt to shift attention from some dimension on which performance appears substandard to some other dimension of assessment. In view of the advantages of having diffuse and multiple goals, why do any organizations have specific and limited goals? The answer is simple. It is extremely difficult to make diffuse goal claims stick. Only under rather exceptional circumstances (for example, widely perceived societal crisis, absence of competition in some period, and so on) would we expect new organizations to be able to activate such diffuse claims for environmental resources. It seems much more likely that successful organizations with narrow goals may attempt to redefine their goals to make them more diffuse when and if they gain substantial control over their environments.

It is similarly difficult to establish a claim to very diverse and large amounts of resources. One of the dimensions on which organizations specialize or generalize in their resource-acquiring strategies is the claim on legitimacy. It is easier to persuade others that your intention is to perform certain narrowly defined tasks than it is to persuade others that you can and will perform every conceivable task. But making such a claim exposes the organization to greater risk. If one organization can make such a claim easily, so can others. And as is usually the case with specialism, the environment may change in such a way that any narrow statement of purpose may be only briefly persuasive.

Survival studies may be scientifically interesting whether or not the theorist believes survival is a goal. (One can assume that organizations are structured in such a way as to increase survival without assuming that all organizations at all times try to survive.) Nevertheless, the analysis of an individual organization's survival, perhaps as a case study, faces all the problems already identified because the survival criterion is itself binary—organizations either survive or they do not survive over some definable time period. Levels of analysis are still problematic because passing the buck up and down the hierarchy is almost certain to obscure the issue of where causal processes are operating. Corporate decisions made at the highest level sometimes manifest themselves at low levels in ways unanticipated by the decision makers. The system boundary problem is exacerbated because failing organizations are likely to form coalitions and other interorganizational associations to provide for a mutual defense. The result is that the separate organizations lose their unit properties and the consequences of their actions are shifted upward toward the collectivity (Hannan and Freeman, 1977; Freeman, 1976). Finally, the endogeneity problem continues, as failure to survive is often anticipated by other organizations, which withhold resources. Bankers and suppliers refuse to extend credit as bankruptcy approaches. Conversely, a history of survival is often the best argument for resource acquisition.

In our view, then, survival studies are different from effectiveness studies (as "effectiveness" is conventionally defined) because they do not directly involve the degree of goal attainment manifested by organizations. In addition, attempts to study survival or failure to survive are beset by many of the same problems encountered by analysts working from a goal-attainment perspective.

Conclusions

Although our discussion has ranged over a number of issues, our main argument is quite simple. Most analysts define effectiveness as goal attainment. We have pointed to well-known problems in conceptualizing and measuring organizational goals. These involve the nonspecificity of most organizational goals with respect to the weighting of multiple goals and the weighting of short-run versus long-run payoffs. We have also discussed methodological problems that commonly arise in comparative studies of organizational performance. These less widely recognized problems include temporal considerations, establishing organizational boundaries, choosing the proper levels of analysis at which to measure outcomes, and the endogenous nature of so many variables typically treated as exogenous.

We believe there is a more fundamental problem. Public goal statements are not specific enough to justify comparisons across organizations in terms of goal attainment. The problem is reminiscent of the difficulties in making interpersonal comparisons of utilities and is so serious that we argue in favor of dropping any pretense to scientific analysis of comparative organizational effectiveness. This conclusion applies only to attempts at constructing and testing abstract theories of organizations. It does not follow that effectiveness considerations should not play a role in engineering or social criticism. We do insist on making clear the distinctions between these types of concerns.

7

Usefulness of the Concept

Jeffrey Pfeffer

In "Obstacles to Comparative Studies" Michael T. Hannan and John Freeman make the case that we can not scientifically study organizational effectiveness. Effectiveness, they maintain, is an engineering, applications-oriented concept and, as such, should be excluded from comparative organizational analysis. Hannan and Freeman have identified several methodological and conceptual obstacles that make studying effectiveness difficult, but their argument rests primarily on two points: (1) identification of comparative studies of effectiveness with a goal approach to organizational analysis; and (2) the distinction between engineering, applications-oriented analyses and scientific, comparative analyses of organizations.

132

The issues raised are not nearly as clear-cut as implied by their essay. The various methodological and conceptual obstacles identified are, in many cases, applicable to any form of comparative organizational analysis and therefore, by themselves, do not inevitably foreclose comparative effectiveness studies. The issue of organizational goals and its place in theorizing about effectiveness or organizations more generally is treated equivocally in the essay and, in any event, does not necessitate the abandoning of efforts to comparatively assess effectiveness. The distinction between engineering and science, with its implications for research, is also open to some debate. We shall deal with each of these issues in turn before suggesting some viable paths to pursue in the study of effectiveness. First, however, it is necessary to clarify what is meant by the concept of comparative studies of effectiveness.

At points, Hannan and Freeman come close to saying that effectiveness is useable as a concept in assessments of single organizations for the purpose of social engineering or criticism but useless as a concept in comparative studies of organizations. Regardless of the purpose of the comparison, I would maintain that effectiveness is assessed—and can only be assessed—comparatively. This is because we are not talking about an absolute, physically defined dimension such as temperature, thermal efficiency, or mass. Rather, effectiveness is inevitably defined only through a process of social comparison (see Goodman, 1977, for a review of this literature). The statement that an organization is effective necessarily implies a comparison with some other organization or set of organizations. Thus, although we may still distinguish between types of application (engineering versus scientific), the assumption must be that effectiveness always implies some comparison with other organizations.

Methodological Barriers to the Comparative Study of Organizations

Hannan and Freeman list a number of methodological problems that render the comparative study of organizational effectiveness difficult. Four problems are identified: (1) the time horizon for evaluation; (2) identification of system boundaries; (3) levels of analysis (a problem related to the second one); and (4) identification of exogenous variables. Each of these problems confronts any comparative research on organizations, and it is not made clear why these difficulties are any more severe in the study of organizational effectiveness.

Hannan and Freeman correctly note that effectiveness assessments depend on the time horizon over which the assessment is made. Organizations or actions effective in the short run may turn out to be very ineffective in the long run. This is nicely illustrated in their discussion of the short-run and long-run consequences of specialization versus generalization. However, the assessment of other organizational properties may also vary as the time horizon varies. Differentiation, the division of labor within the organization, will vary depending upon whether a short or long horizon is employed. Whether people are assessed to be doing the same tasks or different tasks may be a function of whether their behavior is considered over a five-minute or five-week time horizon. Indeed, most organizational properties, including size, complexity, formalization, and centralization, are likely to change over time, which is why longitudinal organizational analysis to identify causal relationships is so desirable. The issue of the choice of an appropriate time horizon over which to assess the variables confronts any comparative researcher, not just those addressing organizational effectiveness.

Boundaries and their definition pose another problem in assessing organizational effectiveness. Again, however, boundary problems arise in other comparative organizational research. Consider the problem of measuring differentiation or complexity. Is a service engineer from a computer manufacturer stationed on site at the customer's facility a member of the customer's organization or the computer manufacturer's organization? When an organization establishes a wholly owned subsidiary with relatively autonomous management to engage in marketing or in exploration for natural resources, should the subsidiary be considered part of the organization and has differentiation increased? Would the answer be different if the subsidiary were partly owned with other organizations as in a joint venture? At what point of joint ownership is the joint subsidiary no longer to be considered a part of the parent organization?

As noted by Freeman (1975), the unit problem is a difficult

one facing comparative organizational research generally. In his own research on the size of the administrative component (Freeman, 1973), one reason why administrative components changed size was the shifting of functions back and forth from the parent organization to the individual facility. The unit and boundary problems confront any comparative research on organizations, including research treating differentiation, complexity, and the size of the administrative component.

Exogeneity, the problem of identifying causally exogenous variables, also confronts all organizational research. For instance, there is a large body of literature relating size to differentiation and formalization (see, for example, Meyer, 1972). But is size truly an exogenous variable? Size is surely not a fixed constraint but rather might be considered as the outcome of actions and decisions taken within the organization (Starbuck, 1965). Hannan and Freeman's comments concerning potential organizational control over inputs, technology, environmental certainty (through choice of domain), and size present problems for the causal modeling of any organizational feature. The specification of causally exogenous variables occurs in the context of some specific theoretical concerns and propositions. Size might be an independent variable in some studies, a dependent variable in others. Hannan and Freeman have appropriately reminded us that our theories are invariably partial theories, leaving some relationships unexplored and undetermined. But, again, this situation is not unique to the examination of organizational effectiveness.

Although the methodological problems enumerated by Hannan and Freeman are important, there is no demonstration that these problems are especially acute for studies of effectiveness compared with other studies of organizational properties. Indeed, Freeman's (1975) own insightful work on the unit problem demonstrates the existence of these difficulties for research that has not treated effectiveness.

Goals as a Basic Problem in Effectiveness Research

Hannan and Freeman emphasize that the problem with comparative research on effectiveness derives from the linkage be-

tween the concept of effectiveness and the idea of goals. One prominent way of defining effectiveness is in terms of the goals of the
organization. The authors claim that goals or preferences are
theoretically irrelevant to developing comparative knowledge of
organizational properties. They further correctly note that there are
many difficulties with the goal concept: (1) there are multiple
and often conflicting goals in organizations; (2) goals are frequently
unspecified and, we might add, possibly unspecifiable, except retrospectively after action has occurred (Weick, 1969); (3) goals involve a time dimension, and the specification of this dimension may
be critical; and (4) goals may be defined only with respect to individual actors and their interests within the organization, such as
the goal of maintaining power or acquiring resources.

It is at this point that some equivocality appears in their
theoretical position. Having thoroughly demolished the concept of
goals, Hannan and Freeman are reluctant to take the next step of
banishing goals (as they have banished effectiveness) from scientific
theories of organization. Rather, they note that many authors (for
example, Parsons, 1956) have used the concept of goals to distinguish organizations from other social collectivities. Goals are
legitimating devices as viewed by Hannan and Freeman, but are
nonetheless essential to the definition of organizations. The authors'
recommended solution to the goal problem also involves some contradiction with positions stated elsewhere in their essay. They
propose using goals as unmeasured causal variables to derive
falsifiable propositions, as the methodology of positive economics suggests the goal of profit maximizing be used in the development of predictions about the behavior of the firm. Earlier,
however, these authors claimed that goals (as normative statements) could not lead to falsifiable propositions. It is clear that goal
preferences can be used to develop falsifiable propositions, as the
authors themselves later recognize. Given a specified goal, we can
assess to what extent other organizational properties are or are not
useful in achieving the goal or can ask whether behavior is predictable assuming the goal. Both forms of the statement are potentially
falsifiable. Whether anyone is interested in the goal is another
matter—we can make statements of the relationship between other
properties and goal attainment, and these statements can be con-

sistent or inconsistent with data. Calling this a study of organizational effectiveness is something else.

One problem noted with the goal concept is the multiplicity of goals and the related issues of the variety of dimensions along which organizational performance may be assessed, the possibility that these dimensions are uncorrelated, and the difficulty of making interpersonal comparisons of utility across the different actors who have different goals related to different dimensions of organizational actions. To use an example in their form, if an organization has three criteria, clearly (2,2,2) is better than (0,0,0), assuming a goal of maximization, but is (2,1,0) better than (1,1,1), or is (2,1,0) equivalent to (1,0,2)? Hannan and Freeman claim one cannot answer these questions without making normative judgments about the worth of criteria and, implicitly, the worth of the various interests that espouse the different criteria. But, in fact, the resolution of this problem does not involve the researcher adopting a specific normative standard at all.

The problem is similar to that faced by a person choosing among products with multiple, uncorrelated attributes. We cannot tell this person how to choose—that depends on the weighting given to the criteria. But once the person has chosen, and certainly after a set of decisions, the implicit weightings of the criteria can be determined, and these can be potentially explained. Indeed, economists measure utility functions by observing revealed preferences— preference functions revealed through just such a series of choices. Therefore, if we follow Hannan and Freeman's suggestion that we imitate microeconomics, we do not have to worry about normatively weighting the various criteria or interests. Rather, we observe the organization and from its actual behavior infer its operating decision rules. Organizations continually make trade-offs among who will be served and what criteria will direct activities. The analyst does not have to make comparisons among utilities or criteria—the organization already makes such comparisons.

Such a strategy, however, does not completely solve the problem, nor does Hannan and Freeman's suggestion to use microeconomic theory as a model. For, if economics is the model, we must be careful not to follow down the path of developing a large literature concerning what the "real" goals of organizations are. In economics, this is the debate between the managerialists and the profit-maximizers—those who argue that organizations seek to maximize something other than profits, such as sales (Baumol, 1959), growth (Maris, 1963), managerial salaries (Reid, 1968), or other managerial perquisites (Williamson, 1964), versus those who seek to account for the behavior of the firm solely in terms of profit maximization. Although such attempts to assess the imputed goals of organizations are becoming increasingly sophisticated, I doubt that Hannan and Freeman believe that organizational behavior is necessarily consciously goal directed, and neither do I. Thus, searching for the true underlying motivation for organizational behavior, attempting to infer goals from actions, is likely to be both scientifically unproductive and practically impossible.

Goals, according to Hannan and Freeman, are legitimating claims to resources. Goal statements are constructed to facilitate the organization's quest for resources and are constructed and changed as required by changing conceptions of social legitimacy, without any necessary direct correspondence with organizational actions. This conceptualization of goals is one that bears more relationship to actual organizational functioning, in which intentions may be loosely coupled with actions, and intentions or goal statements may be used to provide legitimation or enhance the organization's claims to some domain or resources. Note, however, that since goals are decoupled from organizational actions and, presumably, organizational performance, effectiveness can no longer be defined with respect to goals. Thus, the identification of effectiveness with a goal approach to organizational analysis is not necessary and probably not productive. It is possible to view goals just as Hannan and Freeman have, as statements of intent, as claims to social legitimacy, resources or domains, or as retrospective rationalizations to make sense out of organizational actions—but, in any event, with little relationship to future organizational action or performance. As we shall suggest, the concept of effectiveness can still be defined, though clearly not by reference to goals conceptualized in this manner.

Hannan and Freeman's point about diffuse goals making claims to legitimacy more difficult may not be correct. There is no reason why organizations cannot make different claims in different subenvironments, much as politicians do. Furthermore, through a judicious use of secrecy and by asserting professional competence, organizations may obtain positions in which the organizations themselves can affect the definition of the satisfaction of others' demands.

If goals are legitimation, then to what end are organizational activities directed? One answer is survival, and the possibility remains that effectiveness might be defined in terms of the survival of the organization. There are some problems with this also. First, at the point survival becomes considered as an organizational goal, all of the problems enumerated with respect to other goals arise. There is some difference, as it is safer to assume that all members of the coalition that constitutes the organization would prefer its survival to its death. Assuming free movement, the participants must be receiving more benefits within the organization or else they would not participate. Consequently, survival is one organizational goal that is more likely to receive consensus. As noted elsewhere (Hannan and Freeman, 1977), the use of survival presumes the ability to identify the death of organizations, which, in turn, requires the ability to identify distinct organizational forms. Survival is a binary outcome. For some classes of organizations, such as public agencies and many large organizations, death and failure practically never occur (Aldrich and Pfeffer, 1976). Even when failure does occur, the time horizon required to study organizational mortality is likely to be fairly long, except in the case of small businesses, which emerge and fail fairly rapidly. This means that studies of organizational mortality would typically require time horizons of twenty or more years. This is all right as long as historical, archival data are available. But, when the issues to be addressed require new data collection, the problems of undertaking a study of this duration are large.

Distinctions Between Engineering and Science

The third problem with effectiveness discussed by Hannan and Freeman is that it is a term from applications and engineering and is not a concept useful for the development and testing of scientific theory. This position implicitly assumes both the necessity and the desirability of the separation of scientific from engineering or applications-oriented activity. Furthermore, there is some suggestion that a scientific approach to application is inherently a contradiction in terms. Finally, Hannan and Freeman have implicitly assumed that the study of organizations is a pure rather than an applied science and furthermore that the physical science model of theory building and testing is directly transferable to the social sciences.

Each of these assumptions is open to debate, and in no case has the debate been conclusively resolved. No doubt the European tradition in the study of formal organizations would debate the last assumption—that physical science methodologies can be imported with profit for the study of organizations. As a user of positivist methodology, I would accept, with some possible reservations, Hannan and Freeman's position on the applicability of the scientific model and scientific method to the study of organizations. However, I would question their severe separation of scientific from applications activity and argue instead that it is possible to develop a scientific approach to applications or engineering such that each activity, explanation and application, enriches the other. The model for this position is in Simon (1969).

There is little doubt that in the study of organizations the values of the researchers have occasionally interfered with the process of objective investigation, producing results that are neither good science nor good practice. In the study of participative management, for instance, a normative belief in the value of participation has at times interfered with the investigation of the determinants and consequences of particular leadership styles. The question is, however, is such interference inevitable? And is it impossible to merge, at least at some points, the scientific and the engineering approaches?

The argument against the Hannan and Freeman position has been made most cogently by Simon. He has argued that the natural science model has had too much influence on professional education, and that in the course of hankering after academic respectability, the development of a scientific approach to practice— what he terms a science of design—has been neglected. The distinction between the natural science approach and the science of design is this: "The natural sciences are concerned with how things are. . . . Design, on the other hand, is concerned with how things ought to be, with devising artifacts to attain goals" (Simon, 1969, pp. 58–59). Design is the study of the way in which means are adapted to environments. The relationship between science and design is evident. It is difficult to design methods without knowing something about how the system works. At the same time, however, it is possible that in the attempt to apply natural science knowledge to practical applications, new situations will be encountered that test theories in new ways, open up new perspectives for investigating the phenomenon, or in other ways challenge, test, or expand the domain of the natural science form of investigation.

Again, Hannan and Freeman are equivocal in their position, for although they complain about the intrusion of normative and applications-oriented considerations into the domain of scientific inquiry, they hold up microeconomic theory as a model of a desirable approach to dealing with many of the conceptual and methodological obstacles discussed. But if there is one thing true about the theory of the firm, it is that it is a normative theory. Not only does the framework assume a goal of profit maximization and employ this assumption in explaining behavior, in fact, the theory makes normative statements to the effect that profit maximization is the only appropriate goal for business organizations (for example, Friedman, 1962) and that the best environment is a competitive environment. In a competitive environment, individuals and firms each pursuing their own interests will act to achieve the best results for all in terms of resource allocations and production decisions. If effectiveness is too normative for Hannan and Freeman, then so is microeconomics. Microeconomics is at once directly linked with optimization theory and operations research and with theories of competition used to develop public policy toward mergers and other antitrust issues. An examination of Simon's (1969) ideas of what a science of design would look like indicates that management science, developed from microeconomics, is the model implicitly being employed. Thus, there is some indication that microeconomics does provide guidelines for dealing with the effectiveness issue and with the merger of natural and applied social science.

The distinction between engineering and pure science may be overdrawn by Hannan and Freeman. It is inconsistent with their own use of microeconomics as a model of a desirable approach for research. Certainly the assumptions inherent in their position taken here are open to further inquiry.

Where Do We Go from Here?

The question to be answered is, Where do we go from here with the study of organizational effectiveness? The Hannan and Freeman answer is that effectiveness is not a subject appropriate for scientific study, for the reasons just discussed. There are two responses to this position. First, many of the problems enumerated are not specific to effectiveness research, so that unless one is willing to forego all comparative research the problems must be overcome. Also, the identification of effectiveness with the goal approach is neither necessary nor productive, and the distinction between applications-oriented activity and scientific activity may not be a useful one in this context.

Second, the issue of effectiveness will not go away, even if social scientists decide that effectiveness is no longer worthy of study. The fact that organizations are social institutions, using and producing resources, including wealth and personal position, which affect many individuals and other institutions in society, makes it inevitable that those coming in contact with an organization will evaluate it in comparison with other organizations in terms of how well it serves their interests, whether its actions are consistent with their preferences—in other words, how effective for them the organization is. These assessments will be made just as consumers will make assessments about how to spend their limited resources for various bundles of goods and services. Since groups and organizations will make assessments and, furthermore, may be expected to act on such assessments to give or withhold support as the organization serves or does not serve their interests, the assessment of organizations remains an interesting and important social process—a process that has consequences for an organization's ability to acquire resources and legitimacy, and to survive.

The completely nonprocessual, population ecology approach favored by Hannan and Freeman does not treat many of these issues but rather, for analytical convenience, ignores them. There are indeed many interesting issues that are better explored from a population ecology perspective. But what must be recognized is that their position and the position articulated here are not in fundamental conflict—rather, they examine different things. To examine organizational failure and death and not to examine how that failure occurred is to investigate an important, but clearly only a partial, aspect of organizations.

The very things that Hannan and Freeman see as obstacles to studies of organizational effectiveness are, I would argue, some of the more interesting aspects of organizations. Of course, goals are multiple and contradictory within organizations. This raises the issue of how organizational action is determined. One possible answer is that organizations are indeed coalitions and, as such, have political processes within them that mediate contesting points of view. Power, derived from the ability to bring in critical resources or cope with critical contingencies, may be the currency used to resolve conflicting interests in social organizations, just as money is the currency in economic systems that resolves differences about what products are to be built.

Of course, goals are used to legitimate the organization and are not necessarily guides to action. But the use of goals for legitimation poses some interesting questions. What types of goal statements are used, general or specific, under what conditions, with what effects? Instead of taking goals as the independent variables, consider them as dependent, to be explained by considerations of the social context, competition for resources and domains, and threats to legitimacy faced by the organization. Organizations attempt to control others' assessment of them to ensure continued resources and autonomy. This may be done in a variety of ways, including keeping secret the information necessary to evaluate them; claiming special professional competence, which leaves the organization itself, or peer organizations, as the sole judge of its effectiveness; persuading others that they really want what the organization is providing; or reinterpreting the organization's actions so that they seem consistent with the demands of others. Many of these processes are quite visible in school systems, which have tended to release comparative achievement scores only under direct legislative pressure, and which claim unique professional competence to evaluate the educational process. All of these strategies are attempts to build autonomy for the organization by making it more difficult for interested parties to make independent assessments of the organization's performance. Although these processes are widely practiced and important, they have not been much studied. They are an important part of the study of effectiveness, as the processes represent ways in which the organization attempts to achieve favorable assessments by others.

Of course, there are time horizon problems, and unit and boundary issues. Why do some organizations operate with shorter, and others with longer, implicit time horizons? Do terms of office, in the case of political leaders, affect horizons? Does the ownership or control of business organizations affect the length of horizon adopted? Does the budgetary cycle, the time required to obtain feedback on performance, the age or tenure distribution of the organizational members determine time horizons? I suspect that each of these variables may have an effect. This effect needs to be empirically examined. As Aldrich (1971) has noted, some organizations have more permeable boundaries than others. What determines the permeability of a boundary, or the extent to which the organization is open to external influences? The use of selective recruitment and selective exit of members, the amount of information released into the environment—these all vary across organizations. The differences in boundary phenomena are interesting questions to be studied, not issues to be avoided.

It is not only these social processes related to the concept of effectiveness that are of interest. A conceptualization of effectiveness that permits comparative study is also possible and suggests some productive research avenues to follow. Briefly, it seems that the study of effectiveness involves an examination of: (1) the process by which various groups and interests both within and outside of the organization develop and articulate preferences; (2) the process by which the organization comes to perceive the various demands confronting it; and (3) the process by which actions and decisions are finally taken in this environment of frequently conflicting interests and demands. Organizations might be usefully conceptualized as markets in which power and influence are transacted (Pfeffer and Salancik, in press). In such a formulation, activities are determined by the distribution of power and control within the organization and the preferences of those with power and control. In turn, power is closely related to the capability of providing critical resources or solving important organizational problems. Organizations, as open social systems, must continue to transact with their environments, to import resources, and to solicit the necessary support to maintain the coalition. From this perspective, effective organizations are those that accurately perceive patterns of resource interdependence, correctly perceive demands, and then respond to those demands made by those groups that control the most critical interdependencies. One can, of course, ask whether this definition of effectiveness is empirically correlated with other indicators. I suspect it is, particularly with the organization's long-term survival and growth. Furthermore, this definition of effectiveness focuses research attention on the three processes that are embedded in it. The assessment of organizations by social actors and the determination of organizational actions taken in an environment of uncertain and conflicting demands made by these social actors represent important social processes that appear to be fundamental for understanding formal organizations. It is in this sense that the processes implied by the concept *organizational effectiveness* are critical for explaining organizational behavior.

It is possible that the term *effectiveness* itself may be becoming like the term *leadership* in organizational psychology—a red flag that elicits visceral reactions. In that case, we may consider dispensing with the term. I would argue strongly, however, against dispensing with the investigation of the phenomena and processes associated with the conceptualization of organizational effectiveness.

8

Toward a Workable Framework

Johannes M. Pennings
Paul S. Goodman

⫷⫸ ⫷⫸ ⫷⫸ ⫷⫸ ⫷⫸ ⫷⫸ ⫷⫸ ⫷⫸

This essay provides the central elements of a new conceptual framework of organizational effectiveness. The framework developed here is a loosely structured set of statements and propositions identifying salient aspects of organizational effectiveness and suggesting potentially fruitful avenues of research. It is intended to integrate middle-range theories of organizational effectiveness and provide inputs for their further development.

The research on organizational effectiveness so far has been noncumulative, and a framework that integrates and contrasts different theories should help show where future research is needed. In order to do this, this essay will first define organizational effectiveness and delineate its antecedents—that is, the internal and

146

external conditions that determine the organization's well-being. It will also identify the various interest groups that evaluate an organization's effectiveness. This joint consideration of effectiveness preconditions and interest groups requires an explicit view of complex organizations. Therefore, the essay will also discuss the nature of complex organizations, elaborating a view of the organization as an open system subject to conditions that affect its well-being and comprising a set of *determinants* of organizational effectiveness as well as accommodating a set of interest groups, or *constituencies,* that define what effectiveness is. This description is followed by a discussion of organizational environment, which is also seen as a set of determinants of effectiveness and as a set of interest groups or constituencies. The construct of organizational effectiveness and the elements that are attributed to it—that is, goals, constraints, and referents—are discussed next. Finally, a small but representative set of theories will be contrasted with the newly developed framework.

Organizations: A Definition

The recent literature on organizational effectiveness ranges from marketing research accounting for variations in retail stores' sales (Bucklin, 1977), to exploring whether social services agencies perform their intended missions (Litwak and Hilton, 1962), to studying "school effects" on students' aptitudes (Bidwell and Kasarda, 1975), to determining which organizational factors attract new members to voluntary associations (Curtis, 1971). The diversity of this literature may be partly due to the lack of interdisciplinary approaches, which leaves economists, sociologists, and psychologists unaware of each other's contributions. Viewpoints even within the field of organizational theory are widely different and often reveal, implicitly or explicitly, basically different assumptions about the nature of organizations (see Seashore and Yuchtman, 1967, or Price, 1972, for an explicit viewpoint).

These various views are often conveniently classified as either *systems* or *goal* approaches. Briefly stated, the systems approach views effectiveness as the ability to acquire scarce resources that enable the organization to survive and preserve its integration (Seashore and Yuchtman, 1967). Thus, the study on recruitment of members for voluntary associations, for example, illustrates the systems approach. The goal approach views effectiveness as the degree to which the organization attains ideal end states. The studies on social services and school effects reflect this approach.

These two different approaches to organizational effectiveness obviously are founded on different assumptions about the nature of organizations. For example, the systems approach emphasizes functional complementarity among the parts of the organization and stresses the need for maintenance. In contrast, the goal approach sees organizations as rational systems that enable the various parties involved to accomplish certain objectives. Whereas the first approach emphasizes adequate resources and avoidance of undue strain on the system, the second stresses the preferences of interest groups. A comparison between the systems approach of Katz and Kahn (1966) and the goal approach of Cyert and March (1963) or Mintzberg, Raisinghani, and Théorêt (1976) clearly distinguishes these views.

The present framework incorporates both the Katz and Kahn view and the Cyert and March view and follows Thompson's (1967) strategy of combining the open systems notion of complex organizations with the assumption that organizations represent a political arena where different groups try to promote their interests. Thus, organizations are seen as open systems having exchange relationships with their environment and with subsystems that render a contribution to the whole and to each other, show some degree of interdependence, and display some structural arrangement that tunes them in to each other and to the environment. Organizations are also seen as comprising internal interest groups, or constituencies, which make claims on the organization. An organizational consitituency is any group within an organization whose members have identifiable common interests that they try to promote. Such a constituency can be delineated by departmental or hierarchical boundaries or, more generally, by clusters of members that share distinct values and interests. Organizational subsystems, in this open systems view, both determine organizational effectiveness and play a role as constituency in defining its criteria. Likewise, actors in the environment (such as suppliers and competitors) play a dual role of determinant and constituency of effectiveness.

Internal Determinants of Effectiveness

Internal determinants are the factors within the organization itself that enhance or inhibit effectiveness. Organizations are differentiated into subunits, based on a division of labor and subject to the need of coordination. The present framework explicitly adopts this view of organizations to delineate internal determinants of effectiveness. The emphasis is on subunits and the coordination between them. Other determinants (for example, motivational characteristics of employees) are recognized but are not central to the present framework.

Organizations as open systems can be treated as comprising input, transformation, maintenance, and output subsystems. These abstracted subsystems may be paralleled by actual organizational subunits, but many organizations tend to display a higher degree of differentiation. Some subunits have an external mission (for example, sales, placement, personnel); others have an internal mission (for example, training and development, production planning, research and development). Viewing organizations as a conglomerate of subunits has several advantages: It enlarges the *scope* of the concept of effectiveness by not focusing exclusively on output parameters such as sales, patient mortality, or students' aptitude, and it avoids the conceptual difficulties of the systems resource acquisition approach (as Mohr, 1973, pointed out). That is, organizational effectiveness is associated with the contributions of subunits. This view forces one to consider the internal determinants that account for variations in organizational effectiveness. Organizational effectiveness is likely to be a function of the degree to which the subunits meet their task requirements as well as the extent to which their activities are coordinated. Organizations differ not only in their degree of horizontal differentiation but also in the interdependence of their subunits and the corresponding need for coordination (Thompson, 1967; Lawrence and Lorsch, 1967; Landsberger, 1961).

If each subunit were independent, organizational effectiveness would equal the combined effectiveness of all the subsystems.

Interdepartmental relationships are usually characterized by high degrees of interdependence. This line of thinking can be traced to the strategic contingencies theory of organizational power, co-authored by the senior author of this paper (see Hickson, Hinings, Lee, Schneck, and Pennings, 1971), which was developed to account for subunit power—hypothesized to be a function of a subunit's control of contingencies for other subunits due to the division of labor among them. This control was assumed to be some multiplicative function of each subunit's (1) coping with uncertainty, (2) substitutability, and (3) centrality. In conjunction with the nonsubstitutability of a subunit's activities and the centrality of that subunit's work flows, coping with uncertainty gives rise to dependencies of one subunit on another, since the outcomes of one subunit's behavior are contingencies for the activities of another. These three factors are necessary but not sufficient conditions for control of strategic contingencies, but jointly they affect variations in subunit interdependence.

The three concepts just cited can be used to explain the subunits' differential contribution to effectiveness. Since subunits are interdependent, each subunit influences organizational effectiveness—either directly as it affects other subunits' effectiveness or indirectly because of its overall contribution to organizational well-being. Although organizations develop buffering, procedural, planning, and communication devices to optimize the interplay of subunits (Thompson, 1967)—and thus the consequences for effectiveness—it is important to recognize that each subunit's effectiveness by itself plays a primary role in accounting for organizational effectiveness. Therefore, it seems strategically advantageous to focus on subunits' characteristics, including their technological and human resources and the social structure and processes that they have developed. To do so also orients the evaluation of effectiveness toward distinct areas of organizational behavior. That is, this line of thinking helps to avoid excluding from effectiveness considerations those subunits that do not deal with the acquisition of resources or disposal of outputs (compare the earlier mentioned goal and system resource approaches). In fact, output disposal (for example, sales, placement, rehabilitation, and so on) and resource acquisition units (for example, purchasing, recruitment, lobbying, and fund raising) do not represent the only useful areas of effectiveness evaluation. Other traditionally neglected areas such as maintenance and transformation subunits can be evaluated for effectiveness and incorporated into a mosaic of determinants of organizational effectiveness.

These statements suggest that subunits are a central focus of research on determinants of organizational effectiveness. It should be pointed out, however, that the optimization of their interplay represents another set of effectiveness determinants and can provide another area of effectiveness evaluation. It is at this point that the strategic contingencies theory becomes incomplete for effectiveness considerations. Indeed, Hickson and others (1971) explicitly state that the nature of the relationships *between* subunits is not necessarily efficient, rational, or functional for the organization. Such a statement, however, points to the next higher level of analysis, the total organization. The strategic contingencies theory's emphasis of subunit interdependence implies an additional set of determinants of effectiveness in the area of interdepartmental coordination. The importance of coordination for organizational effectiveness is dependent on the nature of the interdepartmental relationships, as elaborated by Thompson (1967), whose influential work has been a central influence on the present framework. The adequacy of coordination is assumed to improve subunits' effectiveness and thus organizational effectiveness.

The present framework stresses organizational effectiveness and especially the distinct areas of its determinants and evaluation. Although this framework does not emphasize technological, motivational, or task variables, these also represent viable areas of effectiveness research. A number of middle-range theories have described variables with demonstrated effects on effectiveness—for example, the organization's reward system, recruitment and socialization processes, and social and task structure. After having defined the construct of effectiveness we shall return to the levels of aggregation issue and make an attempt to synthesize the subunit and organizational levels of analysis.

Internal Constituencies

In addition to *determining* organizational effectiveness, either directly or indirectly, subunits also act as potential interest groups, or *constituencies,* which pursue their own interests—even at the expense of other subunits or the total organization. Hickson and others (1971) recognized this but also acknowledged that organizations as interconnected or strongly coupled systems put limits on how far subunits can go in their tendency to suboptimization. Due to their differential control of strategic contingencies, however, subunits enjoy a certain leverage in setting the criteria of effectiveness; *suboptimization,* then, is defining effectiveness with a bias toward a particular subunit and its goals. Thus, the strategic contingencies theory, which helps explain the determination of effectiveness, is also potentially very useful in conceptualizing the process and the end results of the negotiated definition of the criteria of the organization's effectiveness.

To explain how organizations set their criteria of effectiveness, this paper borrows Thompson's (1967) notion of *dominant coalition.* The dominant coalition comprises a direct and indirect "representation" or cross-section of horizontal constituencies (that is, subunits) and vertical constituencies (such as employees, management, owners, or stockholders) with different and possibly competing expectations. Consensus about the importance of the various criteria of effectiveness is hypothesized to be a function of the relative weights that the various constituencies carry in the negotiated order which we call organization. Consensus among members of the dominant coalition can be employed as a vehicle for obtaining effectiveness data. For example, how important is market share versus employee satisfaction? What should be the trade-off between research and development, between teaching and research, between patient care, medical research, and physicians' education? And so on. The consensus of the coalition allows the identification of such effectiveness criteria. These criteria may have different degrees of importance for the different constituencies in the dominant coalition; but somehow the preferences and expectations are aggregated, combined, modified, adjusted, and shared by the members of the dominant coalition. By invoking the concept of dominant coalition it is possible to preserve the notion of organizations as rational decision-making entities. This is felt to be a more useful approach than one in which an "enlightened" investigator defines effectiveness criteria through induction (because data are conveniently available) or through deduction (because of his idiosyncratic theory). Also, it

makes explicit that our concern is *organizational* effectiveness and
not effectiveness of lower or higher levels of aggregation (for example, individual and industry level or student and school district
level).

The relative influence of a subunit as an effectiveness determinant—although potentially useful in identifying the dominant
coalition—does not necessarily predict whether that subunit will
define the criteria of organizational effectiveness. The earlier assertion that the "votes" of the dominant coalition members correspond
to their control of strategic contingencies may evoke associations
with political models of organizational decision making in which a
number of actors in the dominant coalition, through some majority
rule, define the criteria of effectiveness. Despite this association,
several other scenarios with a lack of correspondence between determinants and constituencies are possible. For example, members
of the dominant coalition might display a tendency toward oligar-
chization similar to Robert Michels' description of party functioning
in *Political Parties*. In a different scenario, the dominant coalition
could be degenerated into some replica of an office of management
and budget that simply reads, encodes, and decodes the information of the various constituencies and incorporates this information
into the definition of organizational effectiveness and the equitable
distribution of inducements. A different scenario would be an
organization dominated by a single individual who enjoys the
general support of the relevant constituencies; this dominant coalition would include one person only. Such departures from typical
strategic contingencies theory expectations are common and represent an interesting research challenge. For example, under what
conditions will the members of dominant coalitions become isolated
from their constituencies and how can they prevent a collapse of
the power structure that would undermine their integrity? To what
extent can their distribution of inducements differ from those that
optimize some welfare distribution?

To review, organizations can be seen as open systems comprising various subsystems that individually and jointly determine
organizational effectiveness and also help (as one set of constituencies) to define the criteria of organizational effectiveness.
These constituencies have competing and potentially incompatible

positions, which are differentially accepted, sanctioned, and represented by the dominant coalition—the ultimate source for establishing criteria of organizational effectiveness.

It should be stressed that determinants internal to the organization and subject to its control are not the only relevant effectiveness determinants. Indeed, this essay will argue that environmental conditions are crucial in explaining interorganizational variations in effectiveness. Furthermore, setting effectiveness criteria is not the sole prerogative of internal interest groups. There are also *external* constituencies that influence the evaluation of an organization's effectiveness. This dual nature of environment with respect to organizational effectiveness requires a further elaboration.

Organizational Environment

The environment of an organization consists of individuals, groups, and organizations that provide resources for organizational input and that are recipients of organizational output. Organizations depend on these actors for both resources and information; this dependence has important implications for effectiveness. The actors, including buyers, sellers, competitors, and governmental agencies, play a dual role as external determinants of effectiveness and external constituencies.

Actors in the environment are *determinants* of effectiveness when they have some control over the focal organization's input acquisition or its output disposal. Organizations either adapt themselves to an existing pool of actors, in turn gaining some control over them, or they select an environment that is congruent with their goals, technology, and structure.

Some actors may also be considered *external constituencies*. Influential organizations such as some suppliers, competitors, or regulatory agencies set constraints and define appropriate referents of organizational effectiveness, which become incorporated in the overall assessment of organizational effectiveness. In this sense, one would view the organizational environment as a political economy composed of constituencies.

To further delineate this dual role of external actors, it is again useful to invoke the strategic contingencies theory. Since these external actors are mostly other organizations, it appears that most exchange relationships can be described on the interorganizational level. However, an interorganizational collectivity is a very loosely coupled "system"—if it is a system at all. The division of labor among buyers and sellers is usually ambiguous (the possible exception being bilateral oligopoly); but on a dyadic level a focal organization's dependence on external actors could be described along the dimensions of substitutability and centrality. As will be discussed shortly, these dimensions are important necessary but not sufficient conditions for external actors to be external constituencies.

The term *substitutability* refers to the replaceability of suppliers or customers from the point of view of the focal organization. The term *centrality* refers to the importance and degree of connectivity of these actors to the focal organization (see Hickson and others, 1971). For example, steel is an important input for firms in the automotive and construction industries (the focal organizations), although a steel supplier may be more critical for the former than for the latter—that is, the speed and severity of disruption of supply may have a greater effect on the automotive firm. However, steel is an undifferentiated product, and there are many domestic and foreign firms that compete with the suppliers of the focal organization. To cite other examples, a power company obtains its inputs from a single coal mine, exemplifying high substitutability but also high centrality; a United Way Fund agency gets virtually all its funds from a single source, illustrating low substitutability and high centrality; finally, a brewery gets its water supply from one source, illustrating low substitutability, unless it can tap other sources. Substitutability and centrality probably have a multiplicative effect on the focal organizations; that is, they both have to be present for the actor to influence the focal organization (see Blau, 1964).

Environmental actors' ability to cope with uncertainty is less important than substitutability and centrality as an aspect of a focal organization's relationship with its environment. This assumption is based on the problematic nature of the division of labor or functional complementarity between the focal organization and organizations in its environment. For example, a failure of the earlier mentioned coal mine to cope with uncertainties will not affect the utility company's effectiveness. Such interorganizational relationships are often characterized by much lower degrees of nonsubstitutability and centrality than internal relationships and therefore are much less subject to the effects of coping. Indeed, it could be hypothesized that this construct of the strategic contingencies' theory has little relevance to analyzing interorganizational relationships and their effectiveness correlates.

In our analysis coping with uncertainty is an important factor at the intraorganizational, subunit level because the division of labor among them induces a functional complementarity. The complementarity creates dependency relationships reflecting a subunit's ability to become an effectiveness constituency. In contrast, at an interorganizational level such functional complementarity is mostly absent. Therefore the differential coping with uncertainty among organizations has often little relevance for a focal organization's effectiveness. However, although coping is not likely to be a major predictor, it can be hypothesized that substitutability carries a great weight in predicting effectiveness. This is based on the assumption that a very loosely coupled system such as a dyad of organizations will prevail only if the exchange relationship provides sufficient incentive for any of the two partners to continue it. Unlike organizational subunits, organizations have great discretion in deciding to continue or to discontinue the exchange relationship. If substitutability increases, the relationship will become more unstable; conversely, a focal organization's effectiveness becomes highly contingent upon external exchange relationships if the external actor becomes nonsubstitutable. Dependency increases and the relationship will become more stable. The dependencies will be reinforced if the actor's goods and services are central for the focal organization.

In addition to these constructs, it is also necessary to incorporate *institutionalization* as a significant attribute for understanding the role of external actors. Institutionalization refers to the level of organization or structuring of the actor. Without institutionalization, environmental groups or corporate actors may lack significant influence on the focal organization's effectiveness. For example, it is only after farmers have formed cooperatives that grain dealers experience constraints on the supply of wheat. Suppliers or buyers may be critical actors, but they often have little countervailing power unless they become organized into, for instance, farmers' cooperatives and consumer associations. The institutionalization will reinforce the effects of nonsubstitutability and centrality.

These three aspects—substitutability, centrality, and institutionalization—indicate the likely influence of suppliers, buyers, or third parties on the focal organization's activities and hence its effectiveness; but influence should covary highly with *awareness* of the relationship between the focal organization and external actors. The external actors must be aware of the magnitude of their influence on the focal organization before they can be expected to exploit their leverage. Influence and awareness among external actors can be assessed by traditional survey techniques or by public and company records.

Figure 1 further clarifies this conceptualization of interorganizational relationships. Each organization has dyadic relationships with organizations in its environment. Figure 1 provides a simplified illustration of such a set of dyadic relationships. The focal organization, X_f, has exchanges with suppliers, buyers, and third parties such as regulatory agencies and professional associations. Furthermore, the focal organization may be a monopolist or an oligopolist, or it may face a large number of competitors. Thus, in Figure 1, X may be zero, a few, or many members. Organizations belonging to an industry or market may be represented in Figure 1 by the symbols X, S, B, or T. Figure 1 gives a representation of the environment from the perspective of the focal organization and is similar to Evan's (1972) *organizational* set and Thorelli's (1967) *ecosystem*. An organizational set consists of all organizations with which the focal organization has exchange relationships. An ecosystem is a collection of all relevant environmental conditions and actors that impinge on the focal organization.

Some actors serve as both a determinant and a constituency with respect to the focal organization. We assume there is a strong correlation between the actor's potential influence on a focal organization's effectiveness and the actor's ability as a constituency to contribute to the setting of effectiveness criteria. That is, an actor has to be a determinant in order to be a constituency. Some orga-

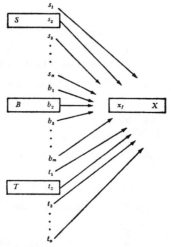

Meaning of symbols:

$x_j =$ focal organization

$x_i =$ member of X

$X = [x_1, x_2, x_3, \ldots x_p]$ competitors of focal organization

$s_i =$ supplier

$S = [s_{21}, s_{22}, s_{23}, \ldots s_{2q}]$ competitors of supplier 2 (secondary environment)

$b_i =$ buyer

$B = [b_{21}, b_{22}, b_{23}, \ldots b_{2r}]$ competitors of buyer 2 (secondary environment)

$t_i =$ third party, for example, regulatory agency pressure group or government

$T = [t_{21}, t_{22}, \ldots t_{2s}]$ third parties associated with t_i, but *not* interacting with x_j (secondary environment)

Figure 1.   Schematic Description of Organizational Environment.

nizations have both the ability to influence the focal organization and the incentive to exploit it; other organizations refrain from their potential role as a constituency. Organizations that refrain from active involvement in the dominant coalition of another organization may do so because they fear legal reprisals (for example, antitrust suits) or simply because they operate with constraints that limit the scope of their organizational activities. In contrast, there are other organizations that have little immediate impact on another organization's input acquisition, or output disposal, but that do serve in a constituency role. For example, many black community organizations have introduced constraints into firms' hiring practices. These constituencies have either worked through other constituencies (for example, government regulatory agencies) of the focal organization or have directly confronted the focal organization. This type of constituency differs from the modal case in that it is not involved in a dyadic relationship with the focal organization over exchanges in inputs or outcome disposal. Its major orientation is to influence the focal organization in adopting a new standard for evaluating effectiveness. This distinction among organizations that serve as both determinants and constituencies, only determinants, or only constituencies is intriguing and needs further exploration.

To summarize, we view organizational environment as having a dual nature. The concept of organizational set may be useful in identifying external actors that affect the organization's input, acquisition, or output disposal. This concept views environment as a set of effectiveness determinants that require organizations to be tuned to the environment so that they can perform effectively. The organizational environment may also be viewed as including actors that play a strategic role in an organization's well-being and thus can be identified as external constituencies. The environment is thus represented as a "political economy" that requires the focal organization to manage interorganizational relationships. This meaning of environment is clearly visible when the focus is on the homogeneous sets of organizations that coordinate their activities because of mutual dependence, as in the case of oligopoly. These two views of environment are complementary in conceptualizing and explaining organizational effectiveness.

This analysis of organization and environment has been at
the level of the organizational set—that is, those organizations with
a direct exchange relationship with the focal organization. Such
organizations do not exist as a collective structure. That is, there
is no collectivity of suppliers, buyers, regulators, and so on, interacting with a particular focal organization. To understand completely
the roles of environment and organization as they bear on organizational effectiveness, one may have to move to a higher level of
analysis such as the market or industry level (represented by the
symbols B, S, T, and X in Figure 1). Unlike organizational sets
(*primary environment*), industry or markets (*secondary environment*) may have distinct patterns of coordination, communication,
and stratification. Organizations in this secondary environment do
not have exchange relationships with the focal organization, but can
influence its suppliers and other actors in the environment. Market
structure of suppliers or buyers may indirectly influence the degree
to which a supplier or buyer affects the focal organization's input
or output subsystem. Thus, it may be necessary to move to the
next higher level of analysis and identify collective structures among
customers, suppliers, or competitors in order to understand fully
their strategic and possible collective relationship to the focal organization (Pennings, 1977; Hirsch, 1975).

Organizational Effectiveness: A Definition

Organizations are effective if relevant constraints can be
satisfied and if organizational results approximate or exceed a set
of referents for multiple goals.

Constraints, Goals, and Referents. Constraints are conditions
that must be satisfied if an organization is to be considered effective;
these conditions are operationally defined by a set of referents or
standards. Failure to meet constraints represents a state of organizational ineffectiveness. Constraints appear in organizations as policy
statements or decision rules that guide behavior. For example,
policies such as maintaining market share at a certain percentage,
maintaining quality at a certain level, and not doing business in
foreign countries requiring political kickbacks all represent constraints on the organization.

Organizational *goals* represent desired end states specified by the dominant coalition. Organizational goals and constraints are similar in that they both are used in the assessment of effectiveness. Also, both can encompass the same substantive dimensions. Organizational goals and constraints differ in two respects. First, goals receive special attention from the dominant coalition. When certain input or output aspects receive special attention because they are more closely related to the motivations of central decision makers and are more often used in the search for alternative courses of action, they are considered organizational goals rather than constraints (Simon, 1964). That is, whether achieving a particular quantity or quality level is a goal or constraint depends partially on which is more central to the organization's dominant coalition. For example, some U.S. universities emphasize the number of students enrolled as a constraint for quality of academic excellence, whereas other universities emphasize high enrollment but are constrained by the need of maintaining a minimum level of academic excellence. A second distinction is that goals may or may not approximate a referent, whereas constraints must be satisfied as a necessary condition of organizational effectiveness. Degrees (or the relative amount) of organizational effectiveness can be assessed by the degree to which a goal approximates or exceeds a referent. For a constraint, failure to satisfy a referent leads to organizational ineffectiveness, meeting the referent imbedded in the constraint provides the necessary condition for effectiveness, and exceeding the referent does not lead to a greater degree of effectiveness. For example, an organization might want to increase profits by a certain percentage and at the same time maintain quality of their services at a given level. If maintaining the quality level is a constraint, it would be a necessary condition for effectiveness. Failing to maintain the given level of quality would lead to ineffectiveness, but exceeding that level would not add to effectiveness. However, increasing profitability beyond a certain percentage would be an indication of a greater level of effectiveness than if the organization simply achieved that level. Similarly, achieving the level would be preferred to achieving a level below it.

Referents are the standards against which constraints and goals are evaluated. That is, the referents imbedded in the constraints and outcomes specify the dominant coalition's standards of effectiveness. The actual results, when compared to these referents, provide a measure of organizational effectiveness. Referents can be internal or external to the organization. Internal referents are standards unique to the given organization, whereas external referents are standards based on information from other organizations. Referents can also be categorized as static or dynamic. A static referent concerns a particular point in time; a dynamic referent concerns rate of change over time. Providing services to a given number of clients would be an example of an internal static referent; comparing the market share of Firm A with Firm B would be an example of an external static referent. If a welfare agency wanted to increase its services to a larger population of clients by 10 percent, this would be an example of an internal dynamic referent. Comparing rates of change in market share between firms would be an external dynamic referent.

Evaluating organizational effectiveness is a complex process, since multiple constraints and goals must be specified. It is highly unlikely that one can evaluate effectiveness with a single referent. For each constraint or goal, multiple referents may be assigned. The task in evaluating effectiveness is one of comparing actual results with the referents imbedded in the constraints or relevant goals. Evaluating effectiveness is an after-the-fact rather than before-the-fact task. It can be argued that the actual behaviors or outputs must satisfy or meet the referents for the constraint in question. For outcomes, the behavior or outputs can meet or exceed the referents as an indication of effectiveness. Evaluating effectiveness is also a relative activity. The closer the organization approximates the referent in the goal, the greater the effectiveness. An asymmetrical relationship for constraints is postulated. Failure to satisfy the constraints leads to ineffectiveness rather than to degrees of ineffectiveness. The process of evaluation is feasible only when referents can be stated in an operational form.

Effectiveness and Efficiency. Efficiency is the ratio of the units produced or obtained to resources or costs required to obtain or produce those units. Efficiency measures the amount of resources used relative to outputs in the processes of acquiring inputs, transforming inputs, and disposing of completed outputs or services. For example, manpower is a resource the organization uses to obtain inputs, to transform these inputs, or to dispose of the outputs. The ratio of supplies acquired over units of labor spent acquiring these supplies is one measure of input efficiency. The number of units produced over labor inputs is a common efficiency measure used in the production or transformation process. The cost of disposing of a product is a measure of output disposal efficiency.

Knowing the ratio of outputs over inputs is not in itself sufficient to evaluate efficiency. The ratio is at best a statement of an actual state of affairs. As was the case with effectiveness, we need to be able to specify constraints, goals, and referents. Thus, we may also establish the dominant coalition's consensus with respect to efficiency goals, efficiency constraints, and referents of efficiency. For example, an organization can try to increase its labor efficiency ratio by 10 percent (internal dynamic referent) while maintaining an accident level (constraint) comparable to other similar organizations (external static referent).

Effectiveness and efficiency are similar in that both incorporate the concepts of constraints and referents. Effectiveness and efficiency differ in that the former refers to input acquisition or output disposal levels, and the latter adjusts those levels in reference to some cost or resource utilization unit. For example, instead of evaluating how many burglaries a police department has solved one might ask how much is spent to solve them. Similarly, it is often more interesting to know the cost of goods sold rather than the actual volume of sales.

This essay views effectiveness and efficiency as complementary—differing only as to whether one wants to investigate input acquisition or output levels alone, or in the context of some cost unit. During the subsequent discussion, reference will usually be made to the first concept alone, although the discussion is also germane to efficiency. It should also be stressed that efficiency can be used to describe input acquisition as well as output disposal processes. Researchers tend to use *organizational effectiveness* rather than *organizational efficiency* since the term *efficiency* carries negative connotations. The fact that the term *effectiveness* seems more palatable than efficiency should not lead researchers to avoid the concept of efficiency. Indeed, *efficiency* may often be a more pertinent construct for the assessment of organizational effectiveness.

Organizational Effectiveness and Time Frame. Another

critical issue is the determination of time periods for assessing effectiveness. The time lags between a determinant and its effectiveness consequences vary widely. In some cases the results of subsystem behavior are known immediately; in other cases consequences are not known for several years. Failure to identify the appropriate period leads to misspecification in assessing organizational effectiveness. Although there is no simple way to specify the time periods, a number of factors can be considered.

The most obvious period to use is the annual fiscal period, since this corresponds to the way most organizations generate their data. On a practical basis, information would be readily available during this period, and most organizations would formally establish new constraints, referents, and goals during this time. Time periods might also be identified by using a variant of Jaques' (1964) concept of time span. Effectiveness could be evaluated within the length of time necessary to determine if a decision (or set of decisions) was unacceptable. Consider, for example, assessing the effectiveness of the input process in acquiring manpower. In this case, effectiveness of the manpower decisions would be assessed in three years, the time period being the length of time it takes to determine acceptable effectiveness.

Changes in major external determinants of an organization's effectiveness can also be used to determine time periods. Whether an organization operates in an expanding or contracting environment clearly affects how well it can dispose of its outcomes. One strategy in defining time periods might be to use major changes in external factors (for example, the period of a contracting market) as a boundary condition. So if one were to evaluate the effectiveness of the acquisition of manpower inputs, the time period would be determined by major changes in the labor market. A swing from relatively low to high unemployment would suggest two time periods for analysis (for example, the low and high unemployment periods). To assess the implementation of a new government policy, one could assess the responsible agency's efforts during the period in which a program is in effect.

Organizational Effectiveness—Aggregation Across Constituencies and Levels. A basic assumption in this discussion has been that organizational effectiveness is a multidimensional concept.

There is no single constraint, goal, or referent to define it. In addition, organizational effectiveness ought to be evaluated with respect to both input acquisition and output disposal units as well as maintenance and transformation units. Within these areas multiple goals, constraints, and referents may be detected. For example, the effectiveness of an airline may hinge not only on number of passengers transported or earnings per share but also on the quality of services or number of accidents per passenger mile. Furthermore, this essay stresses the impact on the organization's well-being of internal and external constituencies that may differentially contribute to the definition of multiple goals, constraints, and referents.

The multiple goals, constraints, and referents provided by various constituencies serve as inputs (about resource acquisition, output disposal, or other areas of concern) into the definition of effectiveness criteria by members of the dominant coalition. The resulting consensus is the outcome of the negotiation over *joint space*—a multidimensional structure representing the weighted preferences of the various constituencies with their goals, constraints, and referents on pertinent areas of organizational behavior. The theoretical reconstruction of how such joint spaces are arrived at is a formidable task. Most of the substantial amount of theoretical work on joint spaces so far has been in the form of game theory (exemplified by pareto optimality, see Luce and Raiffa, 1957). In these game situations optimality represents a point that satisfies the joint utility functions of all the participants. In complex organizations, however, such utility functions are not easily ascertained, nor can we assume that there is a single utility dimension. Most organizations are more complex than two- or three-person games—in fact, there is a hugh gap between the simplified world of game theory and the complex world of organizations. We cannot simply assume that each constituency has a one-dimensional preference that is comparable and isomorphic with those of others.

The combination of goals, constraints, and referents across constituencies is not the only problem that plagues effectiveness research. There are also aggregation problems across levels. That is, the framework has stressed the focus on organizations as conglomerates of subunits, and the strategic contingencies theory was invoked to delineate the subunits' role in determining effectiveness. In addition, however, it was stated that effectiveness considerations on the subunit level have to be supplemented by an organization-level analysis.

The analogy with economic production functions can further clarify this aggregation issue. Each subunit's outputs could be expressed as a function of its labor, capital technology, and material inputs. The framework would add to these components a subunit's coping with uncertainty, its substitutability, and its centrality. Thus, it is suggested to incorporate noneconomic antecedents into a subunit's production function. Also, as implied by the strategic contingencies theory, subunits represent a major additional class of determinants of each other's effectiveness. They differ in their contribution to each others' effectiveness and hence also to the total organization's effectiveness.

As indicated earlier, there are problems in aggregating the resource acquisition or output disposal of subunits to arrive at conclusions about organizational level effectiveness. Except in the case of pooled interdependence, exemplified by bank branch offices or department store units, we cannot simply add the input acquisitions or output disposals of the various subunits. For example, even under a sophisticated transfer pricing system that would assign a uniform currency to the various outputs of the various subunits one cannot simply combine subunit accomplishments to arrive at an organization's production function. Transfer pricing represents an attempt to turn subunits into profit or cost centers by assigning a standardized value to their inputs or outputs. However, it is clear that the effectiveness of a university's library or that of a plant's maintenance department cannot be added to that of other units within these respective organizations. Rather it would be preferable to construct a quasi-production function of the total organization. One component of this production function might be the subunits' functions, but also the coordination patterns among subunits. The magnitude of coordination depends on whether the relationship among subunits is that of serial or reciprocal interdependence. The notions of serial and reciprocal interdependence, introduced by Thompson (1967), indicate exchange relationships between subunits. Subunits exchange information or energy sequentially or reciprocally, or not at all, in which case Thompson refers to the so-called pooled interdependence. Although it is apparent that effectiveness at the subunit level and effectiveness at the organization level stand in a dialectical relationship to each other, it will require a major effort to synthesize these two levels.

In addition to the coordination patterns among subunits, the organization's production function should also include data on external determinants. The role of external determinants is most salient for those organizations with a strong external orientation and high degree of openness as revealed by resource dependence on external actors. External determinants are less salient components of production functions of those organizations that are relatively closed and that put a heavy emphasis on their transformation systems. An organization's effectiveness is influenced not only by dyadic linkages with external actors but also by random external events, and particularly by changes in economic conditions. These determinants as well as the other ones are considered analytically distinct, each independently contributing to an organization's effectiveness and efficiency. Middle-range theories have to be developed to assess the role that each of these classes of determinants plays and to delineate where and how the aggregation levels intersect.

Finally, it should be stressed that the aggregation issues do not center only around economic aspects; there are many noneconomic aspects that could be specified by the dominant coalition. For example, the dominant coalition could define employee satisfaction, patients' well-being, or student athletic performance as a desired organizational outcome. Especially in nonprofit organizations, where economic cost-benefit considerations are less salient, we can expect a stronger orientation to psychological and sociological aspects. Middle-range theories represent the best strategy for dealing with the complexity of aggregation of economic and noneconomic aspects in a wide variety of organizations.

Role of Constituencies in Establishing Constraints, Outcomes, and Referents. The definition of organizational effectiveness has been based on the view of an organization as an open system consisting of subsystems and transacting with the environment to gain inputs, process them, and dispose of newly created goods and services. The definition of organization also includes the concept of constituencies and the dominant coalition. Each constituency is oriented to maximize its inducements from the organization and minimize its contributions. The critical role of the constituencies in our view of organizational effectiveness is in the definition of constraints, goals, and referents. The discussion so far has focused on questions such as, How is organizational effectiveness defined, and what are its aspects? Now it is necessary to consider the agents of evaluation of effectiveness, or more specifically, the actors who define the constraints, goals, and appropriate referents for evaluating effectiveness.

The establishment of constraints, goals, and referents in the focal organization follows from the bargaining process between the constituencies or their representatives in the dominant coalition. Constituencies are likely to bring different preferences to the bargaining process, and conflict is likely to occur. Of interest here is not only the different constituencies' referent preferences but also the process by which the dominant coalition selects referents. The referent adopted by the dominant coalition provides an important guide to behavior.

Bargaining between constituencies has two main effects. First it focuses attention on a specific set of constraints, outcomes, and referents. Why, for example, does the dominant coalition select one set of referents out of a large set of potential referents? One reason is that the bargaining process focuses attention on a specific set. That is, given the limited information-processing capabilities of members of the dominant coalition, some mechanism must exist to select from the large set of potential constraints, goals, and referents. The bargaining process serves as such a mechanism. By focusing attention on a certain set of information, the constituencies create a degree of awareness, a necessary condition for adopting referents. There are many possible examples of how constituencies serve this function. Trade associations require certain types of information and provide comparable information on the industry as a whole. This source of information provides the opportunity for the organization to select external referents by which to assess its effectiveness. Regulatory agencies often require organizations to collect information specific to the regulatory agency's goals (for example, product safety, "equal time" in broadcasting, or effluent standards). This source of information creates a new dimension of effectiveness for the dominant coalition to assess. Similarly, some external constituencies are involved in a direct exchange of resources with the dominant coalition. This exchange often requires the generation of data (for example, number of clients served, proportion of female employees recruited, and change in dividends per share) that can be used to assess effectiveness.

The second effect of the bargaining process is that it requires the dominant coalition to assess alternative combinations of constraints, goals, and referents as they bear on the organization's ratio of inducements to contributions. Organizations select referents that represent the inducement-contribution balance favorably. Similarly, referents that put the organization's inducement-contribution ratio in an unfavorable light are likely to be avoided. The problem for the dominant coalition is to assess the consequences of adopting or institutionalizing a set of constraints, goals, or referents advocated by a constituency. The dominant coalition's basic decision rule is to maximize the inducement-contribution balance in favor of the organization.

The following example illustrates how constraints and referents are established. Let us consider a hypothetical case of a steel company and the Environmental Protection Agency (EPA)—a U.S. government agency. One of the objectives of the EPA is to monitor and improve the quality of the water resources. The more water quality improves, the better the EPA accomplishes one of its missions. One way for the EPA to fulfill its mission would be to get the steel company to adopt a particular effluent level for its discharges. This would represent a constraint for the firm. The firm must satisfy this constraint operationalized with some referent when determining the optimum allocation of resources in its production function. This constraint also represents a cost to many of the other constituencies, since resources (for example, pollution control equipment) are diverted from their own areas of concern. The company's dominant coalition would probably resist the adoption of this constraint. A bargaining process would probably ensue, with the dominant coalition in this case attempting to curtail any actions the Environmental Protection Agency undertakes to minimize the firm's inducement-contribution ratio. The firm in this case can comply by adopting the effluent level, not comply, or propose a new level. The judgment by the dominant coalition will be in terms of the expected cost (for example, fines, court costs, goodwill damage, plant close-down) of complying or not complying. If the firm complies, the new constraints would be incorporated in its evaluation of effectiveness and efficiency. If the firm does not comply and the Environmental Protection Agency does not penalize the firm, then effectiveness would be evaluated without the constraint. Another possible comparison point for evaluation would be to examine effectiveness with and without the constraint. The other option, if the firm does not comply, is that it will be assessed penalties by the Environmental Protection Agency. In this case, the increased costs that would contribute to lower degrees of effectiveness with respect to other goals and their referents would be included in the assessment of effectiveness.

A critical point in this example is that the constraint is adopted by the dominant coalition in light of the assessment of the costs of complying versus not complying. That is, to what extent could the external constituency negatively affect the firm's inducement-contribution ratios? It is not surprising that different external constituencies (Environmental Protection Agency, trade unions, suppliers) would like the steel firm to adopt constraints beneficial to their own interests and would view the relative effectiveness from different perspectives. Needless to state, various internal constituencies contribute another portfolio of perspectives to this set of perspectives so that the end result is a hybrid set of constraints, goals, and referents that forms the basis of evaluating the steel firm's effectiveness. We propose, however, to evaluate effectiveness not in terms of the various constituencies' demands but in terms of the organizational constraints set by the dominant coalition in the light of its interactions with its constituencies.

The discussion of establishing constraints focused primarily on external constituencies. The same analysis would follow for internal constituencies. For example, if prisoners demanded rehabilitative privileges, the prison administration might adopt a rehabilitation policy providing a constraint on the custodial referents of the institution. Whether the monitoring agents or the legislature adopt this constraint depends on their assessment of the extent to which the prisoners as a constituency can affect the prison's operations.

The more expendable the demands of the inmates and the less control they have over enforcing their demands, the less likely the prison would be to adopt rehabilitation policies as a constraint for protecting society against the inmates.

Through a process of bargaining between the constituencies and the dominant coalition, constraints, goals, and referents are established. The constraints and referents are then used by the organization, represented by the dominant coalition, to evaluate its effectiveness or efficiency. Although constituencies may hold many referents and constraints with which to evaluate the organization, it is only to the extent that these constraints and referents can be imposed on the organization that they become useful tools for assessing effectiveness.

Internal actors, by virtue of their complementarity due to division of labor and functional differentiation, represent a well-bounded set of determinants of effectiveness. Their relative importance in determining effectiveness is also hypothesized to affect their influence as constituencies in the formulation of goals, constraints, and referents. However, being a determinant is not a necessary or sufficient condition for affecting the dominant coalition's consensus on effectiveness criteria. For example, an inner circle of coalition partners may emerge from the dominant coalition. Many organizations have gone through a process in which some leading decision makers have acquired additional dominance. Michels' *Political Parties* describes such developmental processes, the results of which may differ from what one would expect of determinants and their relative importance. "Political" processes exist in complex organizations and are crucial in determining what goals, constraints, and referents are adopted for evaluating organizational effectiveness. The interplay of internal and external constituencies will make this task difficult. Even the most inwardly directed organizations may eventually be under external pressures to modify their goals, constraints, and referents; but apart from this it is important to recognize the existence of external constituencies that may modify the view of internal effectiveness.

The present view, then, is of an organization made up of many constituencies that influence the setting of constraints, goals, and referents. Much intriguing research awaits to be done. Some of it may focus on the cycle through which organizational effectiveness gets evaluated. Other research may focus on decisions about referents or goals beyond the main parts of the organization. Still other inquiries might focus on the patterns of decision making of the dominant coalition and what inputs the internal versus external constituencies provide in this decision-making process. These and other research issues are difficult to deal with but are bound to become increasingly salient when an organization's environment challenges the organization's mission and the responses that internal constituencies might provide to such challenges.

Present Framework Compared with the Literature

It might be useful to compare the present framework of organizational effectiveness with others found in the literature in order to identify the extent to which our framework is the same, a synthesis, or a departure in conceptualizing effectiveness. The actual process of comparison is quite complex. In many of the writings on effectiveness, ideas and positions are both explicitly and implicitly stated. The problem in making comparisons is to represent accurately the conceptual papers being compared. To facilitate this process, only major ideas that are explicitly stated will be examined. For example, in reviewing determinants of organizational effectiveness, the writer must specify the determinants and state something about their relationship to the organizational effectiveness criteria. A casual reference or a general discussion of the structural characteristics of organizations (for example, authority, integration) will not appear in this analysis. Although there were a large number of conceptual frameworks that might have been selected, only five are examined here. They were selected because they are frameworks that have been frequently referenced in the literature and also because together they illustrate conceptualizations of effectiveness from both the psychological and sociological perspectives. Table 1 lists the major concepts used to compare the frameworks.

Argyris. For Argyris, organizational effectiveness represents a condition in which the organization, over time, increases outputs with constant or decreasing inputs or has constant outputs with decreasing inputs (Argyris, 1964, p. 123). This definition treats efficiency and effectiveness as the same. That is, effectiveness is defined in input and output terms. Organizational ineffectiveness is a condition in which inputs are increasing while outputs remain constant or decrease.

This abstract definition of effectiveness is then applied to three core organizational areas: achieving objectives, maintaining the internal system, and adapting to the external environment. Effectiveness is the relationship between the outputs in these three areas and the inputs or energy used to perform these activities. For example, consider an organization whose objective is to make shoes. If an increase in shoe production occurs with the same or decreasing inputs, then the organization is said to be effective regarding that particular objective. In the area of "maintaining the internal system" Argyris includes activities such as hiring and training. Effectiveness in this area would be defined in terms of the number of people hired or trained in relation to the resources used to perform these activities. In the third core area—adapting to the external environment—effectiveness would be defined in a similar manner. The more favorable relationships between a company and the government that can be achieved with the same or decreasing resources, the greater the effectiveness in this core area. Argyris also differentiates effectiveness from other concepts such as organizational stress, organizational discomfort, and organizational pseudo-effectiveness. The last refers to a state in which organizational members perceive the system to be effective when it is indeed ineffective. For our purposes, the key contrasts focus on Argyris' definition of effectiveness and ineffectiveness.

Table 1 presents a contrast between this essay's conceptualization of effectiveness and that of Argyris. The elements of the definitions are different: This definition characterizes effectiveness with referents, constraints, and goals; and efficiency and effectiveness are separated. Although both conceptualizations view effectiveness as a concept composed of multiple elements, the substantive elements are different—in this essay effectiveness is defined in terms of resource or input acquisition and output disposal, whereas Argyris defines three core areas.

In his discussion on organizational effectiveness, Argyris briefly lists some potential internal determinants of effectiveness;

however, no systematic discussion of the determinants and their interrelationships is presented. The role of constituencies both internal and external to the organization also is not discussed. Although the importance of the organization's environment is indicated by Argyris' selection of adaptation to the external environment as a critical core area, there is no specification of the role of the environment in determining or defining effectiveness.

Argyris' analysis of effectiveness is clearly at the organizational level. This is a departure from the major level of analysis in his work, which focuses on the effect of the organization on the individual. In terms of the time dimension, Argyris does view organizations and their effectiveness from a dynamic perspective. However, there is no discussion of the time frames that might be appropriate in assessing the effectiveness of the different core areas.

Katz and Kahn. The Social Psychology of Organizations by Katz and Kahn (1966) has been one of the most influential books on organizational theory in the last decade. Katz and Kahn define effectiveness in terms of two components—efficiency and political effectiveness. The greater the efficiency and political effectiveness, the greater the organizational effectiveness. Here, the term *efficiency* refers to the ratio of energic outputs to energic inputs. "Efficiency tells us how much of an input emerges as a product and how much is absorbed by the system" (Katz and Kahn, 1966, p. 170). The greater the efficiency (the closer the ratio approximates 1), the greater the profitability, storage of energy, and long-term survival and growth of the organization. "Political effectiveness consists in the short run of maximizing the return to the organization by means of advantageous transactions with various outside agencies and groups and with members of the organization as well" (p. 165). Examples of political effectiveness would include gaining materials at an advantageous price through superior bargaining or lobbying activities that lead to favorable legislation. Katz and Kahn argue that political effectiveness increases short-term profitability and can provide greater survival and growth opportunities through greater control and adaptability to the environment.

There are a number of important differences between our conceptualization of effectiveness and that of Katz and Kahn. First, Katz and Kahn define effectiveness in terms of efficiency and political effectiveness. Efficiency concerns the transformation process; political effectiveness primarily concerns the input acquisition and outcome disposal processes. Our definition separates efficiency and effectiveness and asserts that both concepts can be applied to any area of evaluation. Second, the use of constraints and referents are integral to our conceptualization of effectiveness. From the Katz and Kahn statement, the best we can infer is that the greater the efficiency—that is, the more it approximates its maximum level (potential efficiency)—the greater the effectiveness. It is our view that we must move beyond the simple assertion, "the more of X, the greater the effectiveness" to a more specific statement of referents and constraints.

The view of an organization as an open system transacting with its environment is accepted both in this version and by Katz and Kahn. Both versions see the organization as an open system; however, the Katz and Kahn view does not elaborate on many other determinants of effectiveness, such as those related with subsystem behavior and the interplay of external actors. In their discussion on determinants, the primary focus is on the psychological determinants of organizational effectiveness.

Although the concept of political effectiveness clearly recognizes the importance of the environment, in Katz and Kahn's view of effectiveness, there is surprisingly little delineation of the nature of the organization's environment and how it interacts with the organization. Specifically, we need to know more about how to describe the environment to identify its role as a determinant and as a constituency in determining constraints and referents to assess effectiveness.

Analysis for Katz and Kahn is at the organizational level. Their discussion of alternative levels of analysis is one of the best in the literature on organizational effectiveness. Similarly, their view of the time dimensions is better elaborated than any of the alternative viewpoints presented in Table 1. The only difference between this essay's conceptualization and theirs, relevant to the time dimension, is our specification of parameters for identifying appropriate time frames in assessing effectiveness.

Seashore and Yuchtman. Seashore and Yuchtman have advocated the "system resource approach" to organizational effectiveness. They define an organization's effectiveness in terms of its bargaining position—that is, how well it can exploit its environment in the acquisition of scarce and valued resources (Yuchtman and Seashore, 1967, pp. 897–898). The term *bargaining position* refers to the ability of the organization to acquire resources. Energy in the form of human activity is an example of a resource. It is scarce, valued, and universally required by all organizations. Other universal resources include physical facilities, technology for the organization's activities, and some commodity, such as money, that can be exchanged for other resources. Seashore and Yuchtman identify other dimensions on which resources can be described: liquidity, stability, relevance, universality, and substitution.

The highest level of organizational effectiveness is reached when the organization maximizes its bargaining position and optimizes its resource procurement. Seashore and Yuchtman here distinguish between the capability of exploiting the environment and the idea of an optimum point in actually transacting with the environment. The latter case is introduced to indicate that drawing too much from the environment can lead to depletion or devaluation of resources and to organizational ineffectiveness. In their conceptualization of effectiveness, the authors suggest that in practice most assessments of effectiveness will be made on a relative basis. That is, it is difficult to identify, in an absolute sense, the maximum bargaining position; therefore, most assessments of effectiveness are derived from comparing the focal organization's bargaining position with that of another organization.

Our definition of effectiveness differs from Seashore and Yuchtman's in that it does not focus primarily on resource acquisition. We have viewed effectiveness as the relationship among goals, constraints, and referents for both input acquisition and output disposal aspects. Their definition focuses primarily on the input acquisition behavior. The concept of constraints and referents other than some comparison organization is not discussed.

Although both concepts of effectiveness are derived from an open systems view of organizations, there are other differences between the two conceptualizations. First, in Yuchtman and Seashore's analysis there is no specification of the determinants of effectiveness. In Seashore and Yuchtman (1967) some psychological determinants of effectiveness are examined, but this category represents a rather limited set of the total set of possible determinants. Second, although there is a strong emphasis on the environment, there is no specification of how the environment serves as a determinant of effectiveness or of the role of constituencies, either internal or external, in establishing referents or constraints.

In terms of level of aggregation, Seashore and Yuchtman's conceptualization is clearly at the organizational level. Also, the dynamic character of organizational effectiveness criteria is explicit in their writings. However, the time dimension is not sufficiently elaborated to identify appropriate time periods for assessing different organizational effectiveness indicators.

Mohr. Mohr's paper "The Concept of Organizational Goal" (1973) provides an extensive discussion of referents, goals, and constraints but deals only marginally with organizational effectiveness, its determinants, and measurement. However, the goal concept is obviously important for organizational effectiveness in that it provides the criteria against which assessment can be accomplished. Mohr's paper deals with many of the issues that were raised earlier and has influenced the development of our work.

Mohr views a goal as an intent to achieve some outcomes, "whose direct referent is either the organization itself as an institution or some aspect of the organization's environment" (1973, p. 475). He goes on to classify goals as reflexive and transitive. The first type refers to inducements being sufficient to evoke contributions from the members; the second type refers to the intended impact on the organization's environment. Referents are further made explicit when he suggests the requirements for pursuing transitive goals and the kinds of inducements to satisfy members. This classification of reflexive and transitive goals is also an attempt to increase the scope of organizational effectiveness beyond the narrow notion of output disposal.

Although his recognition of referents and goals is similar to our concepts of referents and goals, Mohr does stress intent as an essential ingredient of effectiveness. However, he is very critical of Simon's (1964) notion of constraints, which this framework has adopted as an integral element. He views this concept as operationally cumbersome. Furthermore, he alleges that Simon (1964) is vague in providing a rule for determining what is or what is not a constraint as distinct from goal. Although the first criticism is justified, the second is beside the point. When evaluating an organization's effectiveness, it is mandatory to specify both the intended outcomes and the minimum conditions that often are made explicit. Mohr makes such an admission himself when he writes, "When certain sub-objectives have been spelled out, the evaluation may also serve to inform program personnel where *they have failed to achieve a necessary precondition* [that is, a constraint!]" (1973, p. 479, italics added).

Mohr discusses constituencies at length, as well as the existence of a dominant coalition. As a political scientist, he is aware of the potential political processes in organizations as well as of the related difficulty of dissensus about organizational goals and the corresponding problem of aggregating information derived from members' responses. These responses yield information on goals as organizational collective properties. They are collective rather than individual in that they are obtained by aggregating, for example, average intensity or majority opinion. Thompson's (1967) notion of dominant coalition conveys a certain amount of consensus and is proposed by Mohr as a device for conceptualizing collective intent. Mohr further incorporates the idea of program goal to facilitate the search for referents that are pursued collectively. He incorporates Seashore and Yuchtman's (1967) system resource acquisition to further clarify reflexive effectiveness and survival.

Mohr's framework does not, however, distinguish between internal and external constituencies, although these concepts underlie some of his statements. Furthermore, the determinants of effectiveness—internal or external—are not adequately specified in his paper.

Table 1 presents the similarities and dissimilarities between his conceptualization and ours. Altogether, Mohr's paper represents a novel attempt to deal with unresolved issues concerning organizational effectiveness. It links the systems and goal approach and shows why they are complementary rather than alternative ways of analyzing organizational effectiveness. The paper is also unique in that it expands organizational effectiveness to include effectiveness from the perspective of the environment and even the society at

Table 1. Comparison of the New Framework with Alternative Frameworks.

	New Framework (1977)	Argyris (1964)	Mohr (1973)	Price (1972)	Katz and Kahn (1966)	Seashore and Yuchtman (1967)
Concept of Effectiveness						
Definition	✓	✓	✓	✓	✓	✓
Dimensions	✓	✓	✓	0	✓	✓
Constraints-referents	✓	0	✓	0	✓	0
Effectiveness vs. efficiency	✓	0	✓	✓	✓	✓
Concept of Organization						
Systemic determinants	✓	0	0	✓	✓	✓
Constituencies	✓	0	0	✓	0	0
Concept of Environment						
Determinants	✓	0	0	✓	0	0
Constituencies	✓	0	0	✓	0	0
Level of Aggregation						
Individual	0	0	0	0	0	0
Suborganization-organization	✓	✓	✓	0	✓	✓
Societal	0	0	✓	0	0	0
Time Dimensions						
Static vs. dynamic	✓	✓	0	0	✓	✓
Time periods for assessing effectiveness	✓	0	0	0	0	0

✓ = issue is explored
0 = issue is not explored or not explored in detail

large (p. 487) as well as from the perspective of the individual members.

Price. In his monograph *Organizational Effectiveness* (1968), Price is primarily concerned with developing propositions about the determinants of organizational effectiveness. He reviews fifty studies that have attempted to explain variations in organizational effectiveness but does not attempt to conceptualize organizational effectiveness. Degree of goal attainment is used as one general definition of effectiveness. Also, variables such as productivity, morale, conformity, and adaptiveness are viewed as potential indicators of effectiveness. These variables, however, are not integrated into any pattern or conceptual structure. In a subsequent paper (1972) Price discusses the system and goal definitions of organizational effectiveness as well as the distinctions between efficiency and effectiveness. His own conceptualization remains somewhat unclear as to the dimensions of effectiveness.

The major focus of the 1968 monograph is on the internal and external determinants of effectiveness as well as on the role of constituencies. Unfortunately, Price does not clearly differentiate environmental actors as either determinants or constituencies; that is, he tends to merge these two roles, so that an actor making claims on the organization is often also seen as being a crucial antecedent of effectiveness. In particular, the external "components of the political system" are described in reference to their role of inhibiting or enhancing the well-being of the organization. There is little awareness of environment as primarily a set of determinants that are not subsumed under the label of "political system." The organizational components are treated as either determinants per se or as determinants and constituencies.

In the review paper (Price, 1972), there is also a tendency to treat constituencies as determinants. That paper nicely complements the 1968 monograph but fails to deal with relevant issues such as aggregation, time aspects of effectiveness, and multidimensionality of effectiveness. Table 1 contrasts our framework with Price's.

Other Authors. In addition to these authors, there are many more contributions that deal with some of the issues raised in this paper (for example, Friedlander and Pickle, 1968; Steers,

1975, 1977; Mahoney and Weitzel, 1969; Georgopoulos and Mann, 1962; Tannenbaum, 1968; Child, 1974, 1975; Mott, 1972; Caplow, 1964; Neghandi and Reimann, 1973; Pennings, 1975, 1976; Georgopoulos and Tannenbaum, 1957; Campbell and others, 1974; Etzioni, 1960; Hirsch, 1975). As mentioned before, many of these studies and reviews provide little closure, and, on the aggregate, there is insufficient cumulative progress. By developing a conceptual framework, we may alter the present practice and try to steer the efforts in distinct directions.

Conclusion

The usefulness of our framework may be evaluated by developing alternative research strategies. Similarly, it may facilitate the reconciliation of many previous studies in organizational behavior—both those that attempted to measure effectiveness and those that tried to delineate its antecedents. Some of the major traditions in organizational behavior can be viewed as aiming at, explaining, or prescribing conditions that enhance effectiveness—for example, systems theory (Katz and Kahn, 1966), expectancy theory (Vroom, 1964), structural contingency theory (Thompson, 1967; Pennings, 1975), and personality organization theory (Argyris, 1973; Likert, 1967). Some of these theories have gained major status among researchers, but there has been little cross-fertilization. In fact, there is frequent controversy and antagonism, in which adversaries accuse each other of wishful thinking; witness, for example, the debate between Perrow (1972) and Argyris (1973). The framework has stressed organizations as interdepartmental systems. Although the notion of division of labor among subunits and their role of determinant and constituency are the most salient, we believe that the present framework is general enough to be compatible with other effectiveness inquiries. It may even cross-fertilize those inquiries. Indeed, our framework can easily accommodate these positions, thereby enhancing their contribution to the understanding of organizational effectiveness. It also has the potential of pointing to complementarity among various approaches.

The Perrow-Argyris debate provides an interesting illustration of how the present framework can be expanded and exploit complementarity rather than disjointedness among theories. The structural contingency theory, or technological imperative, as embodied in the writings of Perrow, attributes differences in organizational structure to variations in technological and environmental conditions. Organizations must be structurally tuned in to these conditions. For example, if there is uncertainty in technology or environment, organizations must be flexible, decentralized, informal, and participative, whereas the opposite is true whenever the technology or environment is certain, routine, and predictable. Effectiveness, at least implicitly, is a function of the closeness of fit between organizational structure and technology and environment (Perrow, 1972; Mohr, 1971; Hickson, Pugh, and Pheysey, 1969; Pennings, 1975).

There are also viewpoints that ignore technology and environment or that take these factors as givens. The classical scientific management authors are a well-known case in point. Recent contributions by Likert (1967) and Argyris (1973), however, have also aimed at identifying the form of organization that is most conducive to organizational effectiveness. Likert (1967) argues that organizations with System 4 structure have the best performance record. This structure is characterized by participative group management, communication that flows upward as well as downward, peer relationships, and close psychological bonds. Argyris (1973), who takes great issue with authors such as Perrow (1972), is even more explicit in meshing psychological predispositions and organizational requisites to promote effectiveness. Personality characteristics, group dynamics, and interpersonal relationships cannot be ignored. There are also psychological theories, such as expectancy theory, that deal exclusively with individual factors of effectiveness. Expectancy theory focuses on the motivational antecedents of performance; it is a more elaborate version of economic utility theory (Vroom, 1964). The essential ingredients of this theory imply that individuals who are capable of doing so will work harder to increase their performance levels if this effort promotes the rewards they derive from employment. Such a theory would assert that more effective organizations are those that have employees who believe their efforts lead to performance and performance to rewards with high utility. Although more individual than organizational, these theories are compatible with our framework and delineate some of the pertinent psychological determinants of organizational effectiveness. The more sociologically oriented theories are instrumental in identifying organizational, technological, and environmental determinants.

Rather than choosing sides, the framework we propose allows for inclusion of different approaches or theories by stressing their complementarity. For example, Argyris' views have relevance for interdepartmental and interlevel coordination and communication as determinants of effectiveness. They are also helpful in isolating problem-solving areas in which competing constituencies can establish satisfactory relationships and common outcomes. Similarly, Likert's "linking pin" concept provides an interdepartmental coordination device for improving effectiveness and efficiency and alleviates conflict between both horizontal and vertical constituencies. At the same time, our framework may incorporate sociological approaches such as structural contingency theory by its implicit recognition of environmental and technological conditions. For example, uncertainty may be inferred from or may be measured with indices of a subunit's social structure. Thus a high degree of standardization implies low uncertainty. Furthermore, diffuseness of structure may not only entail uncertainty but it may also provide hints about modal ways of coping. More specifically, diffuseness or organicness of structure often facilitates the forestalling of uncertainty by virtue of the flexibility it engenders. Technology and the technology-structure or environment-structure debate can also be linked with the present framework. For example, routinization— one of the most frequently mentioned technology constructs—has implications for various aspects of the approach being advanced here. As Hickson and others (1971) have argued, routinization may either reduce uncertainty directly or it may augment the substitutability of a subunit's output, personnel, or technology. Therefore, routinization has the potential of mitigating a subunit's impact on other subunits' effectiveness. By implication it also has the potential of undermining a subunit's propensity to remain a constituency. Many researchable hypotheses can be advanced here. The framework also fits well with recent trends in organizational sociology, dealing with interorganizational relationships and organizational effectiveness. The framework should stimulate future research; a major hypothesis suggested before is that while coping with uncertainty may be omitted, substitutability among external actors is likely to be of major importance in explaining organizational effectiveness.

Our framework also allows room for effectiveness studies that stress either outcomes or goal achievement versus process. For example, it can be useful for evaluation research on programs such as Head Start, the Tennessee Valley Authority, joint ventures, and intervention by outside consultants. This research is primarily concerned with a priori outcomes or goals. More process-oriented research, for example, on the quality of organizational membership or growth and decline of organizations could also be accommodated by the framework.

Apart from such theoretical versus empirical considerations, the framework may also give fresh impetus to methodological developments. For example, we need to examine how constituencies weight preferred outcomes and constraints. Methodologically, there is a need to combine the different constituencies with their profiles of preferred outcomes and referents into some multidimensional space. Perhaps, however, such an approach is still too ambitious and must be broken down into stages that initially develop composite aspects, mappings of the structure, or pattern-of-effectiveness aspects. We hope that this framework will not only integrate existing approaches and improve research methodology but also generate new propositions and lines of research that will improve our understanding of both the nature and determinants of organizational effectiveness.

9

An Elastic
and Expandable
Viewpoint

Stanley E. Seashore

Johannes M. Pennings
and Paul S. Goodman attempt to create an integrative framework
for theory and research relating to organizational effectiveness. In
doing so they have cast their net widely, employed most of the currently available ideas about effectiveness, and formulated a plausible
although somewhat mind-boggling structure of these ideas. Given
the existing variety of approaches, assumptions, and perspectives that
need integration, and given the tendency of others to adhere ex-

clusively to one or another of several competing conceptual schemes, it would be unlikely for a neat and complete framework to result. That turns out to be the case. There are many loose ends and untreated issues. These loose ends will be deplored by those who regard elegant, simplifying theory as the end product of social inquiry; they will be welcomed by those who regard theory to be most useful when it raises new questions or clarifies unresolved issues in ways that make them accessible for inquiry.

The comments that follow aim to explicate briefly some selected features of the Pennings-Goodman framework, to remark on some of the problematic features of the framework, and then to explore some implications for research strategy.

What are the main structural components of the framework? A listing of the concepts employed would not be of much help, as the list is long and many of the concepts have only a peripheral or elaborative role. The imagery of framework suggested by the essay is not that of the spare classical pyramid, or geodesic dome, but rather that of a tree with central stem, main branches, numerous twigs (some broken), and attractive dangling ornaments.

An organization is said to be effective if it satisfies its constraints and jointly optimizes a set of goals. The relevance of potential constraints and goals is not imposed upon the organization but is continuously evaluated, reaffirmed, or changed by the organization's dominant coalition through processes of bargaining with the various significant constituencies with which the organization is interdependent. These constituencies are both internal and external. The constraints and goals are expressed as formal or implicit policies that identify the constraints requiring attention, the goals that have varying relative priority, and the standards (or referents) by which constraints are to be deemed satisfied and goals optimized. The "organization" is defined somewhat arbitrarily by the observer or participant actor, and may be, for example, a part of a large unit containing nested parts or may be an organizational set comprising semiautonomous units. Constraints and constituencies are recognized, or acknowledged, by the dominant coalition on grounds of their having potentially significant causal influence upon goals; some constituencies are, thus, ignored and some potential constraints are deemed trivial. It is feasible and useful to analyze separately the input, throughput, and output functions of the focal organization, since they involve different sets of constituencies.

Something surely is lost or distorted in thus condensing to a single paragraph an essay of considerable length and high density of ideas. Nevertheless, it is enough to highlight some features of the framework offered by Pennings and Goodman. They embrace open system theory to provide for environmental forces in the determination of referents, that is, standards, for assessing organizational effectiveness, and in noting the significant differences between input, throughput, and output subsystems. They accept the idea of goals, but define the goal set as numerous, transitory, the product of current organizational processes, and unique to each organization. They accept a role for actors (persons or other organizations) representing diverse and often conflicting self-interests, but confine this role to influential bargaining with the focal organization, to the exclusion of their possible roles as independent sources of assessment of the focal organization's effectiveness. Organizational constraints, preferred outcomes, and associated standards are, thus, the products of a continuing political process in which the dominant coalition balances the sometimes conflicting interests of different constituencies by serving as bargainer, mediator, conciliator, and (rarely, one might think) as arbiter expressing self-interests. They allow for the operation of inherent systemic dynamics to toss up standards for assessing organizational effectiveness, but acknowledge that these dynamics are subject to the intervention of members of the dominant coalition, who may intrude with individualistic perceptions and preferences.

Unfinished Business

It is a compliment to the authors that one is induced to focus upon features of the framework needing clarification or elaboration. I expect the further development of this line of integrative theory will turn out to be a cooperative venture with many assistant carpenters. Following are some examples of unfinished business.

The origins of organizational constraints are obscure, multiple, and amorphous. A constraint is so identified by the dominant coalition, assigned some standard or referent, and institutionalized by being made the subject of an organizational policy. But what are the critical sources of information, value perspective, and influence that initiate this process? Are constraints chosen, imposed, discovered, invented—or perhaps all of these? Some constraints clearly have a compulsory character and are imposed: Property taxes must be paid at rates set by others, and discriminatory employment must be eliminated or concealed. Other constraints appear to arise from the forces of interorganizational competition and may be chosen on the basis of negative feedback from markets or by bargaining and anticipatory analysis of competitive conditions. Still other constraints are discovered, as when a mining firm determines the feasible limits of its rate of water usage. But some constraints have the quality of being self-imposed, invented, chosen freely, by the dominant coalition; these may be the most interesting constraints of all to the extent that they reflect changing social norms in conjunction with the individuality of members of the dominant coalition. Perhaps the dominant coalition itself needs to be regarded more explicitly as a constituency whose interests are to be served? Surely constraints of such a diverse nature and origin require differential treatment in the assessment of organizational effectiveness.

The distinction between a constraint and a goal is an uneasy one, made with reference to the "special attention" of the dominant coalition and to the implication of deviation from standard. Although the distinction itself is plausible, and useful in selected illustrative cases, one can wonder whether such a categorical assignment of effectiveness standards will withstand conceptual examination and how it will fare when put to empirical test. Consider that the "special attention" of the dominant coalition may falter or be superseded under the press of unfulfilled constraints; consider that a constraint may be one voluntarily chosen and defined by the dominant coalition itself and, thus, one as singlehandedly ignored as it was invented, without legitimation through constituencies. The press of conceptualization in the social sciences is toward the replacement of primitive categories with multidimensional continua. The domain of goals and constraints may well require that next step in conceptual formulation.

A feature of the Pennings-Goodman integrative framework is that it integrates mainly by addition of components rather than selection or substitution. A complexity results. There is no possibility within this framework to arrive at a definitive specification of the referents (criterion variables) and standards to be used in assessing future organizational effectiveness, even for a single organization. This impossibility arises because the constraints and goals of interest (1) derive their priority in part from sources outside of the focal organization's control, (2) are changing as circumstances change, and (3) are not linked with any fixed framework of value assumptions or of psychological needs of actors or of systemic requirements. This need not necessarily be a flaw in the framework, but it is certainly a distressing feature to a person who wants not only to think about effectiveness generally but also to assess the effectiveness of a particular organization. To make the framework operational, elaborations are needed that will serve to differentiate criteria, on either theoretical or empirical grounds, according to their degree of universality, their stability over time, their susceptibility to clustering and sampling, and the like. Some approach is needed to treat an infinite array of potential criteria (constraints and goals) without imposing assumptions or propositions other than those common to all or many organizations.

Uniqueness is abhorrent to organizational theory just as a vacuum is to physical nature. How, then, is one to think about a framework for viewing organizational effectiveness that emphasizes the unique characteristics of each organization rather than the commonalities? Strictly speaking, the Pennings-Goodman framework denies the possibility of comparing the effectiveness of organizations or of assessing changes in overall effectiveness over time—say, in the context of experimental organizational development programs. Speaking less strictly, the framework would allow comparative assessment only through determination, definitional or empirical, that certain criteria (referents) may be treated as generically alike and comparable *both* as constructs and also as to their priorities, weights, or functional roles in a set of such criteria. We are, thus, led back to some old problems that are not resolved by the proposed framework. What the framework does provide, however, is a basis for identifying significant criterion variables by universally applicable rules of identification; this provides an additional leverage point for empirical inquiry into the degree and nature of the uniquenesses that may exist. It could emerge that our concerns about indeterminacy, value conflict, and transitoriness regarding organizational effectiveness may prove to be excessive.

The thorny problems arising from the presence of alternative, and frequently incompatible, values and perspectives are treated by defining the focal organization's dominant coalition to be the integrating and summarizing agency. This is an attractive notion. It provides a single set of referents for judging organizational effectiveness. It includes consideration for a wide array of value perspectives and special interests resident in the various constituencies. It emphasizes the focal organization's "own" commitments to goals and constraints and thus may distill, from an impossibly complex array of considerations, those that bear most directly upon the critical organizational functions such as allocation of resources, goal-pattern change, internal integration of activity, surveillance practices, and the like. For these reasons, the Pennings-Goodman framework has, in my view, considerable potential as a guide for understanding organizational processes and changes. Nevertheless, this singular focus upon the dominant coalition as the ultimate definer of priority values for the organization may prove to be unduly restrictive. The framework will be unacceptable to those who need to differentiate among value perspectives in order to have a conception of effectiveness that is compatible with other components of their theory.

Directions for Research

The Pennings and Goodman essay is replete with ideas that invite, or even compel, an empirical exploration of the utility of the framework and its fit to the realities of organizational behavior. A few suggestions deserve mention.

A priority question concerns the extent to which dominant coalitions of organizations are indeed dealing with constituencies that present conflicting demands. One can suppose that there exist strong norms regarding the acceptable behavior of organizations, norms that have the power to override short-term bargaining for advantage by constituencies and to govern organizational behavior in areas where the valued outcomes are uncertain or distant. It seems feasible to conduct an initial inquiry to find out whether the several constituencies of a focal organization do in fact present potentially determinant forces that are conflicting or largely compatible. Does consensus or dissensus prevail among constituencies? Is there a patterning of interconstituency conflict issues that would be useful in distinguishing among referents, with some allowing options to the dominant coalition, others allowing no option at all, and yet others becoming the focus for open conflict and resolution through bargaining or coercion?

The central role assigned by Pennings and Goodman to the dominant coalition within the focal organization may require a rationale and technology for identifying the dominant coalition and, in the case of large organizations of nested parts, the network of dominant coalitions. The members of these coalitions would be a source of the information needed to identify referents for the input, throughput, and output subsystems. Alternatively, referents might be identified through organizational member-actors' perceptions of them ("policies") or by analysis of actions and events interpreted to reflect the presence of operational referents. In any case, the application of the Pennings-Goodman framework would require some means to identify referents, and a priority research task would be to ascertain the effectiveness of alternative identification methods. Without such relatively independent means for identification of referents, the framework would have its utility limited to after-the-fact interpretation of actions and events. For example, an observer might note: Critical outcome variables and their referents get special attention from the dominant coalition; X gets such special attention; therefore, X is a critical outcome variable. Finding a way out of such circularity is, in part, an empirical issue.

A crucial feature of the Pennings-Goodman framework is the notion that effectiveness constraints, although identified by the dominant coalition, may in different degrees arise from influence attempts of internal and external constituencies. Should this prove to be the case—and it does appear likely—then the framework provides an additional approach to empirical study of the openness of different organizations to environmental influence, their differences in boundary maintenance strategies, their variations in efficiency that arise from the internal-external balance of constraint determination, and other related issues bearing upon accommoda-

tive processes and upon the conditions that foster or impair successful coping with constraints.

A final example of the research issues brought to prominence
and additional feasibility by the proposed framework relates to the
nature of the dominant coalition. Pennings and Goodman have
returned persons to the scene. Most others concerned with organizational effectiveness have lately been following the strategy of removing persons and individuality. With the role of the dominant coalition given such a prominent and controlling place in the framework,
it becomes necessary to resume a line of research that lately has
been largely neglected, namely, the inquiry into how the attributes
of specific key individuals impact upon the behavior of the organizational system. Attention is reinvited to the perceptions, cognitions,
and affective patterns of those individuals who comprise the dominant coalition.

10

Re-Punctuating the Problem

Karl E. Weick

❧❧❧❧❧❧❧❧

Steers (1975) demonstrates that the problem of organizational effectiveness has traditionally been punctuated into conclusions such as those that the effective organization is flexible and productive, satisfies its members, is profitable, acquires resources, minimizes strain, controls the environment, develops, is efficient, retains employees, grows, is integrated, communicates openly, and survives. I would like to propose a different set of punctuations. Specifically, I would suggest that the effective organization is (1) *garrulous,* (2) *clumsy,* (3) *superstitious,*

Support for this work was provided by the National Science Foundation through Grant SOC 75–09864 and is gratefully acknowledged.

(4) *hypocritical,* (5) *monstrous,* (6) *octopoid,* (7) *wandering,* and
(8)*grouchy.* Any set of punctuations, however reasonable, is arbitrary. Punctuation simply means "chopping the stream of experience
into sensible, nameable, and named units" (Weick, 1976b, p. 280).
In the interest of improving our understanding when we say that
organizations are effective or ineffective, I want to examine some
other ways to carve up the stream of experience from which those
judgments of effectiveness come.

The spirit of these analyses is captured vividly by Ghiselin
(1974), who discusses the problems that can occur when evolution
is punctuated as if it were a game.

> Many kinds of games are possible, and we run
> grave risk of error if we mistake one for another. Actually,
> evolution has no rules at all, in the sense of those that
> govern gentlemanly sport. The best we can say is that
> there are various ways to cheat and that some kinds of
> cheating are hard to get away with. And just as there are
> no rules, there is no criterion of victory. Organisms play
> the game because, and only because, their ancestors did
> not lose. We can keep score, in terms of "fitness" or mor-
> tality, but we must not assume that the organisms are
> striving to gather what we consider points. If we do not
> know the "rules," we may be unable even to identify the
> "players." Many who have written on the "reproductive
> strategies" have been concerned not with the actions of
> individuals but with the good of the species, for no more
> basic reason than the tendency to view the struggle for
> existence as a contest between "teams" rather than "ath-
> letes." If there is any truth in this earlier work, as we
> should admit there may well be, it will not be discovered
> until we have some way to knowing what kind of spec-
> tacle really lies before us [p. 41].

It seems appropriate to examine more closely what spectacle is
unfolding when it is asserted that effectiveness is being scrutinized.

Effective Organizations Are Garrulous

"An explorer can never know what he is exploring until it
has been explored" (G. Bateson, 1972, p. xvi). The organizational

equivalent of that assertion is, "An organization can never know what it thinks or wants until it sees what it does." What organizations say and do provides displays that they can examine reflectively to understand what is occurring.* The sequence in that prototypic soliloquy is crucial. Talk or some kind of action occurs first and provides the occasion for an eventual articulation of cognitions and desires. Organizations talk to themselves in order to clarify their surroundings and learn more about them. Often these soliloquies are closed rather than open systems. They are closed in the sense that organizations examine retrospectively the very displays they created initially as pretexts for sensemaking. Organizations talk in order to discover what they are saying, act in order to discover what they are doing (see Weick, 1976b, for elaboration of this argument).

Organizational talk undoubtedly formulates and constrains effectiveness. How people in organizations invent nouns, connect nouns, and form sentences can influence the probability that their organization is able to "produce, or increase, or preserve, some good in a consistent, dependable fashion" (Diesing, 1962, p. 3). If we examine the garrulity of organizations more carefully, inspecting such things as its form, substance, quantity, and pattern, we should learn more about effectiveness. Two examples of potential lines of inquiry will be examined. Both examples derive from suggestions made by Crovitz (1970) in his charming book *Galton's Walk*. The two examples involve the idea of Poe numbers and the idea of a relational algorithm.

A *Poe number* is obtained by taking a piece of writing such as a brief report in *Science* or an internal memo and crossing out

---

* The unit of analysis implied is a set of contingent behaviors between two or more persons, organized in the pattern of a double interact $(P_1 \rightarrow P_2 \rightarrow P_1)$. Stated differently, the unit of analysis is a plural pronoun (signifying collective activity) inserted in place of a singular pronoun in at least one position in the following sense-making recipe: How can $\left(\begin{array}{c} I \\ we \end{array}\right)$ know what $\left(\begin{array}{c} I \\ we \end{array}\right)$ think until $\left(\begin{array}{c} I \\ we \end{array}\right)$ see what $\left(\begin{array}{c} I \\ we \end{array}\right)$ say. If you and I find ourselves in a relationship portrayed by, "How can we know what I think until I see what we say," we are an organization for the duration of this analysis, capable of unreified seeing and doing.

all words that have to do with content, words that are specific to a particular piece of writing (X words). The remaining words are words that might appear in any piece of writing; they are *form* words and are designated Y words. A Poe number is the number of content words (X) multiplied by one hundred divided by the number of form words (Y). Crovitz argues that when you isolate a set of form words you can drape any substance whatsoever on them and have a sensible display. For example, if you delete the content words in any *Science* abstract and retain the form words, it should be possible for someone in any field to insert the substance words of his own field into these blank spaces and produce a sensible article.

What is intriguing about Poe numbers is that the X words seem to be substances and the Y words seem to be connections. Crovitz argues that the structure of thought is carried by the Y words. Notice that as form words decrease or substance words increase the Poe number increases. Our immediate question is simply, How does an organization generate different Poe numbers when communicating internally and externally, and what is true of a person in general when he constructs different statements that contain different Poe numbers? That last sentence, when stripped of its content words, reads: "Our immediate (1 substance word deleted) is simply, How does (2) generate different (2) when (4), and what is true of (2) in general when he constructs (2) that contain different (2)." That sentence has a Poe number of $1500/22 = 68.18$. The form words in that sentence could also be used to decribe the riddle of Count Basie's piano playing—how can Basie play so simply and yet have a style that defies musical analysis (Hodeir, 1962, pp. 97–108). "Our immediate *riddle* is simply, How does *Count Basie* generate different *melodic inventions* when *playing monotonous simple triplets,* and what is true of *a musician* in general when he constructs *apparent clichés* that contain different *rhythmic experiments?*"

If an organization exhibits a relatively high ratio of form words to substance words in its communications, does this imply that it has a richer set of connections to impose on punctuated displays than organizations exhibiting fewer forms? Are high Poe numbers associated with rigid relational thinking and a preoccupation with specifics such that the organization is capable of tying together variables in only a small number of ways? Given a *constant* Poe number, is a greater variety of form words associated with more adaptability? These and other questions are suggested by Crovitz's analysis.

To examine questions like these, initial research only indirectly related to effectiveness is needed. The initial step would be to develop a more explicit set of rules for discriminating between form and substance words than has been provided by Crovitz. Undoubtedly the reader had some quibbles in the "immediate question" quotation about which words were substance and which form. The only statement that Crovitz makes on this point is the rather disappointing assertion that "there is never total agreement on the problem of distinguishing appearance from reality, or content from form" (p. 65). What we need is a set of rules for distinguishing content from form, after which we can analyze documents for their ratios of content to form words. These ratios, in turn, should relate to other indices of effectiveness and should give us more information about how effectiveness is accomplished.

The second idea from Crovitz that seems worth exploring is the relational algorithm. Crovitz makes the standard remark that invention generally involves putting old things together in a new relation, but then he makes the "wild" remark that in fact there may be no more than forty-two relational words in basic English that can be used to relate two items (p. 100). The prototype sentence for Crovitz is, "Take one thing in relation to another thing." Or more sparsely, "Take one thing (   ) another thing." One at a time, the forty-two relational words (for example, *about, across, after, where, while, with*) are inserted in the brackets to see if they solve the problem. (See Table 1 for the complete algorithm.)

Table 1.   Relational Algorithm.

about	at	for	of	round	to
across	because	from	off	still	under
after	before	if	on	so	up
against	between	in	opposite	then	when
among	but	near	or	though	where
and	by	not	out	through	while
as	down	now	over	till	with

Source: Crovitz, 1970, p. 100.

For example, suppose I am having trouble threading a needle. My two domain "thing" words are *thread* and *needle*. Perhaps I can not thread the needle because I have a relational blind spot. The only sentence I can construct is, "Take a thread *through* a needle." Now, if I run through the other forty-one words I come up with combinations such as "take a thread *among* a needle" (which suggests that I should try to thread several needles at once on the outside chance that one of them might accidentally be threaded), "take a thread *around* a needle" (wrap thread around needle and try to poke it through material), "take a thread *as* a needle" (sew with raw thread that is toughened and sharpened at the end), "take a thread *up* a needle" (move the thread from the base to the top, gradually tilting the needle and thereby spearing the hole). With this example, I can specify some of the problems of bracketing and connecting experiences that relate to effectiveness. The choice of a pair of domain words is undoubtedly crucial. If I had simply reversed the pair, "take a needle *through* a thread," new possibilities (or no possibilities) might have occurred. We need to learn more about how people in organizations choose domain words from a complex display or invent them prior to using the relational algorithm.

Also relevant to the problem of effectiveness is the question, which relational words do people typically use? The question is basically, if people were given any two domain words connected by a blank, what words in their own vocabulary would they use to fill the blank? Presumably, they would use those connectors with which they are most familiar. The questions then become, what relations do they routinely ignore, and, if these relations are ignored, does this mean that these relational words are used infrequently to connect variables in everyday life? If a person connects variables with a limited but overlearned set of rational words, what effects does this have on what he reports, how he connects causal maps, what he notices, how he acts?

For example, if a person uses a finite set of relational words, would he single out from experience only those variables that could be connected reasonably by that finite supply of connectors? Imagine a man who walks through a confusing world and has available only the connectors *against, between, among,* and *through.* On repeated occasions he observes that whenever a person in a stone quarry blows a whistle this is followed shortly thereafter by a blast. Does the whistle "cause" the blast or the blast "cause" the whistle, or are these two events unconnected? Conceivably, the world of shrill noises and thundering noises would neither be labeled with the nouns *whistle* and *blast* nor connected if a person had available only the connectors *against, between, among,* and *through.*

Organizations talk all the time, organizations talk to themselves much of the time, and organizations communicate some of the time. However, investigators have had difficulty incorporating this fact of life into analyses of effectiveness. The garrulous organization serves as a reminder that (1) effectiveness can vary as a function of the conclusions that are drawn reflectively from examination of prior talk and actions; (2) these conclusions will vary as a function of the quantity and quality of the actions and talk; and (3) crucial variables in the talk that can influence effectiveness-related sense-making are the variety of nouns used, the variety of connections imposed among those nouns, and the ease with which those nouns and connections can be reassembled.

Adaptability, which tops Steers' list of effectiveness criteria, can be promoted or hindered by what an organization brackets for further reflective attention and the conclusions that are drawn as a result of this reflection. Therefore, when a Poe number is assigned to an annual report or an assessment is made of the number of words from the relational algorithm that are used in or omitted from this report, we may find a measure of effectiveness that tells as much about long-term adaptability as the report's bottom line numbers tell about short-term adaptation.

Effective Organizations Are Clumsy

A question that lies just below the surface in this essay is, Under what conditions does adaptation preclude adaptability? This question has been raised by people such as Bateson (1963), Dunn (1971), Service (1960), Stebbins (1965), and Stephens (1967). Whenever people adapt to a particular situation, they lose some of the resources that would enable them to adapt to different situations in the future. They sacrifice future adaptability for current good fit. If they try to beat this trap by cultivating future adaptability and sacrificing current adaptation, they are no better off. They live in an eternal state of readiness and loneliness and are able to handle everything except the next customer who walks through the door.

Some people argue that this dilemma is not crucial because when adaptation falters, people can always borrow the solutions being used by those who are successfully adapting. I think that argument is naive. If responses become standardized when organizations merge, if people generally praise their own groups and downgrade others, and if people fear appearing frivolous, then from whom are they going to borrow all of these elegant solutions? We seem to have plenty of parasites, but where is the host?

If borrowing is not all it is cracked up to be, then we must look elsewhere for adaptations. The main alternative place to look is inside the organization. The metaphor here is that we should invent some organizational equivalents of a rain forest (Richards, 1952) and try to describe the conditions under which these forests thrive and produce acceptable inventions. An example of rain forests that preserve mutations for Broadway are the off-off-Broadway experimental theater groups (Lester, 1975).

One way to sponsor rain forests within organizations is intentionally to complicate the organization. And one way to complicate it is to encourage galumphing and purposeful clumsiness. Miller (1973, p. 92) defines *galumphing* as "patterned voluntary elaboration or complication of process, where the pattern is not under the dominant control of goals." He argues that play or galumphing preserves adaptability. "Play is a way of organizing activity, not a particular set of activities; it is a syntax, not a vocabulary" (p. 94). The relevance of galumphing to adaptation is that galumphing provides a way to elaborate means. Play "makes us flexible and gives us exercise in the control of means that we are capable of using but that are superfluous right now. . . . [When people play] they may be mastering incidental skills. But more important, they are using their capacity to combine pieces of behavior that would have no basis for juxtaposition in a utilitarian framework. They are creating novelty. . . . It is by doing things that an organism develops combinatorial flexibility" (p. 96).

From this standpoint, play is not viewed as a means to an end but rather as a crooked line to the end. It gets around obstacles but the obstacles were put there by the player in order to complicate his life. Consider from the perspective of intentional complication this comment by Heinz Werner: "My teacher, Stern, used to say that psychologists were in the habit of putting obstacles in their path and then as they removed them one by one, calling attention to the progress they were making" (Crovitz, 1970, p. 1). Although the sting in Werner's comment is obvious, it is also interesting to think about it from the standpoint of galumphing. Deliberate complication, if it gives the person experience in combining elements in novel ways, can be potentially adaptive for dealing with novel problems. Notice that means activities are given much freer sway. They are not dominated by goals. What play basically does is unhook behavior from the demands of real goals. The person gets experience in combining pieces of behavior that would not be juxtaposed in a utilitarian world.

The heart of Miller's argument is that play is important not because it teaches some new skill. What is crucial about play is that it takes activities that are already in the person's repertoire and gives him practice in recombining those into novel sets. What seems to be implied is a kind of second-order learning. It is not that one learns to recombine a single set of means into a clumsy but passable golf swing; what one may be learning, instead, is that it is possible to recombine the available repertoire of means in novel ways. A person gets repeated practice in doing this whenever he or she intentionally complicates a process.

Several possibilities are implicit in this line of analysis. Less efficient organizations could retain more adaptability than more efficient organizations if the less efficient organizations, which use more complicated means to achieve ends, are actually learning to recombine their repertoire. This would hold true only if they continually reshuffled their modes of inefficiency. Although Miller does not mention it, an additional benefit of galumphing might be that people discover previously unnoticed portions of their repertoires. When people recombine activities, they may clarify just what is being recombined. So deliberate complication might yield better knowledge of the elements in an existing repertoire as well as the discovery that a known repertoire can be recombined in novel ways.

The idea that inefficient organizations preserve adaptability suggests an alternative interpretation of "the privilege of historic backwardness." Service (1960) argues that backward organizations have an advantage because they can profit from the mistakes of "advanced" organizations. For example, the Wankel engine was developed by an organization that had no previous experience with engines. Backward organizations may be able to leapfrog advanced organizations partly by profiting from their errors, but it is also possible that backward organizations cultivate (perhaps unwittingly) a combinatorial flexibility that is unknown to so-called advanced organizations.

The necessity of cultivating diversity and the swiftness with which it can disappear have been illustrated by M. C. Bateson (1972). He noted that:

> the downs of England, on which I collected plants as a boy, had a turf about two inches high, which was a very complex botanical system with forty or fifty species of flowering plants in it. The turf was maintained partly by sheep and partly by rabbits. [Soon, however, the sheep were fenced away from this area and the rabbits died from bacteria.] From there on, the turf started to grow, and when I saw it last summer it was a botanical mess about three feet high. . . . Now what lived in the new botanical mess? A fraction of the original diversity: those plants that were able to survive when the turf was down to two inches and *still* able to survive when the turf was up to three feet. What you get with each change is a slicing down of the ecological diversity. This whole business is obviously a very complex function of rapidity of ecological change and rapidity of evolutionary change working against each other. The generation of new diversity by evolution, or even by diffusion, is necessarily much slower in comparison [p. 274].

Most organizations live in a climate of accountability. Within such climates variability is treated as noise (Klingsporn, 1973), mutations are a nuisance, and unjustified variation is prohibited. The unfortunate effects of these practices may be reversed by clumsy acts that provide excuses to redraw boundaries around elements, recombine elements, and learn more about the activity of combining elements. Thus, organizations that complicate their lives may come to be viewed as more effective than ones that streamline their lives.

Effective Organizations Are Superstitious

As we have just seen, intentional complication of action through galumphing can provide the means for retaining diversity and effectiveness. These same outcomes can be achieved through superstitious acts that unwittingly complicate the actor's tasks and thereby improve adaptability. The argument can be sketched out using Moore's (1957) analysis of divination as practiced by the Naskapi Indians in Labrador. Every day the Naskapi face the question, What direction should the hunters take to locate game? They answer the question by holding dried caribou shoulder bones over a fire. As the bones become heated they develop cracks and smudges that are then "read" by an expert. These cracks indicate the direction in which the hunters should look for game. The Naskapi believe that this practice allows the gods to intervene in their hunting decisions. The interesting feature of these practices is that they work.

To see how these practices work, think about some of the characteristics of this decision procedure. First, the final decision about where to hunt is not a purely personal or group choice. If no game is found, the gods and not the group are to blame. Second, the final decision is not affected by the outcomes of past hunts. If the Indians were influenced by the outcomes of past hunts, they would run the definite risk of depleting the stock of animals. Their prior success would induce subsequent failure. Third, the final decision is not influenced by the typical human patterning of choice and preferences, which can enable the hunted animals to take evasive action and become sensitized to the presence of human beings. The use of scapulas (bones) is thus a very crude way of complicating human behavior under conditions where avoiding fixed patterns of activity may have an advantage. Restated in

Moore's own words, "It seems safe to assume that human beings require a functional equivalent to a table of random numbers if they are to avoid unwitting regularities in their behavior, which can be utilized by adversaries" (p. 73).

My impression is that using tables of random numbers to make decisions may be effective in a broader range of settings than simply those involving adversaries. For example, one reason why adaptation may preclude adaptability is that people remember only those practices that are currently useful. Memory undercuts innovation. It is conceivable that if groups made greater use of randomizing devices, which let them forget current adaptive practices, they might be in a better position to cope resourcefully with change. Notice that an adversary need not be present for this tactic to make sense. For example, if an executive burned caribou bones to decide where to look for new customers or where to relocate his factory, it is not obvious to me that his organization would be any worse off than if he used a highly rational plan to decide these issues. The use of randomizing is equivalent to discrediting retained wisdom (Weick, 1969) and treating memory as an enemy (Cadwallader, 1959; Cohen and March, 1974). There are occasions when this type of intentional forgetting makes sense.

Essentially, any group that solves problems with a randomizing device is in the same position as a "client" in Garfinkel's (1962) and McHugh's (1968) studies of simulated counseling. In a quasi-counseling format the client asks the counselor for advice, using questions that can be answered "yes" or "no." The counselor answers these questions by secretly flipping a coin and answering "yes" if it lands heads and "no" if it lands tails. How does the subject make sense of this random set of answers to his serious questions (for example, "Should I commit myself to an interfaith marriage or not?")? What is striking about the protocols from people who experience this form of "counseling" is the reasonableness they attribute to the random advice. Garfinkel regards this as an eloquent demonstration of how people make do with bits and pieces of information they get in everyday life (which it is); we are interested in additional features of this demonstration. First, continuous practice at making sense out of random inputs could produce its own form of combinatorial flexibility. What the person learns to do is continually reshuffle his ideas about which events are connected to which other events and what the meaning of these events is. Such reshuffling should promote adaptability when it is necessary to notice different things about the world. Second, whatever sense the person makes of the answers, he is in a better position to take action. Even if the action is silly, the person is moved from contemplation to activity. And this action provides new experiences, which are then available for novel retrospective interpretations. Thus, randomizing short-circuits counterproductive planning sessions where people worry about alternatives that never materialize (Weick, 1969, p. 102). Third, randomizing devices break up old patterns of thinking. It is obvious in the Garfinkel and McHugh protocols that the client reexamines his previous experience and finds new implications and connections. The randomizing device may consequently sensitize him to aspects of experience of which he was previously unaware and to which he may have had an imperfect adaptation.

The counseling situation is essentially solitary; we also need to know how group problem solving is affected by a randomizing device. Consider, for example, a group working on one of the survival exercises (for example, Eady and Lafferty, 1973). In these problems people must rank the importance of a set of items, first individually and then in a group, in terms of how well these items would enable them to survive in a hostile environment. These ratings are then compared with expert ratings. The presence of a "correct" answer in these exercises suggests that randomizing would be a silly decision procedure. I am not so sure it is.

Randomizing can be inserted into various portions of these survival exercises. (1) Some individuals can make random rankings and some make rational rankings. The question is, How are these dealt with when the team convenes? (2) A group is told that half of its group rankings will be randomly generated and half will be rationally generated. The question here is, Does this pattern generate significantly less accuracy than rationally deliberating all fifteen survival items? (3) A *specific* environment can be predetermined and the relative merits assessed of the random versus rational ordering for this specific set of problems (the current survival exercises assume a generally hostile environment characterized by averages). (4) Experimenters can vary the experiential background of team members and cross this with random versus rational deliberation. (For example, do people raised in *hot* climates all their lives do any worse on the *arctic* survival problem when they decide their rankings randomly rather than rationally? Under these conditions an interfering set may have to be broken.)

Certain features of organizational life that are relevant to effectiveness include the resourcefulness of humans at making do with incomplete information (for example, see Watzlawick, 1976), the abundance of disturbed reactive environments containing adversaries, and habituation. All three of these suggest that intentional complication through galumphing needs to be supplemented by unintended complication through superstitious acts. Humans' resourcefulness in making sense of their experience further suggests that random superstitious interludes need not be disabling but instead may provide the occasion for a reshuffling of categories and connections.

Isaac Asimov's story "The Machine That Won the War" illustrates beautifully the point of this section. (I am grateful to James Ware for bringing this story to my attention.) Three men are sitting around their huge Multivac computer after they have won a war against the Denebians. While reflecting on the war they become increasingly ambivalent about crediting the computer with the victory. One by one, each man makes a confession. First, the chief programmer, John, admits that the data he was to feed into the machine became more and more "unreliable" so finally he simply "wrote out the necessary data as it was needed." The surprised machine operator then asks, "What made you think Multivac was in working order whatever the data you supplied it?" Answering his own question, the operator then admits to adjusting the output according to his interpretations. Finally, the chief decision maker, Lamar Swift, leans back with the realization that material given to him to guide decision making was a man-made interpretation of man-made data. He says, "Then I perceive I was correct in not placing too much reliance upon it." Both men, trying to avoid an impression of being insulted, reply, "You didn't?" The obvious question then becomes, How did Lamar make his decisions? He finally reaches into his pocket, fingers a coin, and says: "Multivac is not the first computer, friends, nor the best known, nor the one that can most efficiently lift the load of decision from the shoulders of the executive. A machine *did* win the war, John; at least a very simple computing device did; one that I used every time I had a particularly hard decision to make. With a faint smile of reminiscence, he flipped the coin he held" (Asimov, 1969, pp. 326–327).

Effective Organizations Are Hypocritical

Hypocrisy often makes evolutionary sense, and, by implication, it may be a more important component of effectiveness than has been recognized.

In the conventional evolutionary model, consisting of unjustified variations, natural selection, and retention of selected characteristics, the variation process is at odds with the retention process. Thus, in a preliterate society every member who practices a novel variation of customs is one less member who preserves and models the adaptation that has already been achieved. It is for this reason that a common prescription generated by evolutionary theory reads, "Ambivalence is the optimal compromise." Doing what you have always done is necessary for short-term adaptation; doing what you have never done is necessary for long-term adaptation.

Thus, we must conclude that hypocrisy makes evolutionary sense. If words and deeds are contradictory—one perpetuating past wisdom and the other discrediting it—then current functioning should be effective and future adaptation to changed contingencies possible. This is the reason I have argued elsewhere (Weick, 1969) that adaptation requires that organizations follow one of two patterns: Either they should use their old selection criteria but act in continually novel ways or they should do what they have always done but continually interpret those actions using novel criteria. Either pattern provides simultaneous flexibility and stability and avoids the extremes of either total repetition, which fails to detect and respond to change, or total innovation, which fails to exploit the economies of repeating specific efficient actions.

The suggestion that organizations must partially discredit what they know in order to survive has often been misinterpreted by readers to mean that an organization should doubt what it knows for certain. What people have failed to realize is that the suggestion also asserts that an organization should treat as certain that which it doubts. To doubt is to discredit unequivocal information; to act decisively is to discredit equivocal information. When things are clear, doubt; when there is doubt, treat things as if they were clear. That is the full meaning of discrediting.

Discrediting hard-won lessons of experience may seem silly. However, lessons from experience are always dated. They cannot escape this fate because the world in which they were learned changes discontinuously. Thus, discrediting means that every retained experience can be thrown into different figure-ground patterns, that each experience has surplus meaning, and that reinterpreting prior experiences is as warranted as maintaining a constant interpretation.

The argument that organizations will retain adaptability only if they both credit and discredit what they have learned is plausible because two separate processes are influenced by retained content: enactment and selection (action and interpretation). It is conceivable, however, that an organization might accomplish this same split pattern of adaptability by alternating between complete crediting (in both enactment and selection) and complete discrediting. That possibility deserves closer attention.

A closer look at the use of retained content may also be necessary to describe organizational development. If you watch organizations grow, they do not seem to use the split pattern throughout their lifetimes. When an organization is new and vulnerable, complete crediting may be the best way for it to conserve its niche and the wisdom with which it started. Then, as other organizations begin to enter the market and competition increases, the split pattern is often adopted. If that split pattern retains too much of the past, however, we might eventually see total discrediting and the organization starting over.

The usefulness of selective discrediting as an indicator of effectiveness is suggested by several examples. Consider, for example, fire departments that function in areas where false alarms are common. They might be expected to partially discredit an alarm ("This is probably just another prank") and partially credit it ("This could be the real thing"). Thus, when an alarm sounds in an area noted for false alarms the company would answer the call but with less equipment than is usual.

The assertion that scholars are important is often both credited and discredited. Many people assert that scholars are vital but then ignore scholarly inputs. Stephens (1967) puts this hypocritical treatment into perspective.

> To get a horse that will go fast enough, we get one who will try to go too fast, and then we rein him in. To get a man who will do enough for academic subjects, we get a man who will try to do too much, and then we subject him to the necessary constraints. In doing this, we condemn him to a life of frustration. . . . Circumstances invite us to provide less practical support than our verbal protestations would imply. Going farther, survival conditions almost demand that we practice this saving hypocrisy. Verbally we must spur the zealot on. Practically we rein him in. . . . This unlovely discrepancy between word and deed, then, is to be seen not as gratuitous malice but as a survival-favoring device which has evolved as a means of balancing the necessary support of schools with necessary controls that prevent us from becoming dangerously scholar-ridden [pp. 126–127].

Inabilities to discredit should be associated with ineffective action. A possible occasion for this may have been the attempt in 1938 by the Ford Motor Company to introduce a small car that was below their V8 in size and power. They wanted to reach a new group of customers not yet tapped by their $540 car. After several years of development they introduced the car (dubbed 92A), a car that was narrower, shorter, and 600 pounds lighter than the regular Ford. But the small motor cost only $3 less to manufacture than the large engine, and the entire car could be built for only $36 less than the big V8. Ford engineers built the small car the same way they built the big car and saved nothing. Knowing that they could build cars, the engineers failed to act as if this were both true and false. Their inability to make a smaller car that was significantly cheaper than the big car illustrates the argument that a failure to discredit can be a failure in effectiveness. "By mid-April the project was abandoned, signifying that the company would not expand the range of its model downward" (Nevins and Hill, 1963, p. 118).

Effective Organizations Are Monstrous

Evolution often starts with "monsters." This suggests that species that spare their monsters will evolve faster than those that kill them. Thus, it is conceivable that reactions to deformity and deviance may predict the speed of evolution and the probability of effective action. It is uncommon for freak fish to be killed by their parents. But it is more common at higher levels for freaks to be destroyed. This possible relationship between tolerance for deviance and ultimate effectiveness has not been traced systematically in biological evolution, but it seems sufficiently plausible to pursue. Although it is not clear at this stage what constitutes an organizational monster, it should be possible to supply a tentative definition.

Once a monster exists, however, there is still the problem that natural selection takes time. Therefore, one must ask why variations in organizations do not get lost before natural selection has had time to derive from them whatever potential advantages they present. If mutations occur too frequently or are too short-lived, they will get lost in the process of natural selection. Thus, it is not routine for all variations that represent an improvement to be selectively retained. Instead, it may only be those mutations that are stabilized long enough for sluggish selection to occur that have any chance of being retained. Notice that the additional requirement of persistence until natural selection can operate may shrink drastically the pool of mutations available in any organization.

Thus, it may be misleading to use such adjectives as *blind* or *random* to describe variation. First, they imply that the variations are short-lived, transient, fleeting, and accidental, all of which diverts attention from the issue of persistence. Second, the variations technically are not random in the statistical sense nor are they blind in the sense of originating from a *tabula rasa*. To avoid these counterproductive connotations Campbell (1974) urges that we talk about *unjustified variation,* by which he means variation whose truth has not yet been established. What Campbell most wants to forestall is the impression that variations are wise or guided by some kind of foresight. The point is that not only must we account for ways in which unjustified variations can emerge (notice that the word *unjustified* is especially appropriate for organizations where justification and rationality densely overlay many organizational activities), but we must also account for how these variations are sustained over time.

It is also interesting to examine what Darwin had to say about monsters in his major manuscript, *Natural Selection*. Darwin's commentary has a remarkable resemblance to current ideas about deviation amplifying feedback. "Those who have studied monstrosities believe that any affection of a part developed during the early life of the embryo tends to modify other parts of the organization subsequently developed. This seems so natural that it can hardly be doubted; and hence the later formed structures as they are necessarily subjected to the influence of all previous abnormal changes are the most liable to monstrosities and variation. . . . We may infer from these considerations that the same cause tending to produce a monstrosity or variation would produce different results according to the period at which it acted on the embryo" (Stauffer, 1975, p. 302).

When people talk about mutations or unusual influences, they often forget to examine the time in development when those unusual conditions occurred. Given, however, the general idea that the earlier the incursion the more massive the modification, Darwin's suggestion supports those who argue that a small number of positive feedback loops operating over a period of time on very minor deviations can produce remarkably unique entities, some of which may produce significant increments in effectiveness.

Effective Organizations Are Octopoid

"Integration" is argued by Steers and Diesing to be a crucial component of effectiveness. Recent theoretical developments suggest the value of reexamining that criterion. The image of the organization as a loosely coupled system (Glassman, 1973; Weick, 1976a), an empty world (Simon, 1962), a set of weak ties (Granovetter, 1973), or as octopoid (Geertz, 1973) is beginning to gain some prominence. As it does, issues of effectiveness may be recast. "Cultural analysis is as much a matter of determining independencies as interconnections, gulfs as well as bridges. The appropriate image, if one must have images, of cultural organization, is neither the spider web nor the pile of sand. It is rather more the octopus, whose tentacles are in large part separately integrated, neurally quite poorly connected with one another and with what in the octopus passes for a brain, and yet who nonetheless manages both to get around and to preserve himself, for a while anyway, as a viable if somewhat ungainly entity. . . . Culture moves rather like an octopus too—not all at once in a smoothly coordinated synergy of parts, a massive coaction of the whole, but by disjointed movements of this part, then that, and now the other, which somehow cumulate to directional change" (Geertz, 1973, pp. 407–408).

The playful question, "What is an effective octopus?" takes on additional bite when it is broadened to analogous questions such as, What is an effective mob, organized anarchy (Cohen and March, 1974), garbage can (Cohen, March, and Olsen, 1972), or organizational tent (Hedberg, Nystrom, and Starbuck, 1976). What *is* an effective anarchy? Is it a unit that *tolerates* the fact that its technology and goals are unclear and that its personnel are transient; is it a unit that makes do in spite of these circumstances; is it a unit that never raises effectiveness issues or even uses this adjective; is it a unit that *minimizes* the return to the organization, or what? What would one count to find an effective organizational tent: stakes, footage of rope, time or number of people needed to erect it, time needed to strike it, ease of carrying, people it will accommodate, inconspicuousness, capability to withstand elements, odor, longevity, weight, appearance, extent to which it simulates stationary structures, and so on? Many organizations such as orchestras, circuses, entertainers, lecturers, auditors, theatrical companies, carnivals, and prostitutes live a life of one-night stands, in which the organization is built anew and then dismantled within a matter of hours. The transience of these activities suggests the necessity for quite different images of effectiveness. However, despite the widespread incidence of this type of organization and despite the emergence of models that try to capture some of its properties, little is known about how to talk about effectiveness in these settings.

Conceivably, we may need to start our examination of effectiveness in octopoid structures with a laboratory simulation. A possible means to do this would be to create a simulated world modeled after the spirit level task used by Raven and Eachus (1963). (See Figure 1.) Three subjects sit at the corners of a large board in the shape of an equilateral triangle. There is a knob in front of each subject that, if turned, will either raise or lower his corner. Finally, there is a carpenter's spirit level placed in front of each subject. The basic task for each subject is simply to get the bubble in his spirit level into the center of the instrument. The problem is that this task is more or less difficult depending on which way the level is facing. If the levels, for example, are aligned as in Figure 1, it is impossible for the subject himself to center the bubble. Total control of his level is in the hands of the other two players, since they control the relevant plane of the table. The beauty of this exercise is that it is possible to construct virtually any form of interdependence that has been discussed in the literature merely by changing the direction in which the spirit levels point.

The table becomes relevant to an octopoid existence if we add four variables to it. In the Raven and Eachus version, the levels are controlled by turning the knobs. This control becomes complicated if (1) the level itself can be raised or lowered on the table, (2) the viscosity of the bubble fluid varies, (3) the position of the level in front of the subject rotates during the course of the exercise, and (4) the ratio of knob turns to table lowering is variable. To construct an octopoid world, one of these variables could be set so that it maintains a consistent pattern (for example, every ten seconds the level will be raised three degrees, will stay there for ten seconds, and then will be lowered to its original starting position for ten seconds). A second variable could be set so that it has an intermittent regularity, that is, so that a variable set of changes is imposed over a basically orderly pattern. And finally, the other two variables can change randomly. Thus, what confronts the subject is the task of trying to keep a bubble in the center of his spirit level when some features that keep it away from the center vary in a predictable manner and others vary in a random manner.

This provides a fairly good approximation of what a person confronts when he faces an undifferentiated flow of experience. The

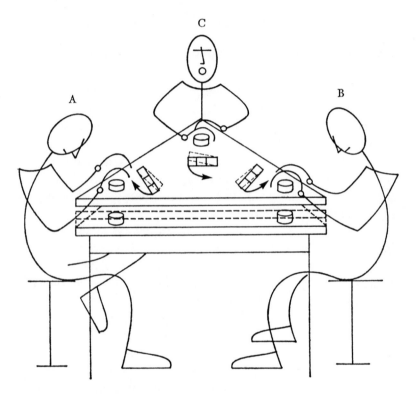

Figure 1.   The Spirit Level Task.

Source: Raven and Eachus, 1963, p. 309.

person does not know which cues are good ones and which are poor; does not see connections and can infer them only after repeated observation; enters this disorderly world with some intention (in this case, the intention to keep the bubble centered); finds that outcomes are often contingent on what other people do; and can make sense of this world in several different, equally reasonable ways. Notice that the spirit table is also a direct example of maintaining equilibrium. Keeping the bubble centered *is* the equilibrium.

Effective Organizations Are Wandering

Some prose and a poem convey the thrust of this argument. "There are means-oriented societies for whom the game is the game; and ends-oriented societies, for whom the game is winning. In the first, if one is happy then one is successful; in the second, one cannot be happy unless one is successful. The whole tendency of evolution and history suggests that man must become means-oriented if he is to survive" (Fowles, 1970, p. 159).

Ithaka

When you set out for Ithaka
pray that your road's a long one,
full of adventure, full of discovery.
Laistrygonians, Cyclops,
angry Poseidon—don't be scared of them:
you won't find things like that on your way
as long as your thoughts are exalted,
as long as rare excitement
stirs your spirit and your body.
Laistrygonians, Cyclops,
wild Poseidon—you won't encounter them
unless you bring them along inside you,
unless your soul raises them up in front of you.

Pray that your road's a long one.
May there be many a summer morning when—
full of gratitude, full of joy—
you come into harbors seen for the first time;
may you stop at Phoenician trading centers
and buy fine things,
mother of pearl and coral, amber, ebony,

sensual perfumes of every kind,
as many sensual perfumes as you can;
may you visit numerous Egyptian cities
to fill yourself with learning from the wise.

Keep Ithaka always in mind.
Arriving there is what you're destined for.
But don't hurry the journey at all.
Better if it goes on for years
so you're old by the time you reach the island,
wealthy with all you've gained on the way,
not expecting Ithaka to make you rich.
Ithaka gave you the marvelous journey.
Without her you wouldn't have set out.
She hasn't anything else to give

And if you find her poor, Ithaka won't have fooled you.
Wise as you'll have become, and so experienced,
you'll have understood by then what an Ithaka means.

C. P. Cavafy

These displays raise two issues concerning effectiveness. The first is the emphasis in effectiveness formulations on instrumental, goal-directed action. The instrumental view of effectiveness is found in all of the standard references, including Price (1968, p. 3), Barnard (1938, p. 19), and Katz and Kahn (1966, p. 161). What is excluded from these treatments is pleasure in the process as a criterion of effectiveness. Doing for the sake of doing, consummatory activity, intrinsic attractions in the process, all seem to be missing as criteria of effectiveness. Organizations keep people busy, occasionally entertain them, give them a variety of experiences, keep them off the streets, and allow them to socialize. If they do that, then they are effective. If the process absorbs time and energy and provides the pretexts for story telling, that is sufficient. This way of talking about effectiveness is unusual, but it has some plausibility.

The scant attention given to process as a criterion of effectiveness may be partially due to the way we have labeled the problem: *organizational effectiveness.* Suppose that we relabel our concern *organizing effectiveness.* What is effective organizing? That rephrasing seems to set the phenomenon of interest in motion. Interactions, sequences of acts, causal circuits, and reciprocities begin to become visible, and one is tempted to talk evaluatively about more and less effective sequences.

As an example of using effectiveness imagery in process descriptions, consider two people having a conversation in search of a topic. As of any particular moment, neither person knows what the conversation is about, where it is going, or how and when it will end. "For the sensible character of an expression, upon its occurrence each of the conversationalists as auditor of his own as well as the other's productions had to assume as of any present accomplished point in the exchange that by waiting for what he or the other person might have said at a later time the present significance of what had already been said would have been clarified. Thus, many expressions had the property of being progressively realized and realizable through the further course of the conversation" (Garfinkel, 1967, p. 41).

People are able to understand and treat an event as informative only after they impute both a history and prospects to the puzzling display. If they can write a history of or tell a story about their process, then it is possibly more effective than if the process leaves them empty-minded. A sequence of topics and turn-taking that can be punctuated into an interesting story having an interesting history is more effective than one that either yields no stories or cannot be historicized. It is not important that the process is somehow instrumental in securing some good for the pair. What counts is that the doing of the process itself provides a pretext for displaying, learning, improvising, practicing, risking, living, feeling, and so on.

Admittedly, that is cumbersome talk that is thin on particulars. I imagine, however, that with concentration, effort, and practice the talk could become more vivid, more accurate, and more stimulating as a means to extract effectiveness themes from process descriptions. My point is simply that the overwhelmingly instrumental quality of effectiveness formulations deters people from working out noninstrumental punctuations.

The second point about effectiveness as process concerns boundaries. The investigator who invokes the imagery of effectiveness usually also assumes that external and internal, inside and outside, organization and environment can be separated clearly. To talk about effectiveness "as the maximization of return to the organization, by economic and technical means (efficiency) and by political means" (Katz and Kahn, 1966, p. 164), the observer has to locate *the* organization and the one from which the return comes.

It is surprising that even though environments appear in all explanations of effectiveness, investigators do not treat environments as problematic. Having drawn lines between those variables that maintain an internal temperature of 98.6 degrees and those that do not, investigators then proceed to describe elaborate transactions across these imposed lines. Furthermore, having set the problem up in that way they look for "properties" of the "entity" rather than raise questions about its presumed existence. Investigators ask, How does an organization discover and persuade those customers who offer the greatest organizational advantage? They fail to ask more basic questions such as, How does an organization decide to punctuate its world into "advantageous customers," "occasions for persuasion," and the "necessity for discovery." That same flow of experience might be punctuated into a different set of connected variables, and the crucial questions for effectiveness would seem to involve how lines are drawn, when they are drawn, in response to what are they drawn, and with what consequences? Boundary-drawing behavior should be treated as a variable rather than a given at this stage of our thinking about effectiveness.

Environments are problematic, but it is not their properties that are problematic, it is their existence. How does it come to pass that an organization finds it useful to say of its flow of experience, We face "an" environment or we face "the" environment? To what questions asked by organizational members is the positing of an environment the answer? Organizational theorists do not often worry about issues such as this. As a consequence, they have overlooked the potential answer, for questions of effectiveness, that the environment is located in the mind of the actor and is imposed by him on streams of experience in order to make those streams more meaningful. It seldom dawns on theorists to look for environments inside of heads rather than outside of them or to ask what happens to effectiveness when organizations and environments are viewed as superimposed inventions rather than underlying structures.

Casting effectiveness issues into the language of instrumentality and means and ends makes conceptual work with complex organizations more manageable. However, if there are unclear goals, if it is possible that much organizational activity is *goal-interpreted* rather than goal-directed, or if there are functions served by rote, nonemotional performance of acts, then our habits of instrumental thinking will obscure them. To see the pervasive grasp of instrumental thought, reconsider the old quip about eating and living: "The creature who 'eats to live' is the highest human; he who 'lives to eat' is coarser-grained, but still human; but if he just 'eats *and* lives' without attributing instrumentality or a spurious priority in time sequence to either process, he is rated only among the animals, and some, less kind, will regard him as vegetable" (G. Bateson, 1972, p. 160).

It is a long way from Ithaka to Bali, where Bateson wrote the preceding comment, but both sites share the crucial element that effective organizations wander. Their destination is secondary, the wandering is primary. If we could categorize properties of traces, trails, and footprints as differential indications of effective process, then our grasp on organizational activities should improve substantially.

Furthermore, if we could articulate means-oriented criteria of effectiveness this might have a very practical effect. Katz and Kahn raise the fascinating point that most discussions of organizational effectiveness assume energy scarcity. We repeatedly try to uncover energy-conserving modes of production; we assume that time and energy must be bought and that leisure is scarce and precious. Suppose, however, that a combination of technical success and automation produces a surplus of energy. "Real affluence creates a situation in which meaningful outlets for human energy are scarce, while available energy abounds" (Katz and Kahn, 1966, p. 169). Organizational effectiveness, in an automated world loaded with surplus energy, undoubtedly will look dramatically different (for example, see Toda, 1970). And it is in such a world that sensitivity to process may be beneficial.

Essentially, what we will need in an affluent world are energy sponges. Where Parkinson's Law was once viewed as the problem, it now may become the remedy. If work expands to fill the time allotted, then it also expands to absorb the energy available. Those who are inefficient may be valued more highly than those who are efficient because they consume more energy. We may need to know

more about over-manned settings (Barker and Schoggen, 1973)
since those will be the sites where energy must be absorbed. The old
days of "uncertainty absorption" as effectiveness may give way to
"uncertainty exudation." When things are clear, there is less to do
than when uncertainty flourishes and consumes the energy of
puzzled people. Pleasure in the process may be a major avenue for
dealing with an energy surplus.

Effective Organizations Are Grouchy

When satisfaction is used as an index of effectiveness, it is
often assumed that as conditions improve complaints will decrease.
Maslow (1971) feels that this assumption is wrong. Complaints
are relatively constant in number but vary in their content. The
content can be categorized as to whether the person is complaining
about lower- or higher-order needs.

The rationale for using complaints as diagnostics is found in
Maslow's need hierarchy, a classification that is useful for pedagog-
ical purposes even if its validity is shaky (see Filley, House, and
Kerr, 1976, pp. 194–195). The needs, ranging from lowest to
highest, are physiological (hunger, thirst, sex), safety (freedom
from bodily threat, security), social (love, affection, belongingness),
esteem (self-respect, self-esteem, desire for achievement, strength,
adequacy, independence, confidence, reputation, attention, prestige,
recognition, importance, appreciation), and self-actualization or
self-fulfillment. Each of those needs can be translated into a complaint. If people in an organization are complaining about cold
and wet conditions, dangers to life, poor shelter, being fired arbitrarily, or lack of job security, then their complaints reflect lower-
order needs. If, however, people are complaining about not getting
praise, not being credited for their accomplishments, and threats
to self-esteem, then the complaints reflect higher-order needs. Finally,
if the complaints focus on perfection, justice, truth, and beauty,
they refer to a very high order of needs, but one that can be addressed by effective organizations.

To complain about the garden programs in the
city where I live, to have committees of women heatedly

coming in and complaining that the rose gardens in the parks are not sufficiently cared for is, in itself, a wonderful thing because it indicates the height of life at which the complainers are living. To complain about rose gardens means that your belly is full, that you have a good roof over your head, that your furnace is working, that you are not afraid of bubonic plague, that you are not afraid of assassination, that the police and fire departments work well . . . and many other preconditions are already satisfied. This is the point: The high-level complaint is not to be taken as simply like any other complaint; it must be used to indicate all the preconditions that have been satisfied in order to make the height of this complaint theoretically possible [Maslow, 1971, pp. 242–243].

The dynamic behind the prediction that complaints will rise in level rather than vanish as conditions improve is the familiar one of habituation and the development of new sensitivities (see, for example, Koestler, 1970; Pribram, 1967; Brickman and Campbell, 1971; Helson, 1964). Brickman and Campbell use the colorful phrase *hedonic treadmill* to specify the inevitable creep upward in aspiration levels, wants, and comparison levels. All of us are familiar with these dynamics and invoke them frequently in discussions of effectiveness. What we may do less often is study changes in content as a way to assess these adaptations. We may also fail to consider what a person is *not* saying and takes for granted when he talks. It is possible that complaints are not the most sensitive indicator of effectiveness. Perhaps the verbal jokes, practical jokes, graffiti, stories told about the organization, gossip, hobbies, doodles, suggestions in the suggestion box, letters to the editor, or even signatures (Swanson and Price, 1972) would be more sensitive. At the very least, these possibilities should be examined.

Conclusion

Erich Heller observed that, "many scientific theories have, for very long periods of time, stood the test of experience until they had to be discarded owing to man's decision not merely to make other experiments but to have different experiences" (Auden and Kronenberger, 1966, p. 332). I have tried to suggest eight different ways that we might change our experiences with organizations and with the concept of effectiveness.

First, I proposed that the kinds of raw materials an organization generates for sensemaking affect effectiveness. Specifically, diversity of linguistic forms, as assessed by Poe numbers and the relational algorithm, was assumed to be positively related to adaptability and to be an index of effectiveness.

Second, novel inefficiencies in the form of galumphing provide information about the contours of resources and about the ways to recombine these newly differentiated resources. The more complete this information, the greater the adaptability and the more effective the organization.

Third, unaccountable interludes of superstitious random activity break the constraints of memory, render adversaries more uncertain (and more persuasible?), and supply novel displays of prior actions that can be punctuated in novel ways, thereby allowing the organization to learn more about itself. This combination of enhanced self-knowledge and loosened ties between means and ends is presumed to increase capacity for effective action.

Fourth, organizations that disbelieve what they know and believe what they doubt retain both stability and flexibility. Presumably, this is the ideal pattern for effectiveness since it indicates that adaptation and adaptability are both being accomplished simultaneously.

Fifth, condoning monsters and preserving them unharmed (and unmutated) are internal processes that create cultural insurance, which buffers the organization from the vagaries (and possible nonexistence) of outgroup "lenders" of solutions.

Sixth, the decoupling of parts and the weakening of bonds between elements serve to localize adaptations and to make systems less vulnerable to the spread of trouble. Although this pattern may have dysfunctions, they are no worse than those associated with dense integration. By implication, weak ties are no worse as indices of effectiveness than are strong ties.

Seventh, evidence that members are preoccupied with means and with consummatory activities to the relative neglect of instrumentalities may index a form of effectiveness that has been obscured because of our concern with organizational rather than organizing effectiveness.

And finally, complaints may be a sign of health as long as those complaints inch upward in their aspirations. The "highly" dissatisfied person may signify an effective rather than an ineffective organization.

Behind the preceding eight points lie several assumptions. One is that conventional effectiveness formulations are shortsighted and are preoccupied with present adaptations to the relative neglect of longer-term adaptability. Repeatedly we have seen that responses that preserve adaptability look ugly and wasteful. What we lose sight of is the fact that apparent waste can be a way of adapting to the next conditions. And capability to adapt to the next conditions should be given as much weight in talk about effectiveness as capability for present adaptation.

A second assumption is that organizations are ineffective more often because of too much organization than because of too little. Organizations emerge spontaneously without managers, and managerial intrusion frequently disorganizes sets of interdependent acts that would otherwise have been stable and deviation-counteracting. Thus, each of the "subtractions" from orderliness, rationality, and predictability implicit in the preceding eight criteria are regarded as having only modest impact on the stable subassemblies that tie organizations together.

A third assumption is based on the finding that as stress increases, people notice less, their views of the world become more simplified and more impoverished, they neglect important variables, and they tend to see the same old things even less imaginatively than they did before. When these things happen, all that managers seem to do is urge people to continue doing what they did before but with more vigor and intensity. This counsel makes the fatal mistake of assuming that quantities can *change* patterns and improve effectiveness. They cannot. If you pour money into a strange system, all you do is reinforce the strangeness. Pouring money, which is a quantity, into a system that has a shape, will not generate a new shape. At best, an infusion of quantities helps you discover the pattern that is already there. If you increase the tension on a chain, you can find where the weakest link is and break that link. But the tension does not create the weakest link.

A particularly good example of the point that quantities reinforce patterns is found in Hall's (1976) analysis of why the *Saturday Evening Post* folded. The demise of the *Saturday Evening Post* is a perfect example of pouring money into a strange system and reinforcing the strangeness. Hall found that the *Post* used the rule of thumb, prevalent in the publishing industry, that the number of editorial pages should match the number of advertising pages. The tight coupling between these two elements means that when advertising shrinks, the magazine's editorial coverage also shrinks, which generates a thinner magazine, which attracts fewer readers, which makes advertisers even more reluctant to purchase ads, and which eventually makes profits vanish. But when the ads increase and editorial pages increase, the expenses of printing the enlarged magazine rise faster than do the revenues, meaning that the profits again disappear. Whether publishers try to cope with this vicious circle by increasing promotional expenditures, cutting advertising costs, or purchasing higher-priced articles, the outcome is the same. Nothing changes.

One way to break this pattern and to insert a *qualitative change* is to control the pages of the magazine so that production costs do not escalate. One way to do this is to control the price of advertising. In the old days, advertising was priced on a per page basis. This means that when the readership increases, the advertiser is getting more people for the same price; consequently the cost per reader goes down for him. If this is changed so that the advertising rate per thousand readers is kept constant, then this removes the lethal linkage and publishing becomes more stable. The important point is that the *Saturday Evening Post* gains its stability not from a quantitative change, not from doing more of the same, not from putting more money in or directing the money to different places. Instead, the *Saturday Evening Post* could have been stabilized if there had been a qualitative change, if the organization had acted in a fundamentally different way than it had on previous occasions.

Prescriptions for effectiveness seem to favor quantitative rather than qualitative change. The prescriptions seldom advise changing the game, inserting a discontinuity, or cultivating deviation-amplification to remain effective. It is this imbalance that this paper has tried to remedy.

11

Effectiveness: A Thick Description

Louis R. Pondy

Karl Weick's prescriptions for effective organization seem odd when viewed against the backdrop of goal-directed, instrumental behavior. One aim of these comments is to resolve that oddity by placing his paper within some other contexts, including that of his other work. This is roughly what Geertz (1973) means by *thick description*—placing observable behavior within a context and thus making it intelligible—when he says, "One starts any effort at thick description . . . from a state of general bewilderment as to what the devil is going on." For example, thinly described, a wink is merely a rapid contraction of the eyelid, but described thickly it might be "practicing a burlesque of a friend faking a wink to deceive an innocent into thinking a conspiracy is in motion" (p. 7). In a special sense of the term "theory," we propose a theory of Weick's paper. But note that "the essential task of theory building here is not to codify abstract regularities but to generalize within them . . . to place them within an intelligible frame" (p. 26). A second aim of this discussion is to raise some questions about what we believe to be the central substantive issue evoked by Weick's paper—whether diversity, randomness, and tolerance of deviance can be carried too far, and how operationally to build the optimal mix of stability and flexibility into the organization.

Loops, Acorns, Eoliths, and Play

As I read and thought about Weick's essay and tried to find a handle somewhere by which to grab hold of it, several metaphors came to mind, each of which seemed to give me access to different facets of what he seemed to be saying about organizational effectiveness. Four metaphors in particular helped me to gain fresh insights into the paper and into effectiveness through the paper: (1) *a loop*, (2) *an acorn*, (3) *an eolith*, and (4) *play*.

The paper is a *loop* in that it practices what it preaches. It exhibits, or displays, the very properties that it attributes to effective organizing. For example, Weick's eight loosely coupled sections constitute an octopoid of ideas that is only weakly coordinated by the introduction and conclusion. And the paper is both hypocritical and monstrous in discrediting the received wisdom about effectiveness and tolerating some pretty strange ideas in its place. Weick's re-punctuation of our talk about effectiveness is a reflexive instance of garrulity. And near the end of the paper he admits that his grouchiness about the literature on effectiveness is a high-level metagripe and therefore should be taken as signifying the "adequacy" of the literature. The upshot of all this looping is that in order to understand more fully what Weick is saying about effectiveness, one should pay attention to how he says it. The paper is not only *about* effective organization; it is also an *analog* of effective organization (Wilden, 1972, p. 155–195). It is a *demonstration* as much as it is a treatise.

The paper is an *acorn* in the following sense: It is a definition of effectiveness in the same way that an acorn is a definition of an oak. Acorns define oaks by communicating rules for their development. They do not contain miniature trees that simply expand in size. To define an oak (or an effective organization) by describing properties of the finished product is to define it *ostensively*. In contrast, a *constructive* definition defines the finished product by listing the rules for producing it, just as a recipe defines a cake. Nowhere does Weick provide an ostensive definition of effectiveness. But his eight characteristics define constructively what he means by effectiveness.

At this point some readers may argue that I cannot have it both ways; I cannot claim that Weick's eight characteristics are used *both* to define effectiveness *and* to hypothesize determinants of effectiveness; that would be circular reasoning. There are two rebuttals to that complaint. First, circular reasoning is problematic only in an Aristotelian logic of linear causality but not in a mutual or cybernetic causality (Maruyama, 1976). Second, there are some time-honored precedents for using the same property both to define a concept and to describe its behavior. For example, Dalton used the observation that chemical elements combine only in fixed proportions both to define and to state a property of chemical compounds (Kuhn, 1970). To return to the main argument, the reader should not look for an explicit or ostensive definition of *organizational effectiveness*. Weick defines it only constructively by specifying behaviors that will generate it.

An *eolith* is a stone implement that is shaped by the uses to which it is put. The eolith in this case is Weick's model of organizing, described most fully in his book (1969). The topic of organizational effectiveness is the most recent use to shape his organizing model. I do not want to suggest that the fit is inappropriate; if effectiveness is a nail, then the organizing model comes close to being a hammer. But it does help, I believe, to see this current paper as an expression of Weick's continuing work on organizing processes (Weick, 1969, 1974a and b, 1975, 1976a and b). That stream of work provides a *context* within which to interpret, make sense of, and attribute meaning to this latest work. And I am arguing here that it is a more fruitful context for interpreting Weick's essay than the context provided by the literature on organizational effectiveness.

It would be extremely difficult to try to summarize Weick's model in a short commentary such as this without doing violence to it. But let me at least outline what I believe to be the most essential elements of that model:

1. Organizations are not material, substantive entities with objective properties; the organization is not an object. That idea is a trap our thing-oriented language has caught us in. Organizations are sets of interlocked organizing processes that create order (remove equivocality).
2. The organization environment is, in part, enacted by the organization itself, not just given in a predetermined, independent variable sense. Some of those enactments are random, and some contradict the retained order.
3. Rational, goal-directed, instrumental behavior plays a relatively unimportant role in organizing. Instead, organizing is treated as an evolutionary process of variation (enactment plus ecological change) and selective retention. Rationales for behavior are developed retrospectively, after the behavior has been completed and is available for "bracketing" and sensemaking.
4. Organizing is primarily an interpersonal process. Realities are *socially* constructed. Therefore, communication and the use of language are important processes. (Language also affects what is selected out for attention.)

A fifth element that is only implicit in Weick's system, but needs to be made explicit for the purposes of this commentary, is that organizations are creative, problem-solving systems, not just performing systems. They have to figure things out, not just execute behaviors.

One might argue, although to my knowledge Weick does not, that the evolutionary model is itself the result of an evolutionary selection process of a higher order. Given a series of random ecological changes, the type of organizing model most likely to survive is one based on evolutionary mechanisms. Within such an evolutionary organizing model, the most natural performance criterion is the capacity for adaptation. Efficiency makes sense as a performance criterion only within a stable, predictable environment.

Thus, when Weick says that effective organizations are "clumsy" and "haphazard," it is merely a reflection of his notion that organizations enact part of their own environments and that by deliberately enacting equivocal environments the organization enriches itself in the process of removing that equivocality, thereby making it more fit to cope with an uncertain future. And when he asserts that effective organizations "wander," he is just saying that effectiveness should be attributed to the process of organizing rather than to some material, substantive entity called *the* organization. In short, much of the fog shrouding Weick's theory of effectiveness vanishes when seen as an application of his general model. Weick's theory seems strange only because we are conditioned to think of effectiveness in the context of instrumental progress toward some preset goal. But evolutionary processes do not evolve *toward* anywhere; they just evolve *away from* where they were (Kuhn, 1970). That is why they are called *e*volutionary (as in *e*ject). If they converged toward some target, they would be called *in*volutionary processes. The direction of evolution is not discovered until after the fact. That is why the evolutionary model and the phenomenological concept of retrospective sensemaking fit together so nicely and why Weick does not worry about how to set criteria of effectiveness before the fact.

It is important to recognize that Weick does not just offer a variation on the instrumental theory of effectiveness, a variation within the same logical type. He proposes an entirely different way of thinking about social processes in general. And the topic of effectiveness has been just one more way of shaping that general model—eolithically.

The metaphor of *play* provides a fourth set of insights into the essay. As Weick points out, play is taking the long way round, deliberately deviating from the most efficient means-end path in order to develop combinatorial skills. But Weick is reflexive in much of what he does. So the essay itself is playful in combining ideas in surprising juxtaposition.

But there is another aspect to play that Weick does not discuss. As Miller (1973) points out, galumphing is not only a way of exploring new behaviors; it is also a *signal* that play is taking place. That is, galumphing is a metacommunication, a statement about itself that the behavior does not have its usual meaning. When puppies play, they nip each other rather than bite. The nip denotes the bite, but does not denote what the bite usually denotes (Bateson, 1972). By not actually biting, the puppy is saying something about the relationship: "This is play." I would like to argue that Weick's use of a strange and seemingly inappropriate vocabulary to talk about purposiveness in organizations is a form of "nip"; it can be taken as a signal that he is playing with ideas. He galumphs with his lexicon. To have said "be playful" in a nonplayful way would have contradicted that message at the metastatement level. But this just loops us back to the self-referencing feature of the essay.

It may appear a bit unorthodox to spend so much time talking about the essay itself rather than about what it says, but doing so, I believe, is necessary for fully appreciating the essay's message. Now I shall comment briefly on one substantive point of Weick's analysis—the need to balance variability with stability.

Limits to Adaptability?

There is some danger of taking Weick's prescriptions too seriously. He is not suggesting that *all* behavior should be random, or that *all* "monsters" should be tolerated, or that the *entire* set of retained wisdom be discredited. But he provides us with very little guidance on how to recognize when the organization is acting too haphazardly, or monstrously, or clumsily. For the evolutionary process to work, there must be a reasonably stable species within which selected variations can be stored. Systems assembled *completely* at random have a very low probability of being adaptive because they have a low probability of working at all.

So there is an optimal level of adaptability, neither too high nor too low, a balance between flexibility and stability. For maximum effectiveness over time, the system needs to be *nearly* organized. Weick addresses this issue only when he describes the hypocritical organization. But I believe that it is so central to his argument that it should be highlighted here. There is another argument for stressing the need to balance *both* crediting *and* discrediting of retained meanings. The value of consistency is deeply ingrained in our models of instrumental behavior, almost at the level of a preconscious assumption. Look at any modern microeconomics text on even the *minimal* requirements of rational behavior. To counteract that restrictive definition of rationality, and the cultural norm that supports it, we need to place special stress on the functionality of hypocrisy.

The value of hypocrisy can be applied to Weick's other seven effectiveness criteria, too. Consider clumsiness. Can a system play continuously and still retain adaptability? No, because the system occasionally needs to stop and retrospectively make sense of what has been done. Play is not just random activity but a deviation away from the most efficient means-end path. It is noteworthy that Weick starts out his paper by identifying a traditional punctuation of effectiveness and then deviating from it. He does not offer just a random punctuation. It is a *deviant* punctuation that honors the traditional by breaching it.

In biology, the phrase *chance and necessity* is used to express the notion that evolutionary processes require both randomness and consistent selectivity to work. Since Weick draws many of his organizing metaphors from the biological literature, it is not surprising that hypocrisy should emerge as one of his organizing principles. It certainly would not have emerged out of the metaphors of classical physics.

Let me close with sketches of three related ideas. First, although Weick rejects what I would call *short-run instrumentalism,* he ultimately defends adaptability in its various guises (for example, diversity, and so on), as the means to ultimate effectiveness. He seems to say that diversity is necessary only because one cannot predict *which* future will need to be coped with. If the future were a constant extension of the past, adaptability would not be needed. But why not value diversity and variety for their own sakes? Why do they need to be defended and justified on some external, ultimately instrumental grounds? If the future threatens to be stable, why not destabilize it so that coping with it will promote internal, qualitative growth—for its own sake, not because it will enhance the system's "capacity for effective (future) action."

Second, the individual organization may be the wrong unit of analysis for assessing and planning effectiveness, especially under conditions of uncertainty. If all organizations were to choose the same solution to achieving effectiveness, and if it turned out to be wrong, then the entire set of organizations would be in trouble. An alternative is to plan ways of achieving effectiveness for the entire collection of organizations. That is, diversity of ways of organizing should characterize the population of organizations, not just each individual organization. If that diversity emerges naturally, so much the better. This provides a novel argument against the traditional "one-best-way" philosophy of organizing. And it also provides a rationale for encouraging distinctiveness of the individual organization, as discussed in the previous paragraph.

Third, none of Weick's prescriptions is contingent on any contextual conditions. Perhaps the mere presence of both crediting and discrediting *automatically* takes care of the contingency, since the organization creates some of its own context and no optimal level of adaptability needs to be designed in. But that is far from obviously true. It would be worth examining in some detail. Short of that, we can begin to specify some of the contingencies on Weick's model of adaptation, specifically the balance between stability and flexibility. For example, my guess is that as systems become more tightly coupled, the optimal balance will shift in the direction of stability and uniformity. But if we do not value stability and uniformity per se, then perhaps we should resist tight coupling. For example, one form of tight coupling is central control and allocation of resources. There are tremendous pressures on decision makers who allocate resources to defend their decisions against criticism. A common defense is to use identical measures of effectiveness that permit comparison among units receiving resources. Both the common definition of effectiveness and the comparison process promote uniformity and interfere with the natural growth processes by which organizational units differentiate themselves from one another. But if resources are controlled in a decentralized fashion, differentiation can proceed more naturally, and the diversity across units needed for survival of the population of organizations will emerge.

A clear value premise present in all three of these ideas is the danger of central control, not just because of the potential for exploitation by those who are in control, but because centralization interferes with the process of individual and organizational development. Perhaps even more strongly than Weick, I value distinctiveness for its own sake. And by "development," I mean the cultivation of distinctiveness and uniqueness inherent in each individual. What is most alarming about a theory of organizational effectiveness is the danger that we may impose a single definition of and a single path to effectiveness. What is most encouraging about Weick's essay is that it helps to keep the theory of effectiveness fuzzy, thereby promoting the diversity and distinctiveness and variety that I value so highly.

The latter section of this discussion is a bit straight compared to the galumphing of Weick's essay. It seems much more appropriate to end on a note that matches the tone of his argument. Spurred on by his eightfold approach to effectiveness, I discovered the following passage from Carlos Castaneda's *A Separate Reality: Further Conversations With Don Juan* (p. 258). It fits nicely with Weick's intention that we "see" effectiveness in a new punctuation. Don Juan is speaking:

> "As far as I know there are only eight points a man is capable of handling. Perhaps men cannot go beyond that. And I said handling, not understanding, did you get that?"
>
> His tone was so funny I laughed. He was imitating or rather mocking my insistence on the exact usage of words.
>
> "Your problem is that you want to understand everything, and that is not possible. If you insist on understanding you're not considering your entire lot as a human being."

12

Organizational Effectiveness: An Overview

Robert L. Kahn

An invitation to provide an overview of anything is in some ways gratifying. It provides an opportunity for lofty observations, integrative pronouncements, and panoramic visions. Of course, there are panoramas that do not lend themselves to easy description, and one such has been created by the ten papers in this book. Nevertheless, the following essay will comply with the requirements of its assignment by considering the following issues, each of which appears as a recurrent theme in these papers, as it did in the conference at which they were discussed: (1) the issue of conceptual utility; (2) the issue of multiple outcomes; (3) the issue of definition versus prediction; (4) some problems with outcomes; (5) the issue of organizational level; and (6) some problems of measurement.

The Issue of Conceptual Utility

To be effective is merely to have effects. The problem is what effects accord with the concept of organizational effectiveness? If some explicit conceptual agreement on that issue were to be reached, or if such agreement could be taken for granted, there would be no problem. In fact, such agreement does not exist, and we are therefore confronted with a scattering of concepts, operations, criticisms, and objections.

Two underlying approaches to organizations (and therefore to organizational effectiveness) seem to dominate: (1) the idea of organizations as natural systems and (2) the idea of organizations as instruments for goal attainment. The first of these approaches defines organizational effectiveness as system survival or viability, sometimes extended to include a number of system properties that are seen as immediate causes of survival. Adaptability, maximization of return, and even integration of subsystems are examples. These properties, like the notion of viability itself, have been difficult to work with.

The definition of organizational effectiveness as goal attainment avoids some of the difficulties of remoteness and abstraction that have troubled the natural systems approach, but it involves difficulties of its own. If effectiveness is the attainment of goals, then goals must be specified; and if there is disagreement about goals, some basis for choice must also be specified. Neither of these requirements has been easy to meet.

Even the partisans of these two approaches, therefore, are dissatisfied with their present state of development and offer various proposals, theoretical and methodological, for their improvement. Other scholars have taken a more radical position and proposed that the concept of organizational effectiveness be dropped.

To question the utility of a concept is good scientific etiquette at almost any time, and at some times it is crucial for theoretical and methodological progress. Those who find the concept of organizational effectiveness wanting in utility point first to the great and persisting disagreement about its definition and next to its confusing multidimensionality. Both points are well taken. *Effectiveness* is what Warren Bennis has called a portmanteau word, implying that it carries a great many things, keeps them in no particular order, and does so in a way that conceals them from view. Empirical studies of variables used as criteria of organizational effectiveness show a discouragingly large number of items and variety of interitem correlations, positive and negative. Therefore, the argument goes, the concept of organizational effectiveness has failed both definitional tests—conceptual and operational—and should be dropped.

Hannan and Freeman put the case well, arguing that effectiveness is a concept that belongs to the vocabulary of engineering and public affairs rather than science. A chemist or physicist might be interested in the properties of metals or even in the relationship between magnitude of force and consequent distortion for different metals; the expression of that interest might take the form of observed data under specified conditions or of a general law relating stress and strain. It would not, however, involve the attribution of effectiveness; that is a judgment that belongs to the world of application. A bridge may be so rated, for example, but it is the engineers rather than the physicists who find the concept useful. Physicians (and patients) may speak of effective and ineffective medicines; journals of physiology and biochemistry use criterion variables of a different order.

The proposal to drop the term *organizational effectiveness* thus refers only to the scientific vocabulary and the attendant operations of measurement. Organizational effectiveness will undoubtedly remain in general usage as a convenient term for a category of research, as a social goal, and perhaps as a useful sort of administrative shorthand where goals are already common and shared. As a research criterion, however, organizational effectiveness might be dropped in favor of more specific organizational outcomes.

Richard Scott, for example, uses patient morbidity and mortality as criterion variables in the study of hospitals. If such specific criteria of organizational functioning are used and if no more generalized meaning is proposed for them, some problems are avoided. We may argue about whether other criterion variables should have been used, but at least we know exactly what was done, and we can interpret the findings as we choose.

Dropping the term *organizational effectiveness,* however, involves losses as well as gains, and the losses are especially visible when we attempt to generalize across different kinds of organizations and different organizational contexts. For example, mortality and morbidity may be criteria well chosen to evaluate the functions of hospitals, but what conceptual common ground do they have with the criteria for evaluating the manufacture of automobiles or the production of high school seniors? And if patient morbidity and mortality have no conceptual common ground with automobile output or achievement scores, must we agree to say little or nothing in the field of comparative organizations?

Hannan and Freeman meet this question head on. They regard organizations as entities involved with a multiplicity of goals, which in turn exhibit only a weak preferential ordering. The underlying preferences they see as depending on the values of the individual, or those of some constituency whose position is accepted by the individual. General statements purporting to relate the performance of an organization to *its* goals they find not scientifically useful, and propositions about the relative effectiveness of different organizations they consider untestable. They propose to treat organizational goals as unmeasured causal variables and get on with the prediction of outcomes from other, more measurable, determinants.

The Issue of Multiple Outcomes

The majority view in these essays, however, is that the concept of organizational effectiveness should be retained for research purposes but given a more satisfactory definition and theoretical position than it may have had in the past. Moreover, it seems to be agreed that assessing effectiveness necessarily involves comparing some aspect of performance with some standard or goal.

If organizations are conceived to have some built-in purpose or goal indicated by original intent or present properties, the attainment of that goal or the rate of progress toward it could reasonably be called effectiveness. Contributors to this book tend to agree, however, that organizations should not be so regarded. No one considered useful the vulgar personification of the organization as a goal-seeking, motivated, humanoid entity, and no one deemed adequate the characterization of organizations in terms of some single dominant goal. We tended rather to accept the formulation of Simon (1964), bringing so-called organizational goals and constraints into the same framework and terms of reference. We recognized that organizations have many outcomes and that research workers must decide which outcomes or surrogates for them they propose to measure and what decision rules they will employ for calling any such outcomes "effectiveness."

To develop an index of organizational effectiveness thus involves at least two preference orderings—one to choose and weight the organizational outcomes to be included in the effectiveness index and another to designate the range or level on each outcome variable that will be defined as representing maximal effectiveness. Preference orderings, in turn, raise the question of whose preferences are to be embodied in the measures—for example, those of the researcher or those of some constituency inside or outside the organization.

We agreed on the fact and importance of such constituencies (members, suppliers, customers and clients, trade unions, regulatory agencies, and various other publics). We recognized also the diversity of interests of such constituencies, the frequent incompatibilities of their preferences for the organization, and their persistent efforts to carry their preferences into the policies and practices of the organization—to make their goals *for* the organization the goals *of* the organization. Here agreement stopped, and several rather different points of view became apparent.

One was quickly disposed of. We considered the utility of a bare-bones operational definition of organizational effectiveness—that effectiveness consists in being good at what is measured—and decided that such definitions begged the question of validity. Indeed, the consideration of this view (in Campbell's essay, for example) was undertaken more for completeness than conviction.

Cummings makes a proposal that is no less radical: that the organization be considered simply as "an arena within which participants can engage in behavior they perceive as instrumental to their goals." This removes the concept of goal from the organization but retains it for the individuals who make up organizational constituencies—at least if they enter the arena. This approach also eliminates the preferential ordering of outcomes: each person gets one vote, and the most "effective organization is one in which the greatest percentage of participants perceive themselves as free to use the organization and its subsystems as instruments." Such familiar criteria as profit and productivity are of interest only as conditions necessary to keep the arena available for use.

Most of the authors represented here prefer to attempt an ordering of organizational outcomes that takes account of constituency differences but includes some integration of them. Pennings and Goodman present a well-developed statement of such an approach, built around the concept of the *dominant coalition* (Thompson, 1967). They begin with the assumption that each organization includes a number of identifiable sets of individuals (constituencies) arranged around the organizational functions such as input, transformation, and output. Each constituency attempts to maximize its rewards or inducements from the organization and to minimize its required contributions to the organization. Each constituency thus has its own standards or referents for preferred organizational outcomes, and each exerts what influence it can to evoke those outcomes. These efforts and the continuing necessity for reconciling them create and sustain a dominant coalition, within which constituencies bargain directly or are represented. The preferential ordering of organizational outcomes is established within this coalition as it accepts, rejects, and redefines the preferences of the several constituencies. Organizational effectiveness thus consists in meeting the constraints and meeting or exceeding the goals (referents) specified by the dominant coalition.

This is a useful formulation, and empirical work along these lines would be welcome. Such work might deal directly with the concept of the dominant coalition itself. Is it an identifiable group of people who are doing for us researchers the difficult task of pref-

erential ordering and standard setting among organizational outcomes? Or is the dominant coalition only an outcome itself, a construct suggested by the fact that organizations do somehow
accommodate their diverse constituencies to some degree and continue thereby to survive and even to prosper?

We may also ask whether—even if dominant coalitions exist
and have ascertainable preference orderings—their preferences and
their referents should define organizational effectiveness. At least
two alternative approaches received considerable discussion: definition in terms of the public good and definition in terms of the preferences of those in power. The definition of effectiveness in terms of
contributions to the well-being of the appropriate public can be
seen, for example, in Scott's paper. Scott recognizes the various
organizational constituencies and proposes a useful schema for
locating them according to their substantive concerns (structure,
process, or outcome) and level (macro or micro). He argues that
social science has been too little concerned with macrolevel external
constituencies, and his emphasis on the public interest can be seen as
an antidote.

Perrow, however, argues that in electing themselves the in-
terpreters of the public interest, social scientists make a number of
mistakes. They forget other and more concrete constituencies, they
neglect the interests and actions of the dominant coalition, and
they impose their own interests on the organization. They are thus
led away from organizational realities and tend to define as goals
many outcomes that those who dominate the organization define
as constraints.

Perrow contends that organizations can be thought of usefully and realistically as the tools of those people who hold positions
of power in them and that we researchers ought to drop our own
preoccupations and find out what the goals of the organizations we
study "really are" (that is, as defined by those in power, those who
benefit in significant ways from the organizational outcome). The
counterargument, developed by Scott and others, is that our various
theoretical frameworks should serve the purpose of freeing us from
the frame of reference of the actors in the organization under study.
It is not only possible but important for researchers to apply criteria

of functioning that the actors in organizations do not themselves use nor perhaps think that others should use in evaluating them.

The Issue of Definition Versus Prediction

Some of the debate over organizational effectiveness could be avoided by distinguishing between variables that *define* organizational effectiveness and those that *predict* it. The issue of definition versus prediction appears in these papers in several contexts, particularly those having to do with methodological difficulties and problems of application.

Hannan and Freeman point out that different criteria of organizational effectiveness present very different methodological problems and that criterion variables of considerable theoretical importance are sometimes neglected because of the difficulties they present for measurement and research design. For example, the criterion of survival is advocated as perhaps the ultimate definition of organizational effectiveness. But the demise of an organization is by definition a unique event in its history, and organizational mortality is a rare event even in most populations of organizations. It follows that we cannot use mortality as a measure of organizational effectiveness unless we are prepared to work with substantial populations of organizations over extended periods of time.

We recognized that the usual way of coping with such methodological problems is to avoid them by using surrogate variables (often chosen as leading indicators) in place of the effectiveness criterion in which one is really more interested. For example, a researcher might use any of a number of indicators of organizational decline (lack of growth, loss of competitive position, and the like) as substitutes for the mortality criterion. The problem with such leading indicators is partly that their use confounds predictor variables with the criteria they are supposed to predict and partly that the prediction itself is less than certain.

The validity of a leading indicator, in other words, depends upon the hypothesis that it predicts an organizational outcome— for example, that lack of growth predicts mortality. Such hypotheses must be tested; if they are not, they become hidden assumptions when the indicators are used and thus increase the likelihood of misinterpretation. Leading indicators, after all, are useful only to the extent that their predictive indications are subsequently borne out, and the present state of knowledge of complex organizations compels modesty with respect to such assumptions.

The preference, therefore, was to define organizational effectiveness in terms of outcomes and to treat the processes that predict those outcomes (and the structures that in turn predict those processes) as hypotheses. It was recognized, however, that practitioners want early diagnoses rather than postmortems and that the tendency to take the predictor as the defining variable is likely to persist. Scott describes this tendency in the field of health care and suggests that it may have the effect of freezing suboptimal procedures and rewarding constituencies already in power. The circle of confusion becomes complete when organizational inputs are taken as criteria of effectiveness without validation of the intervening causal linkage. If licensing and accreditation decisions are made heavily on the basis of per-patient or per-pupil fiscal allocations, the formula for maximizing return to the organization and its elites becomes public policy. Predictive validity must be demonstrated at recurring intervals.

Some Problems with Outcomes

The substantial agreement on outcome variables as the defining components of organizational effectiveness included consideration of their limitations. In addition to the methodological difficulties already remarked, these have to do with the developmental stage of the organization itself and with the context or environment in which it functions. For example, the rate of hiring new salesmen might have very different meanings depending on the state of the organization and its relationship to its environment. The implication is that to make a judgment of effectiveness we need to understand not merely outcomes but outcomes in context. This is not to say that the meaning of every measure is unique to the situation but rather that contextual variables must be conceptualized, measured, and included in our hypotheses. Such contextual specification is particularly important when we are working with leading indicators rather than ultimate criteria. The addition of salesmen, in the previous example, might be either a conservative response to an already increased clientele or a risky attempt to regain a lost market.

A further issue in the understanding of organizational outcomes is their dynamic quality. Most organizations are studied as ongoing systems, and the notion of terminal outcomes (except for mortality) seems inappropriate. Research on organizations has tended to look at comparative outcomes (productivity, attendance, satisfaction, and the like), with the comparison made either between different organizations at the same moment or between different points in time for a single organization. In both kinds of comparison the assumption has been that the greater score indicated greater effectiveness. That assumption seems too simplistic, however, and it might be useful to consider alternative formulations. For example, if survival over the long term is a criterion of organizational effectiveness, does not this imply the attainment and maintenance of certain equilibrium states between the organization and its environment? The providing of organizational inputs at a rate that does not exhaust the environment and the absorption of organizational outputs at a rate that fits the needs of the environment might define such an equilibrium state.

Another alternative to the "more is better" approach to organizational effectiveness would propose a hierarchy of criteria and study the movement of organizations through the hierarchy. This was suggested as analogous to the hierarchy of individual goals and motives described by Maslow (1954). Research along these lines would be concerned with the vanishing goals of organization, on the assumption that we can learn much about the direction and development of an organization by observing the goals that it relinquishes as inappropriate or outgrown.

This discussion led to the still more general proposal that studies of organizational effectiveness should include research on changes in organizational goals. If one defines the goals of an organization as the variables by which its dominant coalition will judge it to be effective, it follows that changes in goals reflect changes in the composition or viewpoint of the people who comprise the dominant coalition. Such changes might be triggered by events of various kinds, including succession in major offices, changes in the external environment, or symptoms of organizational decline. To the extent that such processes are under way in an organization, it is likely that different constituencies will hold different preferences and will make different evaluations of organizational outcomes. Such differences are themselves susceptible to study.

The Issue of Organizational Level

The choice of criteria of organizational effectiveness can be viewed in terms of level—suborganizational, organizational, and supra- or extraorganizational, for example. These essays share a preference for the organizational level, although the assessment of organizational actions in terms of extraorganizational consequences appears as an issue at several points. Scott's suggestion that the researcher can at times take on the role of interpreter of the public good is one example. Another is Pennings and Goodman's inclusion of extraorganizational constituencies (or some representation of them) in the dominant coalition.

The difficult problem of assessing the effectiveness of an organization in terms of its contribution to the larger system (community, society) of which it is a part was considered at length. One possibility is that the organization can be evaluated and judged effective in terms of its contributions to creating a viable environment for other organizations, those that constitute its organizational set, for example. This we found to be an intriguing idea, but in need of specification. Moreover, so nurturant a definition of effectiveness seems to be in conflict with the notion of inevitable competition among organizations and with the notion that an organization is maximally effective when it maximizes return from the environment to itself (Katz and Kahn, 1966) or has the ability to do so (Yuchtman and Seashore, 1967). Nevertheless, the alternative definition of organizational effectiveness in terms of the organization's contribution to the viable environment of its organization set was initially proposed by Seashore. Whether or not it is included in the definition of organizational effectiveness, the contribution of an organization to the larger system of which it is a part must be considered a criterion of importance in its own right. Its importance is emphasized in Parsonian theory and acknowledged in others, but is not often reflected in empirical research, presumably because of the formidable problems of measurement.

The issue of organizational level comes into these essays in another context: the specification of what Pennings and Goodman call referents, that is, optimal points on dimensions already accepted as criteria of effectiveness. It was noted, however, that scores on such dimensions are usually, and inappropriately, treated as if their relationship to overall effectiveness were linear and infinite: The greater the score on the outcome measure, the greater the effectiveness of the organization. In fact, no outcome variable that came into our discussion seemed to fit the unmodified linear model; the turnover rate of highly effective organizations is, for example, likely to be neither very high nor zero. We concluded that most criterion measures would have some point or range at which effectiveness was maximized, with points above and below this range characterized by lesser effectiveness.

The problem is then to specify this point or range, and doing so implies another dimension of values or preferences. If one is to avoid an infinite regression of such dimensions, two courses of action seem possible. The first consists in identifying some constituency whose expressed preferences are taken as definitive. Pennings and Goodman use the concept of the dominant coalition in this way; Scott proposes the researcher as the interpreter of public good, and Perrow reminds us that organizations will be better *understood* when effectiveness is defined in terms of the preferences of those who hold power.

Such differences of opinion are understandable as differences in level. They can be reduced to the question of whether organizational effectiveness is to be defined in terms of outcomes that are intraorganizational (maximum return to those in positions of power, for example), organizational (maximization of resource return to the organization, for example), or extraorganizational (organizational contributions to the community or society, for example). No one will deny the researcher the right of choice. We can ask, however, for awareness of the bases for choice and for explicit statements of the process. Neither has been common in research on organizational effectiveness.

Some Problems of Measurement

The essays deal with problems of concepts rather than measurement. Some issues of measurement nevertheless arose—among them the feasibility and desirability of doing more with behavioral outcomes as measures of organizational effectiveness and relying less on verbalization. The criteria proposed in these essays (from subgroup aggrandizement to societal welfare) are essentially behavioral. It was recognized, however, that direct observations of behavior are, in many instances, difficult and expensive to obtain. It was recognized also that the behaviors that are readily observable are seldom the organizational outcomes in which we are really interested. Observable behaviors are more likely to be surrogates for those outcomes.

Research workers in organizations are thus often in the position of choosing between two types of surrogates for the organizational outcomes they would like to observe directly. One choice is to compromise on method and accept verbalizations rather than direct observations; the quality of patient care is assessed by means of a questionnaire to the patient, for example. No one really thinks that patients are expert or unbiased observers of the behavior of nurses and physicians, but patients are available and docile and more at leisure—although some hospital routines make this last point arguable.

Alternatively, we may insist on the method of direct observation but compromise on the variables observed. It may not be practicable to observe a random sample of care-giving episodes, but we can observe the frequency and duration of physician visits, the level of sedation, or the days of hospitalization for well-established procedures. In doing so, however, we must accept the burden of proof that such surrogate variables in fact accompany the outcome in which we are really interested. A consideration of such alternatives brings to mind Kaplan's (1964) law of operations and concepts, which begins to sound more realistic than cynical: "If you can measure it, that ain't it!"

The goal of this book was to identify the critical issues involved in doing research on organizational effectiveness. The prospect of developing a formal theory or set of propositions is still far away. By delineating the major problems and suggesting some points of resolution, this set of essays should move research on organizational effectiveness in a more systematic and cumulative direction. It is in these terms—appropriately difficult to measure—that the effectiveness of this book should be judged.

References

ACKOFF, R. L. "Science in the Systems Age: Beyond IE, OR, and MS." *Operations Research,* 1973, *21,* 661–671.

ACKOFF, R. L., and SASIENI, M. W. *Fundamentals of Operations Research.* New York: Wiley, 1968.

ALDRICH, H. E. "Organizational Boundaries and Interorganizational Conflict." *Human Relations,* 1971, *24,* 279–287.

ALDRICH, H. E., and PFEFFER, J. "Environments of Organizations." *Annual Review of Sociology,* 1976, *2,* 79–105.

AMERICAN HOSPITAL ASSOCIATION. *Quality Assurance Program for Medical Care.* Chicago: American Hospital Association, 1972.

ANSOFF, H. I., and BRANDENBURG, R. G. "A Language for Organization Design: Part I." *Management Science,* 1971a, *17,* B-705–B-716.

249

ANSOFF, H. I., and BRANDENBURG, R. G. "A Language for Organization Design: Part II." *Management Science*, 1971b, *17*, B-717–B-731.

ARGYRIS, C. *Integrating the Individual and the Organization*. New York: Wiley, 1964.

ARGYRIS, C. "Some Unintended Consequences of Rigorous Research." *Psychological Bulletin*, 1968, *70*, 185–197.

ARGYRIS, C. "Personality and Organization Revisited." *Administrative Science Quarterly*, 1973, *18*, 141–167.

ARROW, K. *Social Choice and Individual Values*. New York: Wiley, 1951.

ASIMOV, I. "The Machine That Won the War." In *Nightfall and Other Stories*. Garden City, N.Y.: Doubleday, 1969.

AUDEN, W. H., and KRONENBERGER, L. *The Viking Book of Aphorisms*. New York: Viking, 1966.

BARKER, R. G. *Ecological Psychology: Concepts and Methods for Studying the Environment of Human Behavior*. Stanford, Calif.: Stanford University Press, 1968.

BARKER, R. G., and SCHOGGEN, P. *Qualities of Community Life: Methods of Measuring Environment and Behavior Applied to an American and an English Town*. San Francisco: Jossey-Bass, 1973.

BARNARD, C. I. *The Functions of the Executive*. Cambridge, Mass.: Harvard University Press, 1938.

BATESON, G. "The Role of Somatic Change in Evolution." *Evolution*, 1963, *17*, 529–539.

BATESON, G. *Steps to an Ecology of Mind*. New York: Ballantine, 1972.

BATESON, M. C. *Our Own Metaphor*. New York: Knopf, 1972.

BAUMOL, W. J. *Business Behavior, Value, and Growth*. New York: Macmillan, 1959.

BECKHARD, R. *Organizational Development: Strategies and Models*. Reading, Mass.: Addison-Wesley, 1969.

BENNIS, W. G. *Organization Development: Its Nature, Origins, and Prospects*. Reading, Mass.: Addison-Wesley, 1969.

BERLINER, J. S. *Factory and Manager in the USSR*. Cambridge, Mass.: Harvard University Press, 1957.

BIDWELL, C. E., and KASARDA, J. D. "School District Organization and Student Achievement." *American Sociological Review,* 1975, *40,* 55–70.

BIDWELL, C. E., and KASARDA, J. D. "Reply to Hannan, Freeman, Meyer, and Alexander and Griffin." *American Sociological Review,* 1976, *41,* 152–160.

BLAKE, R. R., and MOUTON, J. S. *Corporate Excellence Through Grid Orientation Development.* Houston: Gulf Publishing, 1968.

BLAKE, R. R., and MOUTON, J. S. *Building a Dynamic Corporation Through Grid Organization Development.* Reading, Mass.: Addison-Wesley, 1969.

BLALOCK, H. M., JR. *Causal Inferences in Non-Experimental Research.* Chapel Hill: University of North Carolina Press, 1964.

BLAU, P. M. *The Dynamics of Bureaucracy.* Chicago: University of Chicago Press, 1955.

BLAU, P. M., *Exchange and Power in Social Life.* New York: Wiley, 1964.

BLAU, P. M., and SCOTT, W. R. *Formal Organizations.* San Francisco: Chandler, 1962.

BLUM, M. L., and NAYLOR, J. C. *Industrial Psychology: Its Theoretical and Social Foundations.* New York: Harper & Row, 1968.

BRADFORD, L. P., GIBB, J. R., and BENNE, K. D. (Eds.). *T-Group Theory and Laboratory Method: Innovation in Re-Education.* New York: Wiley, 1964.

BRICKMAN, P., and CAMPBELL, D. T. "Hedonic Relativism and Planning the Good Society." In M. H. Appley (Ed.), *Adaptation-Level Theory: A Symposium.* New York: Academic Press, 1971.

BRIGGS, L. J. *Sequencing of Instruction in Relation to Hierarchies of Competence.* Pittsburgh: American Institutes for Research, 1968.

BROOK, R. H. *Quality of Care Assessment: A Comparison of Five Methods of Peer Review.* Washington, D.C.: Bureau of Health Services Research and Evaluation, DHEW publication no. (HRA) 74–3100, 1973.

BROWNING, M. H. (Ed.). *The Nursing Process in Practice.* New York: American Journal of Nursing, 1974.

BRUMMET, R. L., FLAMHOLTZ, E. G., and PYLE, W. C. "Human Resource Measurement—A Challenge for Accountants." *The Accounting Review,* 1968, *43* (2), 217–224.

BUCKLEY, W. *Sociology and Modern Systems Theory.* Englewood Cliffs, N.J.: Prentice-Hall, 1967.

BUCKLIN, L. P. "Structure, Conduct and Productivity in Distribution Systems." In H. B. Thorelli (Ed.), *Strategy and Structure Performance: The Strategic Planning Imperative.* Bloomington: Indiana University Press, 1977.

BURNS, T., and STALKER, G. M. *The Management of Innovation.* London: Tavistock, 1961.

CADWALLADER, M. "The Cybernetic Analysis of Change in Complex Organizations." *American Journal of Sociology,* 1959, *65,* 154–157.

CAMPBELL, D. T. "Unjustified Variation and Selective Retention in Scientific Discovery." In F. J. Ayala and T. Dobzhansky (Eds.), *Studies in the Philosophy of Biology.* New York: Macmillan, 1974.

CAMPBELL, J. P. "Research into the Nature of Organizational Effectiveness: An Endangered Species?" Unpublished paper, University of Michigan, 1973.

CAMPBELL, J. P., and others. *Managerial Behavior, Performance, and Effectiveness.* New York: McGraw-Hill, 1970.

CAMPBELL, J. P., and others. *The Measurement of Organizational Effectiveness: A Review of Relevant Research and Opinion.* Final Report, 1974, Navy Personnel Research and Development Center Contract N00022-73-C-0023. Minneapolis: Personnel Decisions, 1974.

CAPLOW, T. *Principles of Organization.* New York: Harcourt Brace Jovanovich, 1964.

CARROLL, S., and TOSI, H. *Management by Objectives.* Homewood, Ill.: Irwin-Dorsey, 1973.

CARTER, J. H., and others. *Standards of Nursing Care: A Guide for Evaluation.* New York: Springer-Verlag, 1972.

CARVER, R. P. "Two Dimensions of Tests: Psychometric and Edumetric." *American Psychologist,* 1974, *29,* 512–518.

CAVAFY, C. P. *Selected Poems*. (E. Keeley and P. Sherrard, Trans.) Princeton, N.J.: Princeton University Press, 1972.

CAVES, R. *American Industry: Structure, Conduct, Performance*. Englewood Cliffs, N.J.: Prentice-Hall, 1964.

CHILD, J. "Managerial and Organizational Factors Associated with Company Performance: Part I." *Journal of Management Studies*, 1974, *11*, 175–189.

CHILD, J. "Managerial and Organizational Factors Associated with Company Performance: Part II." *Journal of Management Studies*, 1975, *12*, 12–27.

CLARK, P., and WILSON, J. Q. "Incentive Systems." *Administrative Science Quarterly*, 1961, *6*, 129–166.

CLOWARD, R. A. *Theoretical Studies in Social Organization of the Prison*. New York: Social Science Research Council, 1960.

COCH, L., and FRENCH, J. R. P. "Overcoming Resistance to Change." *Human Relations*, 1948, *1*, 512–532.

COHEN, M. D., and MARCH, J. G. *Leadership and Ambiguity*. New York: McGraw-Hill, 1974.

COHEN, M. D., MARCH, J. G., and OLSEN, J. P. "A Garbage Can Model of Organizational Choice." *Administrative Science Quarterly*, 1972, *17*, 1–25.

COHEN, M. R., and NAGEL, E. *An Introduction to Logic and Scientific Method*. New York: Harcourt Brace Jovanovich, 1934.

CRAIK, K. H. "Environmental Psychology." In P. H. Mussen and R. M. Rosenzweig (Eds.), *Annual Review of Psychology*. Palo Alto, Calif.: Annual Reviews, 1973.

CRONBACH, L. J., and GLESER, G. C. *Psychological Tests and Personnel Decisions*. (2nd ed.) Urbana: University of Illinois Press, 1965.

CROVITZ, H. F. *Galton's Walk*. New York: Harper & Row, 1970.

CURTIS, J. "Voluntary Association Joining: A Cross-National Comparative Note." *American Sociological Review*, 1971, *36*, 872–880.

CYERT, R. M., and MARCH, J. G. *A Behavioral Theory of the Firm*. Englewood Cliffs, N.J.: Prentice-Hall, 1963.

DALTON, M. *Men Who Manage*. New York: Wiley, 1959.

DELBECQ, A. L., VAN DE VEN, A. H., and GUSTAFSON, D. H. *Group Techniques for Program Planning: A Guide to Nominal*

Group and Delphic Processes. Glenview, Ill.: Scott, Foresman, 1975.

DIESING, P. *Reason in Society.* Westport, Conn.: Greenwood, 1962.

DONABEDIAN, A. "Evaluating the Quality of Medical Care." *Milbank Memorial Fund Quarterly,* 1966, *44,* Part 2, 166–203.

DORNBUSCH, S. M., and SCOTT, W. R. *Evaluation and the Exercise of Authority: A Theory of Control Applied to Diverse Organizations.* San Francisco: Jossey-Bass, 1975.

DUNN, E. S., JR. *Economic and Social Development.* Baltimore: Johns Hopkins University Press, 1971.

DUNNETTE, M. D. "A Note on THE Criterion." *Journal of Applied Psychology,* 1963, *47,* 251–254.

DUNNETTE, M.D. *Personnel Selection and Placement.* Belmont, Calif.: Wadsworth, 1966.

EADY, P. M., and LAFFERTY, J. C. *The Subarctic Survival Problem.* Plymouth, Mich.: Experiential Learning Methods, 1973.

ETZIONI, A. "Two Approaches to Organizational Analysis: A Critique and a Suggestion." *Administrative Science Quarterly,* 1960, *5,* 257–278.

EVAN, W. M. "An Organization Set Model of Interorganizational Relations." In M. Tuite, R. Chisholm, and M. Radnor (Eds.), *Interorganizational Decision Making.* Chicago: Aldine, 1972.

FILLEY, A. C. *Interpersonal Conflict Resolution.* Glenview, Ill.: Scott, Foresman, 1975.

FILLEY, A. C., HOUSE, R. J., and KERR, S. *Managerial Process and Organizational Behavior.* (2nd ed.) Glenview, Ill.: Scott, Foresman, 1976.

FLANAGAN, J. C. "The Critical Incident Technique." *Psychological Bulletin,* 1954, *51,* 327–358.

FORD, R. N. *Motivation Through Work Itself.* New York: American Management Association, 1969.

FOWLES, J. *The Aristos.* New York: New American Library, 1970.

FRANKLIN, J. L. *A Path Analytic Approach to Describing Caused Relationships Among Social Psychological Variables in Multi-Level Organizations.* Technical Report for Office of Naval Research. Ann Arbor: Institute for Social Research, University of Michigan, 1973.

FREEMAN, J. "The Unit Problem in Organizational Research."

Paper presented at annual meeting of the American Sociological Association, San Francisco, September 1975.

FREEMAN, J. "Defining Organizational Boundaries." Unpublished manuscript, 1976.

FREEMAN, J. H. "Environment, Technology, and the Administrative Intensity of Manufacturing Organizations." *American Sociological Review,* 1973, *38,* 750–763.

FRENCH, W., and BELL, C. H., JR. *Organization Development: Behavioral Science Intervention for Organization Improvement.* Englewood Cliffs, N.J.: Prentice-Hall, 1973.

FRIEDLANDER, F., and PICKLE, H. "Components of Effectiveness in Small Organizations." *Administrative Science Quarterly,* 1968, *13,* 289–304.

FRIEDMAN, M. *Capitalism and Freedom.* Chicago: University of Chicago Press, 1962.

FROMKIN, H., and STREUFERT, S. "Laboratory Experimentation." In M. D. Dunnette (Ed.), *Handbook of Industrial and Organizational Psychology.* Chicago: Rand McNally, 1976.

GAGNÉ, R. M. "Military Training and Principles of Learning." *American Psychologist,* 1962, *17,* 83–91.

GALBRAITH, J. K. *The New Industrial State.* Boston: Houghton Mifflin, 1967.

GARFINKEL, H. "Common-Sense Knowledge of Social Structures: The Documentary Method of Interpretation." In J. Scher (Ed.), *Theories of the Mind.* New York: Free Press, 1962.

GARFINKEL, H. *Studies of Ethnomethodology.* Englewood Cliffs, N.J.: Prentice-Hall, 1967.

GEERTZ, C. *The Interpretation of Cultures.* New York: Basic Books, 1973.

GEORGIOU, P. "The Goal Paradigm and Votes Toward a Counter Paradigm." *Administrative Science Quarterly,* 1973, *18,* 291–310.

GEORGOPOULOS, B. S., and MANN, F. C. *The Community General Hospital.* New York: Macmillan, 1962.

GEORGOPOULOS, B. S., and TANNENBAUM, A. S. "A Study of Organizational Effectiveness." *American Sociological Review,* 1957, *22,* 534–540.

GHISELIN, M. T. *The Economy of Nature and the Evolution of Sex.* Berkeley: University of California Press, 1974.

GHORPADE, J. (Ed.). *Assessment of Organizational Effectiveness.* Pacific Palisades, Calif.: Goodyear, 1971.

GIBB, B. "Organizational Effectiveness: An Open-Systems Perspective." Ann Arbor: Department of Psychology, University of Michigan, 1972 Mimeo.

GIBSON, J. L., IVANCEVICH, J. M., and DONNELLY, J. H., JR. *Organizations: Structure, Process, Behavior.* Dallas: Business Publications, 1973.

GLASER, R. "Learning." In *Review of Educational Research.* (4th ed.) New York: Macmillan, 1969.

GLASSMAN, R. B. "Persistence and Loose Coupling in Living Systems." *Behavioral Science,* 1973, *18,* 83–98.

GLENNON, R. "Issues in the Evolution of Manpower Programs." In P. Rossi and W. Williams (Eds.), *Evaluating Social Programs: Theory, Practice, and Politics.* New York: Seminar Press, 1972.

GOLDSTEIN, I. L. *Training: Program Development and Evaluation.* Monterey, Calif.: Brooks/Cole, 1975.

GOODMAN, P. S. "Social Comparison Processes in Organizations." In B. M. Staw and G. R. Salancik (Eds.), *New Directions in Organizational Behavior.* Chicago: St. Clair Press, 1977.

GOODMAN, P., and LAWLER, E. *New Forms of Work Organization in the United States.* A monograph for the International Labor Organization (ILO). Geneva, Switzerland: ILO, 1977.

GOSS, M. E. W. "Organizational Goals and the Quality of Medical Care: Evidence from Comparative Research on Hospitals." *Journal of Health and Social Behavior,* 1970, *11,* 255–268.

GOULDNER, A. W. "Organizational Analysis." In R. K. Merton, L. Broom, and L. S. Cottrell, Jr. (Eds.), *Sociology Today.* New York: Basic Books, 1959.

GRANOVETTER, M. S. "The Strength of Weak Ties." *American Journal of Sociology,* 1973, *78,* 1360–1380.

GROSS, E. "Universities as Organizations: A Research Approach." *American Sociological Review,* 1968, *33,* 518–544.

HABERSTROH, C. J. "Organization Design and Systems Analysis." In J. G. March (Ed.), *Handbook of Organizations.* Chicago: Rand McNally, 1965.

HALL, R. I. "A System Pathology of an Organization: The Rise and

Fall of the Old *Saturday Evening Post.*" *Administrative Science Quarterly,* 1976, *21,* 185–211.

HANNAN, M. T. "Aggregation Gain Reconsidered." Paper presented at annual meeting of the American Educational Research Association, San Francisco, April 1976.

HANNAN, M. T., and FREEMAN, J. "Environment and the Structure of Organizations." Paper presented at annual meeting of American Sociological Association, Montreal, September 1974.

HANNAN, M. T., and FREEMAN, J. "The Population Ecology of Organizations." *American Journal of Sociology,* 1977, *82,* 929–964.

HANNAN, M. T., FREEMAN, J., and MEYER, M. W. "Specification of Models for Organizational Effectiveness." *American Sociological Review,* 1976, *41,* 136–143.

HANNAN, M. T., YOUNG, A., and NIELSEN, F. "Specification Bias Analysis of the Effects of Grouping of Observations in Multiple Regression Models." Paper presented at annual meeting of American Educational Research Association, Washington, D.C., April 1975.

HAWLEY, A. *Human Ecology.* New York: Ronald Press, 1950.

HAWLEY, A. "Human Ecology." In D. L. Sills (Ed.), *International Encyclopedia of the Social Services.* New York: Macmillan, 1968.

HAYWARD, P. "The Measurement of Combat Effectiveness." *Operations Research,* 1968, *16,* 314–323.

HEDBERG, B. L. T., NYSTROM, P. C., and STARBUCK, W. H. "Camping on Seesaws: Prescriptions for a Self-Designing Organization." *Administrative Science Quarterly,* 1976, *21,* 41–65.

HELSON, H. *Adaptation-Level Theory.* New York: Harper & Row, 1964.

HENDERSON, J., and QUANDT, R. *Microeconomic Theory: A Mathematical Approach.* (2nd ed.) New York: McGraw-Hill, 1971.

HEYDEBRAND, W. *Hospital Bureaucracy: A Comparative Study of Organizations.* New York: Dunellen, 1973.

HICKSON, D. J., PUGH, D. S., and PHEYSEY, D. C. "Operations Technology and Organizational Structure: An Empirical Reappraisal." *Administrative Science Quarterly*, 1969, *14*, 378–397.

HICKSON, D. J., and others. "A Strategic Contingencies Theory of Intraorganizational Power." *Administrative Science Quarterly*, 1971, *16*, 216–229.

HIRSCH, P. M. "Organizational Effectiveness and the Institutional Environment." *Administrative Science Quarterly*, 1975, *20*, 327–344.

HIRSCHMAN, A. O. *Exit, Voice, and Loyalty: Responses to Decline in Firms, Organizations, and States.* Cambridge, Mass.: Harvard University Press, 1970.

HITCH, C. J. *Decision Making for Defense.* Berkeley: University of California Press, 1965.

HODEIR, A. *Toward Jazz.* New York: Grove Press, 1962.

HUMBLE, J. W. (Ed.). *Management by Objectives in Action.* New York: McGraw-Hill, 1970.

JAQUES, E. *Time Span of Feedback.* London: Heinemann-Educational Books, 1964.

KAPLAN, A. *The Conduct of Inquiry.* San Francisco: Chandler, 1964.

KATZ, D., and KAHN, R. L. *The Social Psychology of Organizations.* New York: Wiley, 1966.

KATZ, D., MACCOBY, N., and MORSE, N. *Productivity, Supervision, and Morale in an Office Situation.* Ann Arbor, Mich.: Institute for Social Research, 1950.

KANDWALLA, P. N. "Mass Output Orientation of Operations Technology and Organizational Structure." *Administrative Science Quarterly*, 1974, *19*, 74–97.

KLINGSPORN, M. J. "The Significance of Variability." *Behavioral Science*, 1973, *18*, 441–447.

KOESTLER, A. "Literature and Law of Diminishing Returns." *Encounter*, 1970, *34* (5), 39–45.

KUHN, T. S. *The Structure of Scientific Revolutions.* Chicago: University of Chicago Press, 1962.

KUHN, T. S. *The Structure of Scientific Revolutions.* (2nd ed.) Chicago: University of Chicago Press, 1970.

LANDSBERGER, H. A. "The Horizontal Dimension of Bureaucracy." *Administrative Science Quarterly*, 1961, *6*, 299–332.

LAWRENCE, P. R., and LORSCH, J. W. *Organization and Environ-*

ment: Managing Differentiation and Integration. Boston: Division of Research, Graduate School of Business Administration, Harvard University, 1967.

LAWRENCE, P. R., and LORSCH, J. W. *Organization and Environment.* Homewood, Ill.: Irwin, 1969.

LEMBCKE, P. A. "Evolution of the Medical Audit." *Journal of the American Medical Association,* 1967, *199,* 111–118.

LESIEUR, F. G., and PUCKETT, E. S. "The Scanlon Plan Has Proven Itself." *Harvard Business Review,* 1969, *47* (5), 109–118.

LESTER, E. "Off Off Broadway Takes Center Stage." *New York Times,* August 31, 1975.

LEVIN, H. M. "Cost Effectiveness Analysis in Evaluation Research." In M. Guttentag and E. L. Struening (Eds.), *Handbook of Evaluation Research.* Vol. 2. Beverly Hills, Calif.: Sage Publications, 1975.

LEVINS, R. *Evolution in Changing Environments.* Princeton, N.J.: Princeton University Press, 1968.

LIKERT, R. *New Patterns of Management.* New York: McGraw-Hill, 1961.

LIKERT, R. *The Human Organization.* New York: McGraw-Hill, 1967.

LITWAK, E., and HILTON, L. F. "Inter-Organizational Analysis." *Administrative Science Quarterly,* 1962, *6,* 395–420.

LUCE, R. D., and RAIFFA, H. *Games and Decisions.* New York: Wiley, 1957.

MCHUGH, P. *Defining the Situation.* Indianapolis: Bobbs-Merrill, 1968.

MAGER, R. F. *Preparing Instructional Objectives.* Belmont, Calif.: Fearon, 1962.

MAHONEY, T., and WEITZEL, W. "Managerial Models of Organizational Effectiveness." *Administrative Science Quarterly,* 1969, *14,* 357–365.

MAIER, N. R. F. *Problem Solving Discussions and Conferences.* New York: McGraw-Hill, 1963.

MARCH, J. G., and SIMON, H. A. *Organizations.* New York: Wiley, 1958.

MARIS, R. "A Model of the 'Managerial' Enterprise." *Quarterly Journal of Economics,* 1963, *77,* 185–209.

MARUYAMA, M. "Toward Cultural Symbiosis." In E. Jantsch and

C. H. Waddington (Eds.), *Evolution and Consciousness*. Reading, Mass.: Addison-Wesley, 1976.

MASLOW, A. *Motivation and Personality*. New York: Harper & Row, 1954.

MASLOW, A. H. *The Farther Reaches of Human Nature*. New York: Viking, 1971.

MEYER, M. W. "Size and the Structure of Organizations: A Causal Analysis." *American Sociological Review*, 1972, *37*, 434–441.

MICHELS, R. *Political Parties: A Sociological Study of the Oligarchical Tendencies of Modern Democracy*. New York: Free Press, 1949. (Originally published 1911.)

MILLER, S. "Ends, Means, and Galumphing: Some Leitmotifs of Play." *American Anthropologist*, 1973, *75*, 87–98.

MINTZBERG, H., RAISINGHANI, D., and THÉORÊT, A. "The Structure of Unstructured Decision Processes." *Administrative Science Quarterly*, 1976, *21*, 246–275.

MOHR, L. B. "Organizational Technology and Organizational Structure." *Administrative Science Quarterly*, 1971, *16*, 444–459.

MOHR, L. B. "The Concept of Organizational Goal." *American Political Science Review*, 1973, *67*, 470–481.

MOORE, O. K. "Divination—A New Perspective." *American Anthropologist*, 1957, *59*, 69–74.

MORSE, N. C., and REIMER, E. "The Experimental Change of a Major Organizational Variable." *Journal of Abnormal and Social Psychology*, 1956, *52*, 120–129.

MOTT, P. *The Characteristics of Effective Organizations*. New York: Harper & Row, 1972.

NEGHANDI, A. R., and REIMANN, B. C. "Task Environment, Decentralization and Organizational Effectiveness." *Human Relations*, 1973, *26*, 203–214.

NEUHAUSER, D. *The Relationship Between Administrative Activities and Hospital Performance*. Chicago: Center for Health Administration Studies, University of Chicago, Research Series 28, 1971.

NEVINS, A., and HILL, F. E. *Ford: Decline and Rebirth, 1933–1962*. New York: Scribner's, 1963.

ODIORNE, G. S. *Management by Objectives: A System of Managerial Leadership*. New York: Pitman, 1965.

ODIORNE, G. S. *Management Decisions by Objectives*. Englewood Cliffs, N.J.: Prentice-Hall, 1969.

PARSONS, T. "Suggestions for a Sociological Approach to the Theory of Organizations." *Administrative Science Quarterly*, 1956, *1*, 63–85.

PAYNE, B. C. *Hospital Utilization Review Manual*. Ann Arbor: University of Michigan Press, 1966.

PENNINGS, J. M. "The Relevance of the Structural-Contingency Model for Organizational Effectiveness." *Administrative Science Quarterly*, 1975, *20*, 393–410.

PENNINGS, J. M. "Dimensions of Organizational Influence and Their Effectiveness Correlates." *Administrative Science Quarterly*, 1976, *21*, (4), 688–699.

PENNINGS, J. M. "Strategically Independent Organizations." In P. Nystrom and W. Starbuck (Eds.), *Handbook of Organizational Design*. Vol. 1. Amsterdam: Elsevier, in press.

PERROW, C. "The Analysis of Goals in Complex Organizations." *American Sociological Review*, 1961, *26*, 854–866.

PERROW, C. *Organizational Analysis: A Sociological View*. Belmont, Calif.: Wadsworth, 1970.

PERROW, C. "Review of Neuhauser, D., *The Relationship Between Administrative Activities and Hospital Performance*." *Administrative Science Quarterly*, 1972, *17*, 419–421.

PERROW, C. *Complex Organizations: A Critical Essay*. Glenview, Ill.: Scott, Foresman, 1972.

PFEFFER, J. "Beyond Management and the Worker: The Institutional Function of Management." *Academy of Management Review*, 1976, *1*, 36–46.

PFEFFER, J., and SALANCIK, G. R. "Organizational Decision Making as a Political Process: The Case of a University Budget." *Administrative Science Quarterly*, 1974, *19*, 135–151.

PFEFFER, J., and SALANCIK, G. R. *The External Control of Organizations: A Resource Dependence Perspective*. New York: Harper & Row, in press.

PHANEUF, M. C. *The Nursing Audit: Profile for Excellence*. New York: Appleton-Century-Crofts, 1972.

POPPER, R., and MILLER, W. H. *METRI Personnel Readiness Measurement*. New York: Clark, Cooper, Field, & Wohl, 1965.

PORTERFIELD, J. D. "The External Evaluation of Institutions for

Accreditation." In *Quality Assurance of Medical Care.* Washington, D.C.: Health Services and Mental Health Administration, DHEW pub. no. (HSM) 73–7021, 1973.

PRIBRAM, K. H. "Emotion: Steps Toward a Neuropsychological Theory." In D. Glass (Ed.), *Neurophysiology and Emotion.* New York: Rockefeller University Press, 1967.

PRICE, J. L. *Organizational Effectiveness.* Homewood, Ill.: Irwin, 1968.

PRICE, J. L. "The Study of Organizational Effectiveness." *The Sociological Quarterly,* 1972, *13*, 3–15.

RAVEN, B. H., and EACHUS, H. T. "Cooperation and Competition in Means-Interdependent Triads." *Journal of Abnormal and Social Psychology,* 1963, *67*, 307–316.

REID, S. R. *Mergers, Managers, and the Economy.* New York: McGraw-Hill, 1968.

REINHARDT, U. E. "Proposed Changes in the Organization of Health-Care Delivery: An Overview and Critique." *Milbank Memorial Fund Quarterly,* 1973, *51*, 169–222.

RICHARDS, P. W. *The Tropical Rain Forest.* London: Cambridge University Press, 1952.

RIVLIN, A. M. *Systematic Thinking for Social Action.* Washington, D.C.: Brookings Institution, 1971.

ROEMER, M. I., MOUSTAFA, A. T., and HOPKINS, C. E. "A Proposed Hospital Quality Index: Hospital Death Rates Adjusted for Case Severity." *Health Services Research,* 1968, *3*, 96–118.

ROSENGREN, W. R. "A 'Nutcracker' Theory of Modern Organizations: A Conflict View." *Sociological Focus,* 1975, *8*, 271–282.

ROSSI, P., and WILLIAMS, W. (Eds.). *Evaluating Social Programs.* New York: Seminar Press, 1972.

ROTHENBERG, J. *The Measurement of Social Welfare.* Englewood Cliffs, N.J.: Prentice-Hall, 1961.

SCHEIN, E. H. *Process Consultation: Its Role in Organization Development.* Reading, Mass.: Addison-Wesley, 1969.

SCHMIDT, F. L., and KAPLAN, L. B. "Composite vs. Multiple Criteria: A Review and Resolution of the Controversy." *Personnel Psychology,* 1971, *24*, 419–434.

SCOTT, W. R. "Organizational Structure." In A. Inkeles (Ed.), *Annual Review of Sociology,* 1975, *1,* 1–20.

SCOTT, W. R., and OTHERS. *Task Conceptions and Work Arrangements.* Research Memorandum 97. Stanford, Calif.: Center for Research and Development in Teaching, Stanford University, 1972.

SCOTT, W. R., FORREST, W. H., JR., and BROWN, R. W., JR. "Hospital Structure and Post-Operative Mortality and Morbidity." In S. M. Shortell and M. Brown (Eds.), *Organizational Research in Hospitals.* Chicago: Inquiry Book, Blue Cross Association, 1976.

SEASHORE, S. E. *The Assessment of Organizational Performance.* Ann Arbor: Survey Research Center, University of Michigan, 1962.

SEASHORE, S. E. "The Measurement of Organizational Effectiveness." Paper presented at the University of Minnesota, Minneapolis, 1972.

SEASHORE, S. E., INDIK, B. P., and GEORGOPOULOS, B. S. "Relationships Among Criteria of Job Performance." *Journal of Applied Psychology,* 1960, *44,* 195–202.

SEASHORE, S. E., and YUCHTMAN, E. "Factorial Analysis of Organizational Performance." *Administrative Science Quarterly,* 1967, *12,* 377–395.

SELZNICK, P. *TVA and the Grass Roots.* Berkeley: University of California Press, 1949.

SERVICE, E. R. "The Law of Evolutionary Potential." In M. D. Sahlins and E. R. Service (Eds.), *Evolution and Culture.* Ann Arbor: University of Michigan Press, 1960.

SHEPARD, R., ROMNEY, A., and NERLOVE, S. (Eds.). *Multidimensional Scaling: Theory and Applications in the Behavioral Sciences.* New York: Seminar Press, 1972.

SHORTELL, S. M., BECKER, S. W., and NEUHAUSER, D. "The Effects of Management Practices on Hospital Efficiency and Quality of Care." In S. M. Shortell and M. Brown (Eds.), *Organizational Research in Hospitals.* Chicago: Inquiry Book, Blue Cross Association, 1976.

SIMON, H. A. *Administrative Behavior.* (2nd ed.) New York: Macmillan, 1957a.

SIMON, H. A. *Models of Man*. New York: Wiley, 1957b.

SIMON, H. A. "The Architecture of Complexity." *Proceedings of American Philosophical Society*, 1962, *106*, 467–482.

SIMON, H. A. "On the Concept of Organizational Goal." *Administrative Science Quarterly*, 1964, *9*, 1–22.

SIMON, H. A. *The Sciences of the Artificial*. Cambridge, Mass.: M.I.T. Press, 1969.

SMITH, P. C., and KENDALL, L. M. "Retranslation of Expectations: An Approach to the Constitution of Unambiguous Anchors for Rating Scales." *Journal of Applied Psychology*, 1963, *47*, 149–155.

SOMERS, A. R. *Hospital Regulation: The Dilemma of Public Policy*. Princeton, N.J.: Industrial Relations Section, Princeton University, 1969.

Staff of the Stanford Center for Health Care Research. "Comparison of Hospitals with Regard to Outcomes of Surgery." *Health Services Research*, 1976, *11*, 112–127.

STARBUCK, W. H. "Organizational Growth and Development." In J. G. March (Ed.), *Handbook of Organizations*. Chicago: Rand McNally, 1965.

STAUFFER, R. C. (Ed.). *Charles Darwin's Natural Selection*. London: Cambridge University Press, 1975.

STEBBINS, G. L. "Pitfalls and Guideposts in Comparing Organic and Social Evolution." *Pacific Sociological Review*, 1965, *8*, 3–10.

STEERS, R. M. "Problems in the Measurement of Organizational Effectiveness." *Administrative Science Quarterly*, 1975, *20*, 546–558.

STEERS, R. M. *Organizational Effectiveness: A Behavioral View*. Pacific Palisades, Calif.: Goodyear, 1977.

STEPHENS, J. M. *The Process of Schooling*. New York: Holt, Rinehart and Winston, 1967.

STINCHCOMBE, A. "Social Structure and Organizations." In J. G. March (Ed.), *Handbook of Organizations*. Chicago: Rand McNally, 1965.

SWANSON, B. R., and PRICE, R. L. "Signature Size and Status." *Journal of Social Psychology*, 1972, *87*, 319.

TANCREDI, L. R., and WOODS, J. "The Social Control of Medical

Practice: Licensure Versus Output Monitoring." *Milbank Memorial Fund Quarterly,* 1972, *50,* Part 1, 99–125.

TANNENBAUM, A. S. *Control in Organizations.* New York: McGraw-Hill, 1968.

TAYLOR, J. C., and BOWERS, D. G. *Survey of Organizations.* Ann Arbor, Mich.: Institute for Social Research, 1972.

THOMPSON, J. D. *Organizations in Action.* New York: McGraw-Hill, 1967.

THORELLI, H. B. "Organization Theory: An Ecological View." *Academy of Management Proceedings,* 27th Annual Meeting, Washington, D.C., 1967, 66–84.

TODA, M. "Possible Roles of Psychology in the Very Distant Future." *General Systems Yearbook,* 1970, *15,* 105–108.

U.S. Congress. *Amendments of the Social Security Act,* Public law 92–603, Title XI, 1972, 101–114.

VON BERTALANFFY, L. *General Systems Theory.* New York: Braziller, 1968.

VROOM, V. *Work and Motivation.* New York: Wiley, 1964.

WALLACE, S. R. "Criteria for What?" *American Psychologist,* 1965, *20,* 411–417.

WALTON, J. "Substance and Artifact: The Current Status of Research on Community Power Structure." *American Journal of Sociology,* 1966, *71,* 430–438.

WANOUS, J. P., and LAWLER, E. E. "Measurement and Meaning of Job Satisfaction." *Journal of Applied Psychology,* 1972, *56,* 95–105.

WATZLAWICK, P. *How Real Is Real?* New York: Random House, 1976.

WEBER, M. *The Theory of Social and Economic Organization.* London: William Hodge, 1947.

WEICK, K. E. "Laboratory Experiments with Organizations." In J. G. March (Ed.), *Handbook of Organizations.* Chicago: Rand McNally, 1965.

WEICK, K. E. *The Social Psychology of Organizing.* Reading, Mass.: Addison-Wesley, 1969.

WEICK, K. E. "Amendments to Organizational Theorizing." *Academy of Management Journal,* 1974a, *17,* 487–502.

WEICK, K. E. "Middle Range Theories of Social Systems." *Behavioral Science,* 1974b, *19,* 357–367.

WEICK, K. E. "Is the Evolutionary Model of Organization Evolving in the Wrong Direction?" Paper presented at the Workshop on Radical Approaches to Organization Design, University of Illinois, 1975.

WEICK, K. E. "Educational Organizations as Loosely Coupled Systems." *Administrative Science Quarterly,* 1976a, *21,* 1–19.

WEICK, K. E. "Enactment Processes in Organizations." In G. Salancik and B. Staw (Eds.), *New Directions in Organizational Behavior.* Chicago: St. Clair Press, 1976b.

WEISS, D. W. "Multivariate Methods in Industrial and Organizational Psychology." In M. D. Dunnette (Ed.), *Handbook of Industrial and Organizational Psychology.* Chicago: Rand McNally, 1976.

WILDEN, A. *System and Structure: Essays in Communication and Exchange.* London: Tavistock, 1972.

WILLIAMSON, O. E. *The Economics of Discretionary Behavior: Managerial Objectives in a Theory of the Firm.* Englewood Cliffs, N.J.: Prentice-Hall, 1964.

WILLIAMSON, O. E. *The Economics of Discretionary Behavior: Managerial Objectives in a Theory of the Firm.* Chicago: Markham, 1967.

WILSON, J. Q. *The Amateur Democrat.* Chicago: University of Chicago Press, 1962.

WOODWARD, J. *Industrial Organization: Theory and Practice.* London: Oxford University Press, 1965.

YUCHTMAN, E., and SEASHORE, S. E. "A System Resource Approach to Organizational Effectiveness." *American Sociological Review,* 1967, *32,* 891–903.

Index

267